The Happiness Sutra

How to Live a Heroic Life Free of Stress

Second Edition

By Dr. Rick Levy

Amity University Positivism Series
Volume One

Amity University Press

Amity University Press (AUP) is part of the Amity Education Group, which is dedicated to nurturing youth globally through education to develop leaders for the service of mankind. AUP furthers Amity's objective of excellence in education, research and innovation by publishing world-class books.

Published by
Amity University Press
E-27, Defence Colony,
New Delhi 110024
Email: info@aup.amity.edu

First Published 2012
Second Edition 2017

ISBN 978 81 8011 1655

Layout and Design by: AUP Team

Printed at: Sona Printers Pvt. Ltd. N.D. 110020

Dedicated to
Paramahansa Yogananda

Table of Contents

Part I : Self-Knowledge

Part II : The Methods

Foreword

What is your mission in life? This is a challenge I put before audiences worldwide and one I keep constantly in the forefront for my faculty, students, colleagues and friends. Too few have discovered the essence of their own power and greatness, and fewer still have chosen to apply this power to serve their fellow man.

Our world is passing through an explosive era. To grapple with the challenges ahead and uplift humanity in the process we require enlightened leaders at every level of society: leaders inspired to transform themselves, their families and communities, their nations and the global community we share. Amity – through its universities, schools, institutes, centres of excellence and innovation and philanthropy worldwide – is dedicated to creating this cadre of supermen and superwomen, and to sustaining a living spirit of transformation that will enliven this and every successive generation.

It is therefore with tremendous satisfaction and joy that Amity is inaugurating The Amity University Positivism Series by Dr. Rick Levy, a world-renowned leader in the fields of mind-body medicine, human transformation and enlightened leadership. In this series Dr. Levy provides concise understanding and methods that anyone can use to discover and apply their own infinite potential. Not a philosophy series, Dr. Levy's work consists of specific, proven, scientific mental technologies that deliver results which are nothing shy of miraculous.

It is my greatest hope that you will use this series to discover your own limitless power and greatness, and in so doing, that you will join Amitians worldwide who have taken up the challenge to develop their God-given power to shape their destiny and the future of the world around them. Together we will heal the world and transform it into paradise.

Dr. Ashok K. Chauhan
Founder President
Ritnand Balved Education Foundation – RBEF
The Foundation and Sponsoring body of Amity
Institutions and Universities worldwide

Acknowledgments

First and foremost I want to acknowledge and thank my close associate, Dr. Ashok K. Chauhan, for his most extraordinary vision and commitment. As Founder President of the Amity amalgam of universities, schools, institutions, think-tanks and charities, he is transforming education in India and on his way to transforming education the world over. Divinely inspired, Dr. Chauhan envisions a world in which great opportunities for achievement and fulfillment exist for one and all. His goal is to train the leaders, entrepreneurs, scientists, innovators, educators and healers who will create such a world, and he is qualified to succeed in such a great endeavor. Leadership consultant and author Del Pe describes Dr. Chauhan as one of the greatest leaders in the world today, someone with "the heart of Mother Teresa, the mind of Albert Einstein, the will-power of Mahatma Gandhi, and the philanthropic capabilities of Bill Gates." Only the future will tell just how much this noble son of India will do to change the world. I am honored to be part of the journey.

My deepest gratitude goes to my wife Lisa. Without her constant inspiration and assistance, this book would never have come into being. Lastly I want to thank my daughters Heather and Vicki for all their love and support.

Introduction

Welcome to a unique book whose time has come. It contains a new, scientifically validated world view and advanced scientific methods that will let you lead a heroic, epic life in fulfillment of your dreams, free of stress. Very early in the use of these methods you will prove to yourself that the power of your mind is infinite and that you can use this power to achieve any noble goal. They will allow you to heal yourself, remake your destiny, heal Mother India, and if you so desire, change the world.

The methods in this book are extremely powerful, yet so simple a child can use them. I have taught them on five continents to people of every age, class, gender, culture and religion, from the world's international power-elite to the indigenous peoples of the Amazon and Africa, demonstrating that the methods work universally well and anyone can apply them.

These methods will enable you to achieve enlightened awareness in a fraction of the time that has historically been required. What used to take 30 or 40 years of strict mental discipline can now be accomplished in a few years with relative ease. Use the methods and you will see. They employ state-of-the-art techniques from the field of mind-body medicine to dismantle the mental roadblocks that prevent you from accessing your super-conscious mind (your "soul"). Access your soul force and you can live a robust life of worldly adventure and achievement, accompanied by the power and wisdom of an eternal being. You no longer have to choose between the two. You can have it all, and the world waits hungrily for you to do so. A new world order is at our very doorstep. In order to usher it in we need enlightened individuals at every level within society.

It is my fondest hope you will choose to use the science and methods in this book to fulfill your highest personal destiny and in doing so that you will join me in ushering in the next age of humankind – an age in which people use the power of their minds to create peace, harmony, justice, joy and prosperity for all and for the world we share.

What the experts are saying about Dr. Rick Levy

"In *The Happiness Sutra* Dr. Rick Levy shows how to heal quickly from stress, depression and anxiety and live a healthy, happy life using proven methods from the field of Mind-Body Medicine. A scientist of international renown and a Western yogi who well understands the Indian soul, Dr. Levy says the stresses of modern life exist for a Divine reason: to propel us into a life of deeper meaning and Self realization, and he is right. I highly recommend this book."

Sri Sri Ravi Shankar
Revered Spiritual Leader
Art of Living Foundation

"Dr. Rick Levy's book, *The Happiness Sutra: How to live a heroic life, free of stress*, teaches us how to live a fulfilled life."

Deepak Chopra, MD
Author, The Ultimate Happiness Prescription

"A marvelous book that will touch the mind and heart for those seeking happiness. A blend of science and spirituality to address the Mind-Body complex in health and disease is the essence of this book."

Dr. W. Selvamurthy
President, Amity Science, Technology & Innovation Foundation
Director General, Amity Directorate of Science & Innovation
Former Distinguished Scientist and Chief Controller R&D (LS) (DRDO)

"In *The Happiness Sutra,* Dr. Rick Levy reveals 'We are the architects of our own destiny.' The path of *The Happiness Sutra* is the path of enlightenment, happiness and health . . . I highly recommend this book."

Dr. H.K. Chopra
President, Indian Academy of Echocardiography
Past President, Cardiological Society of India (CSI)
Chairman, World Heart Academy

"Dr. Rick Levy, the internationally acclaimed psychologist of repute, has the rare distinction of not only being a master in his field, but also a truly enlightened soul. This book is his gift to society, a 'How to Change Your Life and Your World' manual, which spells out in a clear and concise manner how to lead a happy, fearless and productive life, free of distress and disease, on one's way to achieving one's highest destiny."

Dr. Vijay Mohan Kohli, MS, MCh, FIACS
Senior Consultant Cardiac Surgeon, Metro Heart Institute
Consultant, Thorax Centre, University Hospital, Uppsala, Sweden

"I have known Dr. Rick Levy and his remarkable work for many years. He is a careful, responsible, and compassionate therapist and healer. In his book *Miraculous Health*...he synthesizes science and mind to provide the reader with valuable exercises that promote the journey of healing. I highly recommend this book."

Brian L. Weiss, MD
Author, Many Lives, Many Masters and Only Love is Real

"Dr. Levy's *Heart Health Kit* (to be published January 2018 by Amity University Press) deals with "healing the heart" through mind-body medicine: strengthening and focusing the mind to promote healing. Other aspects of a heart healthy lifestyle, including diet, exercise, sleep, smoking cessation and weight loss are also well covered. Dr. Rick Levy is an expert and pioneer in the field of mind-body medicine.... I highly recommend his kit to the general public and all professionals interested in fighting heart disease."

Navin C. Nanda, MD, DSc(Med), FACC, FAHA, FISCU(D)
Distinguished Professor of Medicine and Cardiovascular Disease
University of Alabama at Birmingham, USA
Father of the Echocardiogram

"In this series, Dr. Levy provides concise understanding and methods that anyone can use to discover and apply their own infinite potential. Not a philosophy series, Dr. Levy's work consists of specific, proven, scientific mental technologies that deliver results which are nothing shy of miraculous."

Dr. Ashok K. Chauhan
Founder President
Ritnand Balved Education Foundation
The Foundation of Amity Institutions, Universities & Innovation
Incubators Worldwide

"I want to know all God's thoughts. The rest are just details."

Albert Einstein

1

Your Limitless Potential

Your potential is limitless because the power of your mind is infinite. *Any* noble goal can be attained by the person who discovers how to tap the hidden power of their own mind. If you don't believe this is true, it is probably because unresolved stress (from the past or the present) has convinced you – at levels you may not even be aware of – that it's just not possible.

There is a Hindu fable that speaks to this point. There was a lioness who was hunting sheep while she was pregnant. She gave birth and died and the sheep raised her baby. The little lion soon became certain he was a sheep. He would bleat and when there was a threat, he would run away in fright. One day an adult lion came along and said "What are you doing?" He grabbed the young lion by its neck, carried it to a pond so it could see its reflection and said "Look, you are a lion, not a sheep. You are not designed to bleat and run away in fear. You are designed to roar and let the trees and everything else shake in fear of you. Recognize your power. You are a lion."

The moral of the story is: You are a lion, operating under the conditioned illusion that you are a sheep! Like the little lion in the fable, most people are conditioned from the time of their birth into thinking small, limited ideas about who they are and what they can achieve. The most prominent agent at work in this conditioning is fear: fear of death, fear of bodily harm, fear of pain, loss, shame, rejection, loneliness and especially, *fear of failure*. It is fear that causes stress and it is chronic stress that keeps the awesome nobility of the human soul from finding its full expression in each of us.

In this book I will show you how to free yourself from the scourge of fear and teach you how to access infinite levels of power that are secreted away in your own mind – power you can use to pursue your most noble dreams and ambitions, whatever they may be. By employing the tools in this book you will be able to lead a stress-free life without limits.

Let this idea sink in. The average reader will want to resist it owing to the formidable illusion created by our cultural conditioning, an illusion that causes most people to succumb to one of two big lies. The first big lie is "Achieving your dreams and having a wonderful life really isn't possible – it's a myth. Life is hard and everyone has to compromise. A certain amount of misery and sacrifice is normal. You just have to suck it up and endure it." The second big lie is "Oh it's possible to have a great life alright, but not for you because you are just not good enough." These are evil and dangerous lies that create in us a form of conditioned helplessness and susceptibility to fear – the very things that keep stress alive. Stress then perpetuates the cycle, systematically robbing us of our power, our health, our joy, our dreams and most importantly, our highest destiny.

The truth is we are born to discover that we have the power to live out our dreams regardless of our conditioning, regardless of the accumulated stress of a lifetime, regardless of any obstacle that gets in our way. You can do it no matter how difficult your life has been and regardless of your social status, gender or creed, your income or job prospects, or any limits imposed on you by the larger society in which you live. Everyone is born to discover that they possess infinite potential and power, a fact I will prove to you in the pages that follow. For now just consider the possibility that your beliefs and assumptions about who you are, how good life can be and what you can accomplish are way, way too small. You do not have to live with stress, fear or insecurity of any kind. You are a lion.

What Exactly Is Stress?

Stress actually exists to spur us on to the heights of human greatness. It is not designed to harm us, though that is certainly what will happen if we ignore it. If it is properly understood and managed however, it will protect us from harm, help us develop the power we need to realize our dreams and ambitions and aid us in the effort to find ultimate peace and harmony within ourselves and the world around us. Learn how to manage stress – how to use it for what it can teach you about your own infinite potential – and you will lead a miraculous, heroic life.

It is true that if you allow stress to go unnoticed, ignored or unmanaged, you do so at your own peril. If ignored or poorly managed, chronic stress will keep you unhappy, anxious, depressed and confused, rob you of opportunity, ruin your relationships and utterly destroy your health. That is why it's considered to be the biggest nemesis of human productivity, health and happiness.

In the U.S. stress is responsible for about 70 percent of all physical illness and absurdly high rates of anxiety and depression among the populace. For this reason it is considered to be "public enemy number one." We spend hundreds of billions of dollars every year to treat the symptoms of stress but we've done a lousy job of equipping people with the skills they need to transcend it. It is fair to say that in the U.S. we have become an entire nation of sheep! Despite our vast technology and resources, we remain largely alienated from the central purpose of life itself – to discover and live out our highest destiny. In part, I wrote this book so that India could assume her rightful place as a world leader without meeting the same calamitous fate.

The downside of viewing stress as "public enemy number one" is that you fail to learn from it, usually with disastrous consequences. In this book we are taking a different attitude toward stress, one that is far healthier and that delivers profound benefits. We're going to view stress as a friend, a helpful change agent. I'm going to teach you how to recognize it and see it as a sign that something (in yourself or in your life) is out of balance. I'll show you how to jettison stress and gain harmony within yourself and the world around you. Along the way we'll use stress as a springboard that will take you into much higher levels of enlightened awareness. In short, we don't want to annihilate stress so much as we want to use it to your advantage. This approach will lead you over time into levels of personal health, joy, peace, love and power on a scale greater than you can presently imagine.

A lot of people talk about stress, but very few people actually understand what it is. I am going to define it concisely here, because if you understand how it works, you can use this knowledge to great advantage. We begin with a general understanding of what triggers it: **stress arises when there is an unacceptable disparity between our expectations and our actual experience**, as would be the case if you were fired from your job after having been a long-standing, top employee. When something like this happens, we feel threatened and the specter of fear rises. Fear then activates the human stress response – a biological reaction that is a carryover from our primal past as a species.

The stress response begins in the brain, where the hypothalamus – a structure at the top of the brain stem that regulates stress, sleep, body temperature, hunger and sex – gets cued that a threat is imminent. It sends a chemical "alarm" to the nearby pituitary gland – a gland that secretes hormones governing growth, blood pressure, the conversion of food into energy, water regulation, temperature, pain recognition, reproduction and other important functions. The pituitary then releases a hormone that travels through the blood to the adrenal glands located on top of each kidney, triggering the adrenals to release two major stress hormones: cortisol and epinephrine (adrenaline). This three-part network is called the Hypothalamic-Pituitary-Adrenal Axis or HPA Axis and it's the principal pathway through which stress is triggered in the body.

Adrenaline increases heart rate and blood pressure. Cortisol increases blood pressure too and it increases blood sugar and mobilizes fat and protein stores to support high levels of expected energy consumption. Both hormones activate the sympathetic nervous system, which sets off a global body alarm, resulting in immediate changes in cardiovascular, respiratory, gastrointestinal, renal and endocrine functions. Breathing, heart rate and blood flow increase. Blood flows more to the heart and large muscles and correspondingly less to the digestive system, brain and other vital organs. The body concentrates power in the heart and large muscles like this because it "thinks" it has to fight or run away from something. This is the so-called "fight or flight" response. We all recognize the immediate effects: dry mouth, motor agitation, sweating, heart palpitations, increased blood pressure, enlarged pupils, sleeplessness, nausea and mental anxiety.

A single brief episode of fear that triggers the stress response will serve an important function that could save your life if the threat is a street thug, a car about to hit you as you cross the street or a flood bearing down on your home. In cases like this, the stress response would provide you with the power you need to fight or flee quickly from danger. When the threat is passed and fear abates, some of the same hormones that triggered the stress response in the first place act to return the body to normal. This is how the stress response is supposed to work. Unfortunately, there are so many "threats" that prey on the public mind these days that we live in a constant state of fear and the stress response never stands down. The result is that far too many people live with chronic stress, and chronic stress has very dangerous long-term effects.

Indeed, the effects of chronic stress are disastrous for health and welfare. They include poor digestion, autoimmune problems, glandular disease, retarded healing, poor functioning of vital organs like the heart and lungs, sexual impotence, anger, rage, fear, distorted thinking, impatience, erratic emotional states, memory loss and chronic anxiety and depression. Medical research has proven that stress is a significant factor (if not the most significant factor) in the onset and severity of heart disease, stroke, gastrointestinal problems, diabetes, cancer, neurological problems, fibromyalgia, dysmenorrhea and many other illnesses.

"Stressors," the specific events that trigger fear and the resulting stress response, come in many forms. When we think of stressors we usually think of life-threatening or extremely traumatic situations that make us feel like "life as we know it is coming to an end" or "I'm going to die." Obvious examples include: a serious car accident, a life-threatening illness, a terrorist act, war, natural disaster, physical or sexual abuse, a violent crime, or the death of a dearly loved-one. Events like these constitute immediate threats to our survival and our way of life, cause great fear, and can have catastrophic consequences, not only for individuals but for their families and entire segments of society.

Stress actually arises from numerous sources. Heavy responsibilities are at the top of the list: unpaid bills, a chronically ill family member, many children to care for on a fixed income, meeting important deadlines at work when there are too few resources to get the job done and so on. Difficult relationships are also a culprit – few things in life will stress us more than dealing with an abusive parent or sibling, an unfaithful or deceitful partner or an enraged boss.

All major life events – a move, a death in the family, a change of employment, a divorce or the break-up of a long-term relationship – are stressful. Even positive events like a wedding or the birth of a baby can cause stress because they introduce a high degree of uncertainty about the future. Advanced age and chronic illness are stressful for obvious reasons: as the body fails to rise to the challenges of day-to-day living, the gap between one's experience and one's expectations widens. Chronic pain also causes stress, and acute (intense) pain of the type experienced during childbirth, injury or surgery will also trigger the human stress response.

Stress can also result from poor nutrition, too little sleep, too little exercise and even from imagined experiences or frightening images like those in dreams and movies. Our environment can also trigger stress, in the form of too much harsh sound, pollution, rush hour traffic and long queues (not to mention rude people). There is almost no end to the things that stress us out.

There is an entire category of stressors I have left for last – a category that affects more people in the post-industrial world than *any* other stressor: *the fear of failure*. Stress is endemic to post-industrial, technological societies partly because of the pace we keep and partly because of the endless opportunities at our disposal – opportunities that create very high expectations. Here the explicit social expectation is that people will make constant gains in wealth, power and prestige. This expectation is drilled into children from a tender age by their parents (who usually want their children to achieve more than what they themselves have achieved) and bolstered over time by commercial media, the entertainment industry, educational and social institutions, peers and the business sector.

In technological societies, stress is almost exclusively a problem of opportunity and competition is king. Social expectations end up becoming our own, so we strive hard to earn a decent salary, live in a good neighborhood, wear attractive clothes, own the right car and be actively involved in the affairs of school, temple, mosque, church and community. When we fail to achieve these goals, or even if we *think* there is a possibility of failure, we succumb to fear and the stress response kicks in.

It is a well-established scientific fact that how you feel is governed by what you think. Your thoughts about the risk you are facing and the consequences of failure will determine the degree of fear you experience and therefore your susceptibility to stress. In the chapters that follow, we will take a close look at the relationship between thought and feeling and I will show you how to master your thinking so you can keep fear and stress at bay.

Interestingly, in indigenous poor rural societies where opportunity is nonexistent, people live without many necessities and often endure great hardship, death and disease, yet they live with little stress because they have no expectation that life should or could be different. The research on this subject is clear: a person living in a fashion consistent with his or her own personally accepted expectations has no stress, even if living conditions are extremely adverse. This concept is worth exploring and we will come back to it. For now, it is important for you to realize that your expectations play a very critical role in your susceptibility to stress.

One last thing about the hazards posed by chronic stress: its effects over a lifetime are cumulative and insidious. We humans have a way of acclimating to high levels of stress right up until we succumb to mental disability, bodily dysfunction, serious illness or all three. Stress begins in childhood and mounts on us gradually, so gradually we don't notice it until it starts to make us ill. This effect is reminiscent of the old parable about the frog in the pot of water. According to the parable, if you drop a frog in boiling water it will jump out immediately. However, if you put a frog in a pot of cool water and slowly heat the water to boiling, the frog will stay in the pot and cook to death. Unfortunately the same is true with us and stress.

Given that life is becoming more stressful and we human beings are so inclined to endure chronic stress over long periods, we are now observing a substantial rise in rates of depression, anxiety and neurological problems like Multiple Sclerosis, Alzheimer's and Parkinson's Disease among post-industrialized nations. This is happening because, if you do nothing to reverse it, chronic stress will change your brain chemistry and physiology over time, making you prone to serious illness. This is another reason to liberate yourself from chronic stress once and for all. Armed with the tools in this book, you can do just that.

Everyone carries some degree of unresolved stress from events in their past. There is plenty of suffering to go around and some of us have had more than our fair share. Perhaps you had to endure the death of a parent when you were a child, or one of your family members abused you, or you were locked in a loveless marriage at a tender young age. Maybe you were shunned because you were born with a disability, or you couldn't go to school because you had to support your family, or you had to bear the brunt of racism or sexism or homophobia. Maybe your family home was destroyed in a typhoon. Events like these create profound mental and physical stress which, if not resolved, will remain hidden deep in the mind, sabotaging our happiness, distorting our thinking, damaging our self-esteem and strongly predisposing us to stress in the here and now.

There are a host of early-life stressors that are far more subtle than the examples I just gave, and therefore more insidious because people tend to ignore them. For example, consider the daughter who hungers for love and attention from a father who is emotionally distant and uncaring, or the second son who grows up in the shadow of his more accomplished older brother in a family where the parents dote exclusively on their oldest child. The young mind is invariably scarred by such events. The resulting stress can be just as profound as stress caused by major life-threatening trauma, the results just as catastrophic.

The good news is, no matter what you've had to endure it is possible to free yourself from the stress of a lifetime and completely heal your brain, mind and body. I will show you how to do it. You will be surprised and delighted with how much better you feel.

Stress Is Actually Good for You

The preceding discussion is designed to drive home what has now become obvious to the reader: persistent stress that is not resolved eventually causes significant harm to mind and body, so you must learn to manage it effectively. The upside is that you *can* manage it well, and if you do, you will be vastly much happier, healthier, stronger and more successful.

It is a medically proven fact that stress is actually good for us because the challenges posed in our lives have the potential to enhance our physical, mental and spiritual power. In 1975 Hans Selye, a noted endocrinologist and chemist who pioneered research on stress, published a model that divides stress into two camps: **eustress** and **distress**. Eustress is "good" stress that enhances human performance and wellbeing. It is a term given to stressful events that result in increased strength (physical, intellectual or spiritual power and endurance), gains in knowledge, feelings of fulfillment, increased confidence and other desirable benefits. "Distress" is the term Selye gave to persistent stress that is not resolved and leads to dysfunction and illness (the type of stress I've been describing in this chapter so far).

Selye was the first researcher to demonstrate that we cannot grow, as individuals or as a species, without stress. His early research proved what every athlete already knows: our muscles atrophy if there is too little physical stress imposed on our bodies. Subsequent research proved that low levels of stress are not good for the mind either. When people go on long vacations for example and really relax, studies show their self-esteem goes up and their stress levels go down, but their intelligence quotient goes down too! Perhaps you know someone who has led a pampered life with very little stress, one in which everything they wanted was handed to them on a silver platter and they didn't have to work for anything. Such people often turn out to be aimless ne'er-do-wells who are emotionally and intellectually challenged.

Studies in anthropology and sociology prove the same thing is true for our species: stress is the catalyst for the evolution of human culture. Ancient mankind made its greatest evolutionary leap forward following the stress of the last Ice Age, when the challenges posed by the harsh climate spurred the development of larger brain size and tool construction. We stopped being hunter-gatherers then and formed collective social structures that would ensure our survival as a species. Likewise, any social historian will tell you that most of modern man's greatest social and political advances have occurred on the heels of cataclysms like war, natural disaster or severe economic crises.

There is a well-known true story that speaks to this issue. A biologist working with majestic Emperor butterflies decided to conduct a small experiment. As one of his butterflies began to emerge from its chrysalis, he took a fine pair of scissors and carefully snipped the hard casing away, saving the butterfly from having to struggle out on its own. The freed butterfly made one huge effort to open its shriveled wings, which remained limp and useless. It then died. Only the effort required to break out of the chrysalis would have provided the vital circulation and strength needed for the butterfly to develop properly. Without that effort the butterfly lived a short sorrowful life, unable to fulfill its destiny.

The bottom line is this: without stress we human beings would not progress, either as individuals or as a species. We do not need freedom from stress: what we need is the ability to manage distress (so it gets resolved) and cultivate eustress (use stress as a tool for constant gains in self-understanding and self-expansion).

The distinction between distress and eustress is an important one I will refer to often in the pages that follow. For the remainder of this book I will consistently use the term "stress" to refer to the basic biological reaction described earlier in this chapter. I will use "eustress" to refer to stress that enhances your understanding and personal power and I will use "distress" to refer to harmful mental and biological distress that remains unresolved and leads to dysfunction and illness. Don't worry, I'll remind you of these distinctions as you read on.

Your Mind is the Key

One fascinating thing about Selye's research is that he proved the same stressor can trigger distress (a bad outcome) or eustress (a good one). What this means is you can expose two people to exactly the same stressor and one person can be deeply wounded by it (distress) while the other person becomes stronger for having had exactly the same experience (eustress). The difference is to be found in the individuals: the psychological and spiritual resources they have at their disposal, their thoughts and expectations, and how they perceive the stressor.

In the fall of 2008 through the good graces of the Deepalaya Foundation, I toured the slums of Delhi. The sewage in the streets, the pestilence and disease would have stressed most people – certainly most Westerners – but it didn't bother me. The only thing I perceived was the extraordinary potential in the young students who attend Deepalaya's schools and the dedication of their teachers. I was not stressed at all. To the contrary, I became steeped in awe as I took in the power of the human soul in that place. I was so blind to the surroundings that I failed to notice my pyjamas had gotten soaked in excrement! I share this simple example for the obvious reason. It illustrates the point that one person's stressor can easily be another person's Nirvana – the difference is in the mind of the beholder.

Hans Selye was the first researcher to prove that any individual's response to a stressor is governed by what he or she thinks, not by the stressor itself. Richard Lazarus, a psychologist and professor at the University of California, later built on Selye's research. Lazarus showed that cognitive processes (how we perceive and interpret our experiences) will determine our reaction to a potential stressor.

Lazarus demonstrated that when we're faced with a potential stressor, we analyze the situation to determine whether it is a threat or whether it contains promise – a process that usually takes place in a matter of seconds. In the blink of an eye, we ponder whether the situation has a high risk of harm, is a challenge we can undertake and overcome, if we can benefit from it, or whether it is simply benign (a non-issue). It is this analysis that determines whether we react to a potential stressor with fear and trepidation, outrage or anger, courage or optimism, intrigue, endurance, faith or a combination of these.

An important thing to understand about this analysis is that all or part of it occurs *unconsciously*, which means it's conducted at levels in the mind that are hidden from our awareness. You are only aware of the end-product of the analysis – your feelings on the matter – which spring into your awareness seemingly "out of nowhere." The trouble with unconscious thinking is that it's often inaccurate, because the unconscious mind is full of distorted thoughts and feelings we carry from encounters with stressful events in our past. In this book I will show you how to bring this "hidden" thought process into the light of day. You will be able to analyze your own logic much more effectively then, and free yourself from distorted thinking and feeling of the type that keeps you susceptible to fear and distress.

Stress as a Springboard to Your Highest Destiny

Stress is not some random phenomenon. It has a Cosmic purpose grounded in Divine love. It is designed to help you fulfill your highest destiny. It is a fact that the power of your mind is infinite. There are higher levels of thought and awareness (consciousness) in your mind that you have not sufficiently explored – enlightened levels of mind that will enable you to free yourself from distress and conditioned ways of thinking entirely, give you the power to fulfill your destiny and ultimately lead you into unity and harmony with God and all that is. This is the very purpose of life itself.

Almost everything that has happened to you so far, including the suffering and the stress you've had to endure, has been designed by your soul to bring you to God. Unresolved, negative stress (distress) prompts us to resolve our lack of internal harmony and seek deeper for the meaning and purpose of life. Positive stress (eustress) helps us make the gains in psychological and spiritual wisdom we need to liberate ourselves from the illusion that we are "confined" by our lives to begin with, and to remake ourselves. Enlightened awareness is the natural goal of both these dynamics. Attain it, and you will experience the end of all sorrow. When seen in this light, stress turns out to be nothing more than a helpful companion on the road to enlightenment – a Divine gift.

I will show you how to access enlightened states of awareness in this book, and we'll do it using easy methods that deliver very rapid results. It is no longer true that enlightenment is reserved only for swamis, sadhus, teachers and saints. In the West, traditional meditative methods have been supplemented by western science to create techniques that anyone can use to attain enlightened awareness almost overnight. What used to take decades of mental discipline can now be accomplished in a few years, sometimes in a few months if the student is hungry enough.

Right away using the methods I provide in this book, you will be able to experience the intuitive intelligence of your soul. Even a little soul awareness will enable you to examine the hidden workings of your own mind – the anxieties, fears and things in your culture and history that are holding you back – with extraordinary levels of insight and compassion. You will be able to purge your mind of the thoughts and feelings that keep you distressed and unhappy, come into a very high degree of internal harmony and joy, and pursue your own highest personal destiny for this lifetime.

Soul awareness will provide you with the ability to perceive the deepest meaning hidden behind the tapestry of your experience and open you to the fullness of possibility at your fingertips. In this state of awareness, you will see that your possibilities are endless. Your response to life's stressors will seem of little consequence to you. Much more important to you will be your *Story Behind the Story*.

The story of your life consists of your history – the events and people you've known, your actions and what you think and feel about your experience. Your *Story Behind the Story* runs much deeper: it consists of **who you are trying to become** within your history. From person to person the plots vary widely, leading us through the extremes of poverty and wealth, triumph and despair, love and loneliness, strength and weakness, illness and health, grace and shame. Everyone's lessons in life are different, but everyone's journey has the possibility of a miraculous outcome if they can discover their *Story Behind the Story* and live it out authentically.

Rumi said, "Everyone has been made for some particular work, and the desire for that work has been put into his heart." Each of us is born with a soul-inspired, entirely unique set of deeply held longings and dreams designed to bring out our most noble qualities. From the time of our birth however, we are taught to suppress these longings as "unrealistic" and to conform to limited social expectations. As a result we end up suffering from an anxious tension between who we have become and who we dream ourselves to be at the deepest levels of self (the soul). If we continue to live this way, we become alienated from our own soul and therefore alienated from God. This is the ultimate cause of distress, the one source of distress from which all sorrows flow. Alienated in this manner and assaulted by the stress of day-to-day living, we have no internal harmony with Spirit from which we can draw insight, peace, healing and power. We then succumb to chronic mental distress, serious physical illness, and worse yet – the death of our dreams.

The *Story Behind Your Story* – your own highest personal destiny for this life – can only be known through the self-reflection of the soul. Using the methods in this book, you will be able to directly experience the intuitive intelligence of your soul. At that point it will become quite clear that you are living a unique, epic adventure in self-discovery designed to bring you into enlightenment. As you continue to move forward, you will find that your noblest, most deeply held dreams and longings are actually God calling you home.

Most people agree: the purpose of life is to find happiness. If we think material success will make us happy and if we expect it will be hard to get it, we will be maximally stressed. If instead we focus on achieving enlightened harmony within ourselves and with God as the ultimate source of happiness, our experience will be very different. *As expectations go up or down in relation to current conditions, we do not succumb to stress because we are not attached to our expectations for how events will unfold – we measure our success based on the intuitive awareness of our own soul.* Our super-conscious awareness provides us with the power we need to pursue our goals for worldly success with greater ease and efficiency and actively assists us with the realization of our own noble longings. In the end, we discover that this approach brings the death of distress, and more happiness than we dared dream of.

What I bring to you is a series of simple, highly effective methods that will allow you to discover the truth as I have outlined it in this chapter. If you came to this book because you were looking for a fast, easy way to deal with stress you will not be disappointed. You can pick and choose from the methods in the same way you would choose appetizers, salad and a main dish from your favorite menu. My guess is, once you've experienced the power that comes from the methods, you will want to know more. I'm not asking you to trust me now, I'm asking you to trust your own experience after you've gained some familiarity with the methods.

On the other hand, if you are a seeker of Truth you will not be disappointed either. The methods in this book will allow you to reprogram your thinking so it is free of distortion, completely liberate yourself from fear and anxiety, live out your chosen destiny and enjoy the myriad benefits of enlightened awareness.

This book is a roadmap for coming into peace and harmony within yourself, with God and with the world around you – the ultimate stress management strategy – the only strategy that will let you live your life as a heroic adventure filled with joy, able to overcome any obstacle that stands in your way.

Serenity Now – The Stressbuster

Your mind is infinite. Once you experience this you will rapidly free yourself from fear and distress and, if you so choose, gain the power to fulfill your highest destiny. Let's begin right now with a simple yet convincing demonstration of the power you possess within your own mind.

There are many ways to manage harmful stress (distress). The method I'm about to show you will reduce the amount of distress you carry by as much as 50 percent in just 15 minutes. Use of this method will provide you with immediate relief and also illustrate just how much control you can exert over your own wellbeing in a short time.

To understand how this exercise works you need to understand how best to minimize stress. Two common responses to stress simply won't work. The first of these is trying to "think" your way out of a stressful situation. This can be helpful occasionally, but you can't fix every problem with logic. Let's say your problem persists no matter how you analyze it and respond to it rationally. If you keep applying logic to an illogical problem, your thinking becomes distorted. At that point, you become like the man who is lost on the unmarked dirt roads in the Bandhavgarh preserve, driving left and right, trying to find your way out of the park with no map and a broken compass.

The second response that rarely delivers a result is trying to "tough" your way through a stressful situation using willpower. This approach might help you survive the current crisis but it will cause even more stress in the long run. If stressful events crop up frequently for you (as they do for most of us), you can't keep overcoming them with willpower alone. At some point, the accumulated stress will catch up with you and break you down mentally, physically or both. You must slow down long enough to deal with it.

To get free from stress quickly, you have to stop thinking altogether. Where does stress come from? It comes from fear-based thought, belief and expectations – things like "If I don't make that deadline, I will lose my job," or "If the economy declines further, I'll have to fire my staff," or "What if my surgery is unsuccessful," or "If I don't pass this exam, I won't have a future."

To stop thinking altogether you have two healthy options available to you. You can use scientific meditation to access your own higher states of consciousness (which I discuss later) or you can use imagination and imagery to access the power of the subconscious mind. Right now we're going to do the latter. This experience will free you from stress measurably and *immediately*. You will come out of this exercise feeling unbelievably better. In fact you'll end up saying, "I had no idea I was *that* stressed to begin with." That's how much better you'll feel.

To use this exercise find 15 minutes when you can have some privacy and quiet. Place the CD that accompanies this book in a CD player or if you are using an electronic version, queue up the first audio method on your device. Then turn off the phone, dim the lights, lay back on your bed, couch or chair, get comfortable and play the first track titled **The Stressbuster**. All you have to do is listen as I guide you through a simple process of mental and physical relaxation, then take you on a mental holiday from stress.

When you come out of *The Stressbuster* notice how you feel. You should feel significantly better. Most people report a 50 percent decrease in stress. If you keep doing this exercise over time, its healing power will gain in potency. Use it once or twice a week to keep stress at bay.

Part I
Self-Knowledge

If you wanted to take a cross-country road trip, you would first have to learn how to drive a car. Similarly, if you want to live life like an adventure, free of distress, you must first learn how to "turn on" your mind and steer it where you want to go. In this part of the book I describe the structure of the mind and show you how to access its hidden power. I also help you analyze just how much stress you're carrying and its cause. Along the way, you'll learn a great deal of valuable information about yourself, and your own *Story Behind the Story* – your highest destiny for the incarnation. You need this knowledge to take advantage of the powerful methods contained in Part II.

2

The Story Behind the Story

I first met Ann when she brought her 14-year-old nephew to see me for help. She had adopted him and his younger sister after their parents died two years earlier. Unmarried and 33 years of age, Ann was now trying to be a good mother to two needy children while she met the demands of her job as a White House policy advisor. During our first interview, two things were clear. The first was that Ann, though poised and outwardly calm, carried enough distress for 20 people. The second thing, directly related to the first, was that she lived in excruciating pain. Her story is a case study in how early life distress can establish patterns of thought, belief and expectation that keep us mired in distress for years, destroy our health and blind us to our own greatness.

Ann was one of four daughters born to a fairly affluent and influential family. Her father, and his father before him, were men of distinction in U.S. politics and business affairs. Her mother was a stay-at-home mom who kept a perfect home and was devoted to her children, their church and community. Her mother's nickname in their neighborhood was "The Saint."

It sounds like a good enough start in life, with one exception: Ann could never seem to get the love she needed from her father. He was often working, and when he was home he was concerned only with whether she was performing well. He had always wanted a son and Ann learned as a tiny child that he would dote on her only if she excelled at the things he cared about: academics, sports, current affairs, social savvy, and above all a *"be tough and never complain"* attitude. Only if she was "perfect" in these ways could she win her father's attention and approval. She succeeded at it too, to the point that her father came to refer to her as "the son he never had."

Then the unthinkable happened: when Ann was eleven years old, her mother died tragically of heart failure. Her mother was seven months pregnant at the time and the unborn child also died. Ann's father was inconsolable after he lost his wife. It became usual for him to drink an entire bottle of whiskey after he came home from work at night. The slightest normal turmoil (a problem with homework, a spill in the kitchen) would launch him into a fit of rage. If everything wasn't perfect there was hell to pay, so Ann bent over backwards to placate him. She became very good at being precisely the way her father wanted her to be *all* the time. If she didn't succeed, she was punished.

Desperate to find a mother for his daughters, Ann's father was quick to remarry – too quick. Unfortunately, the girls' new stepmother didn't live up to his expectations. She was selfish and grasping, and resented his children. She especially didn't like Ann, because Ann resembled "The Saint" who had died.

Forced to leave home at a young age, Ann worked her way through college, then a Master's degree in management. She got the Masters in part because it was what her father had desired and partly because it was one of few good options available. Managerial jobs in the U.S. were male-dominated at the time, but social and political pressure to hire women was strong and well-qualified women were few in number.

Ann did very well in graduate school. She had a job offer from one of the most prestigious consulting firms in the world before her diploma was awarded. She got along with everyone, worked hard, out-performed her male colleagues and never complained. She became the youngest person, man or woman, to hold a senior executive post in the U.S. government and at 32 she became an advisor to the White House and the U.S. Congress. She also had her own consulting business and earned an annual income in the top 5 percent of all female wage earners. She was intensely involved in the affairs of her church and community, had a robust social life and could afford to travel for leisure and adventure. Owing to her father's influence growing up she was an avid scuba diver, skier and markswoman. She was also beautiful, with a string of long-term romantic relationships behind her and several proposals of marriage – all of which she had said "no" to. She seemed to lack for nothing.

That was Ann's story. Most people would envy the life that Ann had built for herself. There was only one problem: the stress of it was killing her. Eight months before Ann walked into my office she had undergone emergency surgery. Too much stress over too many years had lodged in her neck and caused a condition called degenerative disc disease: an irreversible, progressive disorder in which the discs between the vertebrae in the spine break down – a condition that always involves advancing pain and disability.

Owing to the "be tough and don't complain" attitude Ann inherited from her father, she didn't think of seeing a doctor until the pain got really bad and unfortunately, it was too late. Even as the doctors were running their diagnostic tests, two discs in her neck collapsed and cut into her spinal cord, severing the nerves that ran down her spine into her right arm and leg. At that point she became hemiplegic – paralyzed on the right side of her body. Emergency surgery followed. The doctors were unable to reverse the damage done to the severed nerves in her spinal cord. Her neurosurgeon told her she would never walk again.

Through faith in God and lots of willpower and physical therapy, Ann eventually got herself walking again. The doctors at The Washington Hospital Center where she was treated called her "the miracle patient." However, her right leg and arm remained almost useless. Her leg would give out from under her as she walked, and her right hand and arm were so weak, she couldn't carry a small bag of groceries or open a jar. Post-surgery, she continued to live with excruciating pain in her neck and spine that no physical therapy or prescription painkiller could touch. She had been like this for nearly 6 months prior to our first meeting. I had great compassion for her. Like every well-intentioned person, she got in all this trouble just trying to do her best under stressful circumstances.

Immediately we went to work, applying the skills in Part II of this book to help Ann heal herself and obtain the quality of life she was looking for. In the first stage of our work, we focused on discovering the distortions in her thinking that were driving her outrageously high stress levels. Remember what I said in Chapter One – your stress level is determined by what you think (your beliefs and expectations), not by the stressor itself. It doesn't matter whether the stressor is a series of terrorist attacks, a disgruntled mother-in-law, your inability to get a job, a boss at work who is the world's biggest loser, a chronically ill child, an abusive boyfriend or girlfriend, your failing health or something else. What you think, believe and expect are driving your susceptibility to stress, not the situation you are in.

Very quickly Ann was able to identify a handful of distortions in her thinking (false, harmful beliefs and expectations) that were keeping her stressed-out, unwell and unhappy. They were all located in her subconscious mind where she didn't even know they existed. The subconscious mind is where we store our memories, powerful thoughts and feelings associated with memory and a deep, profound sense of who we really are. It is a level of mind that is usually hidden from our day-to-day awareness, yet it is extraordinarily powerful – nearly three times more powerful than your "mind" as you presently know it. I gave Ann the tools she needed to access her subconscious. What she found there was nothing shy of life altering.

Ann discovered three closely related distortions in her subconscious mind that were driving her stress and destroying her health. The first was "If I am perfect enough, everything will be alright and I will be happy." This idea wasn't true for Ann and it's probably not true for you either. It is usually a mistake to think you can rid yourself of stress by working harder and smarter or in some other way "being perfect." The only exception to this rule exists for people who are lazy. Clearly, Ann had learned this distortion in her thinking from her father, who withheld his affection unless she performed at the superior level. In Ann's case this distorted thought was disastrous because she had also adopted her father's exaggerated, absurdly high ideal as her own (i.e. a good, successful person worthy of love is able to do everything perfectly, without failure or complaint).

Ann might have rejected this absurd ideal if it hadn't been so firmly cemented in her mind by the culture in which she lived. In her culture women were expected to be smart, thin, beautiful and sexy. They were also expected to be loving wives and mothers, maintain a perfect home and manage successful careers. This stereotype of the "perfect woman" was on every billboard and television show, in every magazine, newspaper and online feature. It was buttressed by Ann's teachers, mentors and friends, reflected in the attitudes of the business world, the retail market, even her church community. Everything in Ann's environment growing up had conditioned her to believe this ideal was right and true.

Ann had quite naturally succumbed to a falsehood that preys on everyone: as a youngster she was conditioned to believe that the distorted ideals and expectations of the culture she was born into were real, virtuous and much-to-be-desired. There isn't a person on the planet who hasn't succumbed to the conditioning effects of the family in which they were born and the culture in which they live. It's human nature. Cultural norms – and our inclination to adopt them – exist for a reason as old as life itself: they ensure the survival of the species. Not all cultural norms are virtuous however, and as Ann discovered, they can be wildly destructive to individual wellbeing.

Another distortion hidden in Ann's subconscious mind was the expectation "If I am not perfect I will fail and be punished." If you were driven by the same beliefs and expectations, you would do just what Ann had done:

every moment of every day you would try very hard to measure up to an impossibly high standard of perfection, and be chronically fearful about the consequences if you should fail. It was this chronic fear of failure that was driving Ann's intense distress. Because of it, she lived in a constant "fight or flight" mode and drove herself way too hard.

The important thing to understand about Ann's experience – something all of us have in common – is that she was unaware of how her subconscious mind had latched onto these distorted ideas. At a conscious level she was smart enough to understand that the media-driven social norms of her day were exaggerated and harmful. In fact women's health was one of Ann's professional specialties. Her subconscious mind however, had a strongly different opinion. It had established what is known as a "subconscious repetition compulsion."

Subconscious repetition compulsions are endemic to human experience and everyone suffers from them. They occur when one or more distorted ideas in the subconscious mind cause us to repeat the same harmful patterns of behavior, thought, feeling and expectation. In Ann's case, the distortions "If I am perfect enough, everything will be alright," and "If I am not perfect, I will fail and be punished," would compel her to drive herself too hard, and if things weren't going well, to drive herself even harder in order to "make everything alright."

Ann's job wasn't helping her. It was her responsibility to advocate for the needs of the poor against powerful political interests. Every gain Ann made for the poor was the result of a long, hard-fought political battle and she was often under attack from unscrupulous adversaries. In this environment the distortions in her thinking played heavily against her because the consequences of failure went way beyond her own welfare: if she failed at her job, millions would suffer. She was constantly "sticking her neck out" on behalf of the poor. This is why her distress ended up concentrating in her neck. The subconscious mind will place unresolved mental distortion *symbolically* in the body in just this way as a means to communicate that something is wrong that needs our attention. In Ann's case, her mental impression that "her neck was on the line" had focused her excessive distress on her neck, where it caused her degenerative disc disease. When stress somatizes (becomes cellular) in the body as a means to communicate like this it is called "symbolic somatization," an important subject I return to in Chapter Four.

As soon as Ann discovered the distorted thoughts in her subconscious mind that were driving her distress, she was quick to let them go. In fact they struck her as absurd when she found them. Ann had never been in denial about the trials she encountered growing up. She was well aware she carried an emotional burden and had made good strides toward healing herself. She worked with a psychologist after graduate school, studied a number of good self-help guides and was part of a women's group at her church. It was just that the subconscious distortion in her thinking was deeply buried with a thousand memories in a place where she couldn't access it using ordinary means.

The simple fact is that *everyone* has distorted beliefs and expectations secreted away in their subconscious mind – thoughts that are driving their stress levels in the here and now, thoughts they aren't even aware of. People who have endured obvious tragedy early in life are not the only ones who suffer from this phenomenon. If you have done any living at all you have at least a few hidden, subconscious distortions in your belief system that are keeping you needlessly distressed. Indeed, it is often people who've had a seemingly "normal" life who suffer in silence from subconscious distortion, because they have little or no basis upon which to question their experience or even wonder if things could be different. The vast majority of people lead lives of quiet desperation. That's too bad. Life can always get better.

Ann also suffered from a sinister form of spiritual distress that affects a majority of people. She was devoted to God, like her mother before her. Though born a Christian, she was schooled in the philosophy of the world's great religions and meditated daily. She wanted to attain enlightened awareness and was certain it was out there to be had – a noble and realistic goal. Unfortunately, she hadn't been able to achieve her goal because of a third distortion in her thinking, one that was hurting her the most: deep down in her subconscious mind, Ann held the distorted belief that her father and God were alike.

It is universally common for young children to pattern their concepts of God on the example set by their parents. This tendency will work in your favor if your parents are saintly, but for Ann it was a disaster. God is always unconditionally loving and nurturing. As a perfect respecter of our own soul-inspired free will, God is eager to help us explore the limitless possibilities at our disposal, happy to help us make our own noble dreams come true, always compassionate and unconditionally loving. Ann's father had been the opposite of the Divine reality.

See the bind that Ann's subconscious distortion had set up for her? In the first instance, instead of pursuing God's standard of perfection, Ann was pursuing a "worldly" standard of perfection she inherited from her father and the culture she grew up in. This is always a mistake. In the second instance, every time Ann didn't quite measure up to this artificial standard, she worried that God would withdraw His care and affection, or worse yet punish her, just as her father had done when she was a little girl. When life was difficult, Ann assumed (based on the distorted logic in her subconscious mind) that she was a failure in the eyes of God and alienated from Divine grace. At a conscious level she knew this belief was ridiculous. At the subconscious level however, the stress she carried because of this distortion in her thinking was staggering – it was literally paralyzing her.

It was easy enough to dismantle the distorted thoughts that were causing Ann's spiritual stress. She used the tools in this book to achieve direct communion with God. There is a level of your mind – the super-conscious mind – where you are always in unbroken, constant unity with the intelligence that undergirds the universe. When Ann experienced this reality, she was easily able to break down her remaining delusion and fear. She found, contrary to what she had thought for decades, that God adored her just the way she was – always had and always would.

Ann came to understand herself at very deep levels – levels of herself she never even knew existed. She freed herself from the delusions that were imposed on her by her upbringing and cultural conditioning and as a result, leapt into a fairly high degree of enlightened awareness in a very short period of time. Then she began to delight in discovering who she really was. At the age of 35, having been a corporate success, a top-notch government executive and a powerful lobbyist, Ann discovered she really wanted to be a healer. If you knew Ann you might have concluded this was true by simply looking at her past – she was always taking care of people. It was one of her defining characteristics. She came into this life to be a healer. It was just that her early life conditioning had temporarily clouded her understanding of her own highest purpose for the incarnation.

Every stressor, no matter how formidable it may seem, contains endless potential for self-understanding and growth. On the strength of the self-knowledge Ann gained she returned to graduate school for training as a clinical pastoral counselor (a priest who specializes in healing). Her degenerative disc disease arrested and began to reverse, the pain went away, the strength in her right arm and leg returned, and she became truly happy for the first time in her life. She also became a truly gifted healer, author and public speaker. A fabulous new man came into her life who loved her for exactly who she was and they married. From this point on she began to live out her highest personal destiny and her distress became a thing of the past.

Why Are You Here?

If we were friends and I asked you to tell me your story, what would you say? In all likelihood you would tell me where you were born, where you went to school, where you work, how many children you have, and so on. You might mention some major accomplishments you can call your own. If there was something really significant that happened in your past you might tell me about that too, along with what you thought about it, maybe even how it changed your life. If you had strong beliefs about something like the state of the economy, the plight of the poor, international affairs, or women's equality, you might share these too. You might even share your hopes for a better future.

If, after you were finished, I asked you to tell me your *Story Behind the Story*, what would you say then? I might clarify: "So far you've told me about your history, but what I really want to know is who you are trying to become within your history? What have you learned about your own nature and the deepest meaning and purpose of your life? What are your own noblest hopes, dreams and ambitions and are you fulfilling them? In short, what is your soul-inspired mission for this incarnation and are you living it out?" At this juncture most people would say nothing because most people do not know the answer to the question.

When you end this life and look back on it, most of the things that stressed you out while you were alive will have no meaning to you whatsoever. Your mistakes and failures along the way will not be important, nor will your trials or losses, nor will the amount of money you earned, what house you lived in or how much influence and power you wielded while you were here. The only thing you will care about will be your *Story Behind the Story*: your own soul-inspired dreams and aspirations, and whether or not you were able to live them out.

Your life has a Divine purpose and you came to earth to discover what it is and live it out. No doubt you have glimpsed it now and then – everyone is inspired occasionally. However, you can assume that your experience in life so far and the conditioning imposed on you by your upbringing and your culture have obscured it, at least somewhat if not entirely.

What is the *Story Behind Your Story*? This is a question you must answer. If you can pursue it you will be able to fulfill your dreams with little or no distress. If you fail to pursue it you will endure internal strife, distress and hardship. Living outside your *Story Behind the Story* – by not learning the lessons that life is trying to teach you, misunderstanding or repressing your experience or allowing your cultural conditioning to obscure your own noble dreams and desires – is the root cause of distress.

The vast majority of us are guilty of all the above, and not because we're dumb or in denial. We human beings tend to ignore or "ride-over" experiences we find painful, frightening, difficult, shameful or otherwise challenging, so we can move on in life. We do it unconsciously, without even "thinking" about it. We do it because we have to in order to maintain our forward momentum – we have jobs, school, children and other important responsibilities that need our attention. We are quick to sacrifice our needs and our personal quest for meaning in exchange for the limitations imposed on us by the society in which we live. It's human nature. It's just not why we're here.

The good news is, if you can identify your own *Story Behind the Story* and live it out authentically, you can unleash miraculous mental power and attain great health, peace and joy. Your age, station in life, race, culture, gender or how much suffering you've had to endure don't matter. It really is that simple. Everyone's life has the potential for a supremely happy and noble outcome if they can discover their highest destiny and live it out.

Your *Story Behind the Story* is yours and yours alone. It cannot be compared with anyone else's. It is a function of three things that are entirely unique to you: your experience, how you think (your thoughts, feelings, attitudes, beliefs and expectations) and the degree to which you've chosen to exercise your free will to find ultimate meaning and purpose in life. You are an eternal soul that has traversed many lifetimes in search of ultimate truth. In this lifetime, as in every other, your soul has set you upon the stage of life on earth to find it.

Of course you were born with a long, rich history of experience behind you already. Whether you are aware of it or not, some of what you've known in this life is a direct function of thoughts, feelings, desires, beliefs and expectations that you carried forward into this incarnation from past lives. Because of what I do, people from all over the world often ask me to help them discover their past life experiences. Sometimes it is wildly helpful and I will show you how to do it in a later chapter. However, it is also true that your past life experience and the tendencies of thought, feeling, attitude and expectation you have as a result of it, are right under your nose.

If you want to understand your past and the degree to which it is informing your experience today, you can look in the mirror. You just need to learn how to look very deeply into levels of your self that most people never see or try to understand. Your self (your consciousness or mind) is literally infinite and immortal, so obviously there's a lot to discover here. Can you say you have any real understanding of what it means to be "infinite" and "immortal?" It is not enough to understand these terms from a philosophical perspective. I know many people who have an enviable grasp of the highest, purest philosophy passed down by the enlightened masters of their respective traditions. But it is not enough to "think" about supernal realities. You must directly experience Truth, know it in your bones, live it out, become it.

What You Think Is Governing Your Reality

Everyone's lessons and challenges in life are unique and each person's *Story Behind the Story* is their own. However we all share one universal goal: to discover what Jesus meant when he said "Ye are gods." What he meant is that we have the power to heal from all forms of distress and attain extravagant, super-human levels of peace, love, wisdom and joy. We have the power to live out our noblest dreams and aspirations and the power to remake our destiny if we so choose. We have the power to change not only ourselves and our own lives, but the lives of those we love, our community, our nation, our world. In short, we are gods.

If we are gods, why isn't life on earth some kind of Nirvana where everyone has the resources they need, justice and freedom prevail for all and each of us is busy living out our own dreams in joyous communion with everyone else? The answer is simple: we haven't created Nirvana on earth because the vast majority of the 7.4 billion people on the planet don't believe it is possible. This is why Vivekananda said, "All the powers in the universe are already ours. It is we who have put our hands before our eyes and cry that it is dark." The vast majority of individuals in the world today have succumbed to the conditioned illusion that they are sheep – just fallible, weak mortals. The fact is, if you knew for certain you were a god and had the power to make it happen, you would be living in Nirvana right now, because what you think (your attitudes, ideas, beliefs and expectations) are actually scripting your experience as you move through space and time.

Contrary to what many people believe, your thoughts are not confined to the privacy of your own mind. They exist in the form of subtle quantum (subatomic) energy – waves of electromagnetic energy – that broadcast through your body and out into the world over phenomenal distances, at superluminal speed (in an instant, with no time lost at all). Like energy attracts like: negative thought and feeling attract stressful events and troublesome people our way, while harmonious thought and feeling attract love, joy and success. This is a scientific fact substantiated over a century of research in the fields of quantum physics and subtle energy medicine and validated through recent brain imaging studies at Johns

25

Hopkins University. This is why The Buddha said "The mind is everything. What you think, you become." The Greek philosopher Socrates and his famous student Plato agreed. Their simple maxim was "As you think, so shall you be."

What the ancient Rishis and Rishikas knew 5,000 years ago has been proven by science beyond a shadow of a doubt: matter is made of energy and energy is governed by thought. Your thoughts about your own nature, the nature of the world and your prospects in life, are creating the very future you are experiencing as you move through time. Small thoughts about who you are and what you can do will create a small future and boatloads of distress. Larger-than-life thinking, as long as it is accurate, will create a destiny consistent with your highest aspirations and beyond.

This simple fact – matter is made of energy and energy is governed by thought – is the engine that drives karma. Master your thinking and you'll be able to control your karma. Direct your thinking in the right way and you will live out your highest hopes and dreams for the incarnation, free of distress. The truth really is that simple. The human mind however, is not that simple. It is a complex machine, one in which the vast majority of your thoughts, feelings, beliefs and expectations are going on "behind the scenes" at levels of your mind that you can't access without the right tools. That's where my methods come in.

Some years ago a book called *The Secret* became a worldwide bestseller. *The Secret* is based on the same scientific premise: matter is made of energy and energy is governed by thought. The Secret claimed that you can manifest what you want by thinking and imagining that you already have it. *The Secret* was a deep disappointment to its readers however, who gave their all to "think positively" about obtaining the objects of their desire (health, wealth, love and so on) without results. If *The Secret*'s premise is correct, and I assure you it is, why did these readers discover that positive thinking alone didn't deliver the desired results? The answer is simple: the only level of mind they were bringing to the task – the conscious mind – is the weakest, smallest part of the mind. If you want to realize your dreams, you need to be able to access and direct your thinking at *every* level of mind.

Most people are only aware of their conscious minds (their everyday thoughts, feelings, beliefs and attitudes) but there are other levels of the mind far more powerful, levels at which you are constantly "thinking" but unaware of it. Hidden behind the conscious mind is the subconscious mind. It is two and a half times the size and power of the conscious mind and you are living out much of your story there. Then there is the vastness of the super-conscious mind – what people commonly call the "soul" or "Spirit" (more on this in the next chapter). Every human being possesses super-conscious awareness and it is infinite in power. Here your story is being lived out in the form of your highest aspirations, the "knowledge" of why you came and your yearning for what is sacred.

For each of us, the resources in the subconscious and super-conscious minds constitute a limitless storehouse of insight and energy that can heal the body and mind, conquer the challenges of day-to-day living and sustain an extraordinary life of fulfillment and joy. The tools in this book will let you get in touch with these hidden dimensions of your mind. Armed with these tools, you will be able to do three things that are essential to your ability to live out your own *Story Behind the Story*, free of distress:

1. **Maintain the Right Attitude** – You must dare to dream. You are a god who was born in human form for the purpose of living an epic, heroic adventure – a life characterized by nothing less than total fulfillment, harmony, love and joy.

2. **Gain Your Freedom** – You must understand the themes, buried memories and unacknowledged lessons you learned from others that have distorted your beliefs and expectations about who you are, what you can do and how good life can be. These distorted, conditioned habits of thought are driving your karma, keeping you susceptible to distress and prohibiting you from realizing your awesome potential.

3. **Claim Your Power** – You must access the super-conscious dimensions of your mind, where you will find insight into your highest destiny and the power you need to create it. With this power you will be able to achieve any noble aspiration and conquer any obstacle that stands in your way, including your distress.

3

Miraculous Mind–Infinite Power

Learn how to master the power of your own mind and life will become your playground. There are actually four levels to the human mind, each more powerful than the last, rising all the way up to infinity. If you learn how to access and steer your thinking at all four levels you will gain astounding benefits. You'll be able to free yourself from distorted logic of the kind that keeps you susceptible to distress and limits your ability to pursue your dreams. You'll gain tremendous insight regarding your own destiny and the power you need to make it happen. Distress will be nothing more than a distant memory and every challenge will become a cause for eustress – the opportunity to make gains in understanding, progress and power.

In this chapter I describe the four levels of the human mind. Each level has different content and capabilities, each is accessed using a different type of "thinking" and each is susceptible to a different type of stress. The four levels of the mind are arranged in a hierarchy. I'll discuss each level, beginning with the weakest.

The Conscious Mind

The first tier of the mind is the one you are most familiar with and have the easiest access to: the conscious mind. It consists of your everyday thoughts, feelings, beliefs, perceptions, attitudes and expectations – the facets of your mind of which you are very aware. It is however the weakest, smallest part of the mind.

During the course of our waking hours a myriad of thoughts pass over the radar screen of our conscious minds. It's usually in an analytic mode – "Why am I stuck in this dead-end job? . . . Which dress should I wear to Verma's party? . . . How can we lower infant mortality in the slums? . . . Is this where I turn right to get to the university?" The conscious mind is also where we maintain our mental to-do list and it is usually awash with things like "Don't forget to pick up groceries for dinner." Occasionally the conscious mind is in the affirmative mode – "I'll finish this project on time no matter what!" Sometimes it is just observing – "I can't believe Sudha thought it would be a good idea to dye her hair red." Once in a while the conscious mind gives voice to powerful emotion – "If he doesn't stop flirting with my girlfriend, I'm going to punch him!"

Even though the conscious mind is the weakest, smallest part of the mind, it still packs a lot of power. At least up until now in the history of humankind, it's the part of the mind that is principally responsible for getting us where we are today. Just think of what we have accomplished by relying on it: the Internet, space travel, the United Nations, satellite communication, laser surgery, cell phones, 3-D printers. Almost any advance you can think of over the last 10,000 years of human history owes its existence in large part to the insight and power of the conscious mind.

Despite all that we accomplish using the conscious mind, it has limits and it is important to understand what they are. For one thing, the conscious mind is not as reliable or as objective as you think. What you "think" at the conscious level is actually a product of your conditioned habits of thought and the workings of your brain, all of which are highly subjective. Consider the mechanism by which we "see" an object – a new car, for example. A light wave from the car hits a receptor nerve cell in your eye. At the same time, electrical energy is running from your brain into this nerve cell. The two currents of energy meet and an electrical signal goes to the brain. Then the mind has to perceive or "interpret" the signal that's being received by the brain. That's where a lifetime of conditioning – your experience, education, belief system and general level of awareness – comes in.

At any step along this process, there is room for substantial error. If you have too little energy in your nerves – as would be the case if you are exhausted, sick or taking certain medications – you won't actually "see" correctly because insufficient electrical current is going to the brain. Or perhaps this is the first "car" you've ever seen, in which case you still won't "see" it accurately because your belief system provides no model for interpreting the signals received by your brain.

In 1998 I joined a humanitarian mission to heal the Shuar, a tribe of headhunters in Amazonian Ecuador. Most of the Shuar had never seen any form of modern technology. A Shuar colleague of mine on that expedition had left her native Shuar village years earlier to go to "the big city" to get an education. She described her experience the first time she encountered a door. Since the Shuar don't have doors on their grass huts, she stood for a long time in front of the door, pushing it, kicking it and growing increasingly frustrated. She did not "see" the doorknob because her mind had no basis for perceiving what she was looking at.

Before you say, "Well, those were a very primitive people . . . I'm not that unaware of things in my environment," think again. Research proves that the modern human brain receives more than eleven million sensory inputs every minute and that most people are only aware of about 2 percent of this massive wave of data! Clearly, the thing to take from this discussion is that your conscious mind is not as aware as you think it is. It is a part of your mind that is easily conditioned by the limits imposed on you by your upbringing and the larger society in which you live. It is therefore very limited in what it is able to perceive and do – something to "keep in mind" as you move forward.

The type of thinking that allows us to access and govern the conscious mind is analytic thinking: ordinary logic and reason. Logic and reason arise in your mind in your native language or perhaps two languages if you are bilingual. If you "think" about this for a moment you will realize that your conscious thinking, by definition, is accurate or inaccurate in direct proportion to your language skills. If you are poorly schooled or if your native language provides no conceptual basis for perceiving and understanding the world around you, your conscious thinking will be prone to distortion.

I defined the type of stress that preys on the conscious mind in Chapter One but the key concepts are so important that they deserve another mention here. To begin with recall that stress is triggered whenever there is an unacceptable disparity between our expectations and our actual experience. When this happens, fear arises and activates the biological "fight or flight" response.

Any event that triggers fear and sustains it in the mind, even imagined events, will activate the biological stress response. There are "classic" stressors like war, terrorism, natural disaster, economic or political oppression, racism, sexism, crime, psychological or physical abuse, the death of a loved one, chronic illness, acute pain and heavy responsibilities. There are also a host of more "subtle" insidious stressors that prey on people in modern, highly technological societies, all of which fall under the category of *fear of failure*.

The Subconscious Mind

Hidden behind the conscious mind is the subconscious mind – a storehouse of memories, deep feelings, desires, motives and knowledge of which you are not usually aware. It is gigantic in size and power compared to the conscious mind. Sigmund Freud provided a simple but accurate model for understanding the size-power relationship between the two levels of mind: "the iceberg model." The conscious mind is the tip of the iceberg, the part you see above the water. The subconscious mind is the part of the iceberg that's submerged and hidden, which is always many times larger than the "tip" you can see above the water line.

The subconscious mind has numerous functions. It plays a significant role in guiding your heartbeat, circulation, immune functioning and so forth. In fact, one of its principal jobs is to keep you alive. The subconscious mind also contains a library-like catalogue of your life experiences (including significant past-life experiences), along with the thoughts and feelings associated with important events from your past. You probably can't recall what you were doing, feeling and thinking during Diwali when you were three years old, but your subconscious mind has it all neatly tucked away in high definition.

There is still more to the subconscious mind. Carl Jung, Freud's colleague, first coined the phrase "the collective unconscious" to describe an aspect of subconscious memory that includes a storehouse of traces from man's ancestral past – the whole history of our evolution. Included in the collective unconscious are "archetypes," or basic human personality patterns that we live out – things like warrior, statesman, caregiver, seeker, sage, fool, teacher, artist, musician and so on. How many people do you know who live life like a battle that needs to be won, or are always taking care of everyone, or always playing practical jokes, or always on an adventure? In doing so they are fulfilling their own archetypal roles.

Over the course of many incarnations you will develop the gifts and talents associated with numerous archetypes. Some of these will evolve over millennia and are part of your "core" eternal nature. These are holy – God's way of expressing Himself/Herself through you. Even after reaching full enlightenment your "core" personality features will be preserved.

Sometimes your soul will decide to pursue an archetype simply because you want to have the experience of what it feels like. The reasons are two-fold. First and foremost, the soul is interested in obtaining a variety of experiences and it will drag us through numerous lifetimes until we check off all the items on our cosmic to-do list. The second reason is karmic – a choice you made in order to learn and evolve. Let's say in a past lifetime you were a wealthy Maharaja who owned hundreds of slaves you held with callous disregard. You might choose to be born a Dalit in a future incarnation just to gain the experience of what it feels like to be oppressed – a pathway to compassion for almost everyone!

Owing to these Divine dynamics, everyone possesses at least one major archetype in any given lifetime. Most people have a primary archetype and a secondary archetype and sometimes these can appear widely disparate: the statesman who is an avid gardener, the nurse (a healer archetype) who enjoys mountain climbing (the adventurer archetype). A few people are living out the gifts and inclinations of multiple archetypes. These people tend to be entrepreneurs who simply cannot be nailed down. It's not unusual for them to have multiple vocations and intense, diverse interests they pursue with gusto across their lifespan.

If you can access your subconscious archetype(s) you can better pursue your *Story Behind the Story* – your highest personal destiny for the life you're living. Living in a manner that's consistent with your natural archetype(s) will help you keep distress at bay. Imagine how it would feel if your primary archetype was "Adventurer" and you'd spent thirty years working at a desk in front of a computer in a small glass cubicle. You'd be so distressed you couldn't see straight!

Another very important characteristic of the subconscious mind is that it's *extremely aware* – far more aware than the conscious mind. Have you ever pulled up in front of your house after driving home from work and wondered just how you got there because you don't remember the drive home? Your conscious mind was so focused on something, a report that's due tomorrow for example, that you made the entire trip thinking only about your report. So who was driving the car? Your subconscious mind was driving it.

In fact your subconscious mind is in charge of everything you do by rote memory – standing, walking, brushing your teeth and so forth. Every time I drive through the streets of Delhi I'm reminded of this particular talent of the subconscious mind. Most drivers in Delhi have a lifetime of training behind them and they negotiate the congestion and mayhem with relative ease. I however, find the experience daunting because my subconscious does not have the benefit of years of practice.

The content of the subconscious mind is accessed using a type of thinking that is radically different from the "logic" we use to access our conscious minds. The subconscious mind is operated using symbolic thought – deep feelings, imagery, symbols, stories, myths and metaphors.

The type of stress that preys on the subconscious mind is *historical distress that has never been resolved*. Unresolved distress from events in our past causes sustained distortion in the thoughts and feelings that reside in the subconscious. This distortion will keep the biological stress response active in the here-and-now, even in the absence of current stressors. Perhaps you've had the experience of going on vacation with the express intent of getting away from your hectic, stressful job and getting some rest. You arrive at your dream destination and find your mind won't stop racing, you can't sleep and you can't enjoy the trip. In cases like this, your conscious mind may be on vacation but your subconscious mind is still at the office and has trouble letting it go.

When subconscious distortion is intense it can establish a repetition compulsion – a repetitive pattern of destructive thought, feeling and behavior. I introduced this topic in the last chapter. Remember Ann's compulsive drive to be perfect? Granted, her situation was complicated by the trauma of losing her mother and her father's subsequent bout with alcoholism. Much more often however, a subconscious repetition compulsion takes hold in the mind due to distortion that arises because of difficult but fairly commonplace events. As a case in point I recall a 55-year-old man named Ed who came to see me for help with chronic anxiety and anger. Ed also had a bad case of diabetes that he'd been unable to control with diet or insulin.

As I've mentioned, the subconscious mind will lodge unresolved distress in the body symbolically as a means to communicate that something   is wrong that deserves our attention. Diabetes is well-known to be stress-induced and it typically afflicts people who "have trouble digesting the sweetness of life." A quick conversation with Ed indicated this was very likely in his case. He pushed himself hard, worked nonstop and always kept his emotions at bay. He was also cynical and he didn't get much joy out of life.

I gave Ed a method he could use to access the content of his subconscious mind, the same method I provide for you in Chapter Eleven. Using this method Ed went back to a time when he was just four years old. Something had upset him and he'd started crying. His father took him aside and very sternly upbraided him. "Be a man," his father said harshly. "Boys don't cry. Emotions are for women." Feeling very frightened and intimidated by his father in that moment, Ed developed the attitude that it was whimsical and improper to feel and that he should always set his emotions aside and "be a man."

As soon as Ed found this episode in his subconscious memory bank, he also found the distortion in his thinking that resulted from the experience. He had compassion for himself as a little boy, rejected the tough lesson his father taught him decades before and decided he could open himself

33

more fully to the sweetness of life. Sure enough, he started enjoying things – sunrises and sunsets, the taste of a good meal, taking long walks holding hands with his wife – the pleasures of using his heart as well as his head. His blood glucose levels fell close to the normal range. He was able to quit his insulin and keep diabetes at bay just by monitoring his diet. He overcame his anxiety and anger and became happy for the first time in his life.

I share this true story because it illustrates an important point: the distortions in thought and feeling that lay hidden in the subconscious can be very subtle. You do not have to have suffered from obvious trauma in order to carry harmful distortions in your thinking at this level of mind – after all, Ed's distortion in thought was based on the conscious logic of a four-year-old! Remember what I said earlier in the chapter about the limitations of the conscious mind? In this case Ed simply wasn't intellectually or emotionally mature enough to understand what was going on when he was four. His father had in fact been a stern man who himself was raised with the credo "Boys don't cry." On the other hand he loved his son and would never have purposely harmed him. On this day however, Ed's father was maximally stressed and lost his temper – something that is fully understandable to the adult mind but utterly incomprehensible to a four-year-old.

Getting in touch with your subconscious mind will help you accomplish two things. First, you can discover and release old trauma, distorted beliefs and emotional pain that are fueling your distress in the here and now. Second, you can access your archetypes – the gifts and talents most endemic to your essential nature. If you live your life in a way that builds on your archetypal understanding of self, you can access the full potency and insight of your subconscious mind and use this powerhouse to your advantage. If you want to succeed in life, you have to acquire this level of self knowledge and fulfill its purpose. Only after you've done this are you free to decide whether you want to stay with the archetypal tendencies you've got or change them – something we do effortlessly by accessing the content of the next level of mind: the individual super-conscious mind, or soul-level awareness.

The Individual Super-conscious Mind

Hidden behind the subconscious mind is a third level of mind called the individual super-conscious mind. Most people know it by its popular name: the soul. It is here that we are most directly aware of our *Story Behind the Story* – our personal highest destiny for this life – and possess the power to make it happen. This level of mind is exponentially more powerful than the conscious mind and possessed of abilities that defy most people's imagination. It is for this reason that the nature of the soul is usually relegated to the realm of scripture and poetry.

To understand the power you possess at this level of your mind you have to have a basic understanding of how the universe is structured and how it works. To comprehend it let's look at it first through the lens of science, then through the inspiration of faith – two different means of comprehending the same extraordinary reality.

For the scientific perspective, we turn to the work of the world's great physicists. Most people today have a Newtonian view of the world, named after Sir Isaac Newton, the father of modern physics. He thought the world was made of discreet physical objects with empty space in between – but Newton was wrong. To understand how the world works, we have to look instead to the work of Albert Einstein, Neils Bohr, John Stuart Bell and a host of other great scientists who came after Newton. They proved beyond a shadow of a doubt that absolutely everything in existence (your body, flowers, air, sunlight, your computer, our planet and everything else in the universe) is made of energy.

Recall from your schooling in physics and chemistry that everything in the physical universe is composed of atoms or collections of atoms (molecules). What may appear to be solid – a table top or a mountain or your body – is actually composed of infinitesimally small atomic parts (protons, neutrons and electrons), which in turn are composed of even smaller subatomic parts (quarks and leptons), which in turn are composed of waves of quantum (subatomic) energy. Even things that have no measurable solid mass like the vacuum of empty space, exist as quantum energy.

Anything made of energy has its own electromagnetic energy field, so there is a unique energy field associated with every person, place and thing in existence. All of these fields overlap with and influence one another. Furthermore there is a single vast quantum energy field that exists behind the myriad number of individual energy fields that make up the entire universe. Within this universal field everything in the universe is instantaneously connected to and reacting with everything else, faster than the speed of light, with no time lost at all (what the physicists call *superluminal*). The universal field acts as if it were governed by one organized thought or "intelligence" to guide the energetic forces that make up our universe.

The universal field goes by several names in the scientific literature. Einstein called it "The Unified Field" and since his era a host of researchers and international scientific bodies have been hard at work refining our understanding of it. The average reader probably doesn't need or want to know the detail, but the reader who follows the field of theoretical physics will be aware of evolving models of understanding with names like "Superstring Theory" and "M Theory."

Our knowledge in this field is not just theoretical either. Studies in quantum physics, biophysics, neuroscience and subtle energy medicine over the last 25 years have proven that quantum energy is affected by thought (sometimes called *consciousness* in the literature).

Our ability to use "thought" to direct quantum energy is well-documented in the field of quantum physics, beginning with groundbreaking research at Stanford's National Accelerator Laboratory, which has produced six Nobel laureates in physics since 1962. The Stanford accelerator breaks apart atoms so the quantum energies that make up subatomic parts can be harnessed and studied. In the early 1990s Stanford researchers were among the first to document that quantum energy trapped within their accelerator was behaving in whatever way the researchers expected it to behave. This is well-known in the study of quantum physics today and contemporary research is done by scientists who observe these quantum energies 'from a distance' using sophisticated remote-sensing technology.

Our ability to use "thought" to direct quantum energy to effect change in ourselves or another person, group or situation has also been well-documented. A great deal of research is focused on improving our understanding of precisely how it works and how to increase its use in mainstream medicine. In the U.S. the National Center for Complementary and Integrative Health is actively conducting research in this area. If you want to know more about the science and current studies globally, visit the website of the International Society for the Study of Subtle Energy and Energy Medicine at www.issseem.org. We will revisit this subject in Chapter Nine where I teach a simple method you can use to move energy with your mind – a method that will help you achieve your dreams and desires more quickly.

The foregoing discussion leads me to the scientific definition of the individual super-conscious mind: a level of mind capable of sensing and influencing quantum energies. Whether you know it or not, your own super-conscious mind is at work in this moment influencing the energy fields associated with your body and the events you encounter in your day-to-day experience. It also influences other people, places and events, even those half a world away. Super-conscious thought travels at superluminal speeds so it is instantaneously able to influence space, time and matter anywhere. Likewise you are being affected by the thoughts of your family, your countrymen in India and the other 6 billion people on the planet.

Now let's turn our attention away from science and onto the religious view. Here we look to the teachings of the great enlightened Masters: Krishna, Mohammed, Buddha, Guru Nanak, Jesus, Mahavira, Moses and many others. They all taught the same basic truth: the universe is a manifestation of the mind of God, Brahman, Jehovah, Allah, Adonai, Sat, Nirvana, Tao, Spirit or other names appropriate to your religious perspective. As God "thinks" the universe comes into being and is sustained by God's intelligence, which is omnipresent within creation. We human beings are made in the image of God – each endowed with an immortal soul which is of the same substance as God and united with it, in much the same way that a wave is one with the ocean it rides on and shares its essence. The soul is God (Atman is Brahman).

Mahavira described the soul as "perfect knowledge, perfect power and perfect bliss." At the level of soul we are co-creating our experience in tandem with the universal, cosmic mind of God. As soul, we have the power to create our own future, to influence the collective future of the culture in which we live and to effect the future of the entire human species. Gain the actual perception of your own soul-consciousness and you will gain the power to heal and transform yourself, your life and your world based on how you think, pray and act. It has been said that all creation waits with eager longing for the sons and daughters of God (us) to realize our Divine nature and bring heaven on earth.

We do not have to look far for an example of the power of the soul. Mahatma Gandhi freed India from the British Raj through the use of what he called "non-violent soul-force." That same force is available to you, to be used for any soul-inspired purpose. People have a strong tendency to look at a Mahatma, idolize him and say "*That* individual was a fully enlightened being who was sent by God but I am just an ordinary human." This is a mistake. If Gandhiji had felt similarly, India might still be under the thumb of British colonial rule. Instead she is the largest democracy in the world and gradually becoming a world super-power. You should never think small, limiting ideas about who you are or what you came on earth to do. A Mahatma comes not just to illumine the path, but to show us how to embody it: your soul is God; you are not a mere mortal.

Your personal destiny for this life may not involve the liberation of millions of oppressed people, though you are free to choose such a destiny if you desire it. You may have come on earth to help create the next generation of the Internet or develop a water filtration system for the Ganga that runs on sunlight. You may have come to raise happy, visionary children who will usher in the enlightened age of humanity. You might have come to be a great teacher, musician, artist or statesman. Whatever your personal destiny may be, I assure you that you possess enough soul force to fulfill it. Learn how to tap the power of your own soul and the entire universe will mobilize to help you achieve your dreams.

The thing to take from the prior discussion is that science and religion are converging, with science now confirming what the ancient Rishis of India knew 5,000 years ago: we are all part of the same vast soup of intelligent energy, energy that is governed by super-conscious (soul-level) thought – yours and God's. Never forget that at this level of your mind, you and God are literally one. You are God come to earth disguised temporarily as a physical being in order to learn, evolve, play and love until such time as you gain enlightenment. You came on earth to live life as a god who is on a heroic, epic adventure. The universe is happy to give you anything your soul desires as long as it is consistent with your reason for being here. This is why God created the universe in the first place.

Now that we've canvassed the scientific and religious background, let's take a closer look at the characteristics of the individual super-conscious mind. It may surprise you to know how much scientific study has been applied to it over the last decade with the advent of new brain imaging technology. The science is very clear: when people enter the individual super-conscious mind (soul awareness) they know it. It doesn't feel at all like the ordinary stream of thought and feeling that flow through the conscious mind and it looks very different in brain imaging studies.

The individual super-conscious mind (soul awareness) is a state of consciousness in which the attention is highly focused and enhanced, one in which stressful everyday thought and feeling are set aside and a much more accurate level of insight and mental power emerge. Advanced meditators can enter this state with relative ease and high-tech brain imaging studies show specific changes in brain activity that result: brainwaves smooth out, left-right and front-back brain hemispheric communication increases, electrical activity and cell growth increase in the pre-frontal cortex and other critical brain areas, the emotional centers of the brain become relaxed and better regulated and the entire body enters "the relaxation response" (the biological opposite of stress).

I will come back to this subject – what it's like to experience the individual super-conscious mind – in subsequent chapters. Right now I am simply distinguishing it from the conscious and subconscious minds. The type of thought that allows us to access it and "steer" it is *intuitive thought* – a deep, immediate and accurate sense of knowing something that we could not necessarily know using simple logic.

Everyone has multiple intuitive experiences every day, it's just that they are very subtle and they often get "lost" in the frenzy of thought, feeling and sensation that is flooding through a person's mind. For this reason people tend to overlook or dismiss them. Sometimes they are not so subtle, however. If you are a parent, perhaps you've awakened in the middle of the night with a nagging fear that something is wrong with your son who is attending university far away. You call him on the phone and find out he's sick or very upset because he just broke up with his girlfriend. If you've had an experience like this you've directly experienced the intuitive knowledge of your super-conscious mind, which was simply reading the information in the energy fields associated with your son and his distress – knowledge that came to you as "instantaneous knowing."

The fact is intuitive awareness can be developed to a very fine art by anyone. I give you the skills you need to do it beginning with Chapter Seven, and if you use them consistently your intuitive awareness will become sharp and accurate. Very early in your efforts you will find that life gets a lot easier. You will know at a gut level for example, whether or not a person can be trusted or if they have harmful motives – an invaluable skill. You will be able to discern the subtle energies associated with any endeavor, understand why things are happening the way they are and accurately forecast future outcomes. You will just "know" whether to embark on a new business venture, if now is the time for a career move, whether your child should see a doctor, which classes to enroll in, or whether to feint left or right on the football field to make the goal. No issue is too large or too small for the soul. More importantly, you will be able to do something to change a situation just by "thinking" intuitively about it. There is nothing the super-conscious mind can't penetrate, comprehend and change for the better.

Develop your intuitive awareness and your compassion for others will increase because you'll be able to sense the nobility of their soul, which like yours is striving to find fuller expression. You will directly experience your essential oneness with other people and with the world around you – an experience that delivers a breathtaking sense of belonging, awe and joy.

While the gifts of intuitive awareness are many, it exists for one reason only: to help you pursue your *Story Behind the Story* – your highest personal destiny for this lifetime. Once you gain intuitive awareness of your path, you can choose to stay with the destiny you plotted out before you were born or change it. Remember Ann? She was well into her profession as a public health official when she developed soul-level awareness. Clearly, she carried the archetype of "warrior for the oppressed" in her subconscious mind because she was good at it. However, after she attained soul-level awareness she discovered other gifts and tendencies at work in the depths of her mind. At that juncture she was free to change her vocation and lifestyle in keeping with a different ideal. You can do this too. Attain super-conscious awareness and you can choose to do either: stay with your current destiny and make it better or script-out a new destiny altogether, one that's more to your liking than the one you are living out now.

The type of stress that can assail the individual super-conscious mind is much more serious than the stress that plagues the mind at lower levels. It arises when we ignore our *Story Behind the Story*. The reason this is true is that when you fail to pursue your own soul-inspired personal destiny, your soul and its power will remain essentially hidden and unavailable to you. If this happens your internal harmony will remain elusive and distress will run rampant at lower levels of your mind (the conscious and subconscious levels of the mind I discussed previously).

In the end it turns out that you cannot violate your own soul's highest purpose for the incarnation without enduring substantial distress. It may sound harsh but it's true: your soul doesn't actually care whether you are healthy, happy, earn a good salary, have a great love life or own tickets to the World Cup. It is delighted for you to have these things and more but not at the expense of your primary reason for being here.

The thing to take away from this discussion is that persistent failure to pursue your *Story Behind the Story* will alienate you from the power of your own soul, with disastrous consequences. By contrast when we dare to "live life large" by going after our noble dreams and deepest longings, our soul is delighted and God Himself will bend the very laws of the universe to give us what we want and need.

The Universal Super-conscious Mind

Individual super-conscious mind (soul-consciousness) is a gateway to universal super-conscious mind (God), which is infinite. It is impossible to describe infinite mind to someone who has not experienced it. There are no words, no poetry that can do justice to it. Lao Tzu, the fully enlightened master who founded Taoism, once said "He who speaks does not know, and he who knows does not speak." Trying to imagine universal super-conscious mind for someone who has never experienced it would be like an ant trying to imagine what it's like to possess the mind of a human being.

To understand the nature of universal super-conscious mind (God) we'll come at it using the same approach I used in the last section, by looking at it first through the lens of science, then through the teachings of the great masters.

For the scientific perspective we turn once again to the world's great theoretical physicists (Michio Kaku, Brian Greene, and others) who study Cosmology – the nature of the universe. Very recently scholars in this field discovered "the missing link," the knowledge that had eluded them for the last two decades. It turns out the mathematical equations that explain how our universe works only make sense if they account for a near infinite number of alternative universes. Some of these universes are physical (like our own) and some consist of energy. Some are larger than ours and some can fit on the head of a pin.

The ordinary mind cannot begin to imagine the magnitude or implications of this reality. The key word here is infinite: these universes go on and on, spanning multiple dimensions of time and space. Many coexist in the same physical space, if indeed you measure "space" the way most people do, using the dimensions of length, width and height. At last count however, physicists have identified 13 discrete dimensions. What this means is that there are multiple universes occupying the space where you sit as you read this book, and still the scholars are certain there is only *one* intelligent logic that explains how it all functions perfectly to sustain life as we know it.

The view from the standpoint of religion, though it predates the latest scientific discoveries by millennia, takes the science into account and goes beyond it. The highest teachings describe God as the source or "mind" which is projecting all of creation – an *infinite* number of universes, some physical and some made of energy (the heavens). God is creating all that is and is also that from which everything is made. In addition God exists "outside" of creation, where God's nature is pure cosmic consciousness – the essence of awareness itself. Outside of creation, God is that which cannot be described and cannot be delimited: infinite, eternal, omniscient (all knowing), omnipotent (all powerful) and all-loving.

The soul, being of the same substance as God, has one purpose: to traverse many lifetimes within the worlds of matter and energy until it evolves to the point where it can return to full, conscious merging in the cosmic infinite mind of God outside of creation.

You can attain universal super-conscious awareness (God awareness) via meditation: a form of highly focused concentration. Recall my statement a few pages back: your soul is one with God and of the same substance as God, much like a wave is one with the ocean it rides on and made of the same substance. In meditation the soul acts as a portal through which your mind expands to merge with the entire ocean. With this merging comes the experience of ever-new peace, joy and love that keep expanding without end – an experience known as *bliss* in the East and *ecstasy* in the West. When you gain this level of consciousness you will know the meaning of Paramahansa Yogananda's poetry, "I, a bubble of laughter, have become the sea of mirth."

The type of stress that plagues us at the level of the universal super-conscious mind is caused by spiritual ignorance: a failure to become consciously aware of our oneness with the Universal mind (God) or in other words, a failure to attain enlightened awareness. True, you are already one with God but for so long as you remain consciously unaware of it, you endure the stress of being *mortal*. This is the most lethal form of stress because as long as we think we are mortal we are susceptible to fear in all its forms – fear of death in the particular.

Just for argument's sake, try to imagine you've attained enlightened awareness for a moment. You could start by recalling the happiest you've ever been in your life. Maybe it was the birth of your first child, your wedding, college graduation or the first time you bought your own home. Then imagine multiplying that feeling a hundred times. This would be your starting baseline for the bliss that comes with awareness of the Universal mind, but it doesn't stop there. Next you have to imagine that this feeling of joy, peace and love keeps expanding, on and on without end. You are infinite energy, knowledge and power, one and the same with an infinite number of beings on an infinite number of worlds, all of which you cherish as a part of your own Self. On a whim you can savor any experience of your choosing. If there isn't a universe where you want to play, you simply create a new one just by thinking about it.

Get the picture? While this imagined scenario falls far short of the actual experience of enlightenment, it isn't wise to dismiss it as fanciful. The simple fact is that you just don't know how good life can be until you've achieved universal super-conscious awareness. Until you have it, you can't know how bad it is to live in the "mortal" consciousness you reside in now. Many people are ambivalent about attaining enlightenment for just this reason – they have no idea what they're missing. If they did, they would gladly give up everything they have or desire to obtain it. This is why Ramakrishna said, "If you are fortunate enough to be born in human form, and do not find God, you have wasted your life." Sure, you can re-incarnate again and again until you find enlightenment. You'll find it eventually. But the point is you can have it now. You can have the most wonderful, fulfilling life possible, a life so far beyond your wildest dreams you cannot imagine it, right now.

It's simply not that hard to come into enlightened awareness. You can do it and you will. It is your own true nature actually. You just need the right tools to get there and the right tools have only recently become available. The reason why they are available now is that God is ushering in the next age of humankind: an enlightened age wherein human beings use the power of their minds to manifest harmony and prosperity for all people – a topic I will revisit in the last chapter.

The Hierarchy of the Mind – A Reprise

It was upon the direct experience of his own mind's wondrous abilities that The Psalmist of the Hebrew Bible proclaimed "I am fearfully and wonderfully made." In this chapter I described the four levels of the human mind – a limitless storehouse of awe, knowledge and power. For each level I defined the type of thinking used to access and "govern" it and the type of stress associated with it. I've summarized this content in a table at the end of the chapter for your easy reference. As you move through the book it will help you to remember a few important characteristics of the hierarchy of the mind and how it operates.

The first characteristic is that the amount of power you can wield increases dramatically as you move up through the hierarchy. The first level, the conscious mind, is the weakest part of the mind. The second level, the subconscious mind, is almost three times more powerful. The third level, the individual super-conscious mind (the soul), is exponentially more powerful than the conscious mind, and the last level, the universal super-conscious mind (God), is infinite in power.

The second characteristic of the hierarchy is that the type of stress gets more serious as you move up through the ranks. The conscious stress you endure in your day-to-day experience is not as detrimental as the unresolved historical stress carried in your subconscious. Worse yet is the stress carried in the individual super-conscious mind by people who are ignoring their *Story Behind the Story* (soul-level stress). The worst form of stress is carried at the universal super-conscious level by people who have no interest in attaining any degree of enlightened awareness. This stress is lethal because it will keep you bound in the consciousness of being mortal and prevent you from experiencing your own eternal, infinite nature – the only thing that will make you absolutely impervious to fear.

The third characteristic of the hierarchy is not discussed extensively in the chapter though it is important to know. It has to do with how your mind was created in the first place and how it is being sustained. Your mind is actually "birthed" out of the mind of God so its starting place is at the top of the hierarchy – the only part of your mind that is eternal. To create you as an individual human being, universal super-conscious mind expresses itself as your soul. Your soul then expresses itself as your subconscious mind, which then expresses itself as your conscious mind. So the hierarchy of mind actually flows from the top down, not the bottom up. As a practical matter this means that universal super-conscious mind (God) must pass through your individual super-conscious mind (soul), then through your subconscious mind, in order for you to become aware of it at the level of your conscious mind. If your mind at lower levels is loaded with conflict and distress, your super-conscious mind will have trouble punching through it. This is why you must be concerned with stress – it can effectively cut you off from the God-given power you need to live a heroic life in pursuit of your highest destiny.

In the chapters that follow, I'll help you assess just how bad your stress is at every level of your mind – information that will be invaluable to you, your self-understanding, and your ability to live a life without limits.

Structure of the Mind – A Summary

	Level 1	Level 2	Level 3	Level 4
Scientific Term	Conscious Mind	Subconscious Mind	Individual Super-conscious Mind	Universal Super-conscious Mind
Popular Term	Ordinary self	Hidden self	The Soul	God
Type of Thought	Analytic	Symbolic	Intuitive	Meditative
Susceptibility to Stress	Arises when there is a disparity between our expectations and our actual experience	Historic distress that remains unresolved	Failure to pursue the *Story Behind Your Story*	Lack of awareness of the Universal Mind/ Alienation from God

4

Your Current Stress Rating

You can pretty much count on the fact you are more stressed than you realize. Studies show that people under-estimate their stress levels by about 50 percent on average. If you are a parent, you should know that parents tend to under-estimate their children's stress levels by nearly the same factor, or 43 percent to be precise.

The reason we tend to under-estimate our stress levels is that, by and large, we're all born into stressful circumstances. Then with every new stressor that comes our way we simply accommodate it. Most of us don't even know what it feels like to be free of stress because stress has characterized our life as far back as we can remember. This inclination of ours – to endure stress over time – is dangerous. Sure, you can endure for a while under chronic stress but not forever. It will eventually take its toll in the form of mental instability and physical illness. Way before it retards your health however, chronic stress will keep you unhappy, hurt your prospects and prevent you from realizing your dreams. For these reasons it is important for you to know just how much stress you're carrying.

In this chapter we take a closer look at the signs and symptoms of stress and how stress leads to illness. First I'll help you assess how much stress you're carrying in your conscious mind based on recent exposure to obvious stressors. Remember, there are four levels to the mind. Ranked in ascending order these are: 1) the conscious mind, 2) the subconscious mind, 3) the individual super-conscious mind (the soul), and 4) the universal super-conscious mind (God). Each level of mind is susceptible to a different type of stress and the stress associated with each level becomes more severe as you move up through the hierarchy.

I'm going to help you evaluate how much stress you carry at all four levels of your mind. When you're finished you'll have a complete profile that will give you valuable insight into your own *Story Behind the Story*. Your profile will help you target the issues that stand in your way and let you implement a strategy that will ensure you live out a destiny consistent with your noblest dreams and aspirations.

Current Stressors

The classic rating scale in the field of mainstream medicine is the Holmes-Rahe Stress Scale. It rates how stressed you are right now based on how many stressful events you have gone through in the past year. Then it correlates your level of stress with your risk of illness.

Before you take the test, ask yourself whether you think your stress levels are low, moderate or high. This is your pre-test self-assessment. Then take the test. It's easy. If an event on the list has happened to you in the past year, put a check mark in the column for that event. When you're finished, fill in the relevant number of "Life change units" for each event you checked. Then add them all together. The total you get will be your stress score – an indicator of how vulnerable you are to illness due to stress. There are two scales provided: one for adults and one for people 17 years old and younger.

Pre-test Self-Assessment

I think my current stress level is: Low   Moderate   High   (circle one)

The Holmes-Rahe Stress Scale for Adults

Life Event	Life Change Units	Check here if this event has happened to you in the last year	Life Change Units for every item you checked
Death of a spouse	100		
Divorce	73		
Marital separation	65		
Imprisonment	63		
Death of a close family member	63		
Personal injury or illness	53		
Marriage	50		
Dismissal from work	47		

46

Marital reconciliation	45		
Retirement	45		
Change in health of family member	44		
Pregnancy	40		
Sexual difficulties	39		
Gained a new family member	39		
Business readjustment	39		
Change in financial state	38		
Change in frequency of arguments	35		
A major mortgage undertaken	32		
Foreclosure of mortgage or loan	30		
Change in responsibilities at work	29		
Child leaving home	29		
Trouble with in-laws	29		
Outstanding personal achievement	28		
Spouse starts or stops work	26		
Begin or end school	26		
Change in living conditions	25		
Revision of personal habits	24		
Trouble with boss	23		
Change in working hours or conditions	20		
Change in residence	20		
Change in schools (you or your children)	20		
Change in recreation patterns	19		
Change in temple/mosque/church activity	19		
Change in social activities	18		
Undertook a minor mortgage or loan	17		
Change in sleeping habits	16		
Change in number of family reunions	15		
Change in eating habits	15		
Vacation (did you have one)	13		
Diwali or other festival participation	12		
Minor violation of law	11		

Total number of Life Change Units	XXXXXX		
(This is your overall stress score)	XXXXXX		

The Holmes-Rahe Stress Scale for People 17 and Younger

Life Event	Life Change Units	Check here if this event has happened to you in the last year	Life Change Units for every item you checked
Getting married	101		
Unwed pregnancy	92		
Death of a parent	87		
Acquiring a visible deformity	81		
Divorce of parents	77		
Fathering an unwed pregnancy	77		
Becoming involved with drugs or alcohol	76		
Jail sentence to parent for over one year	75		
Marital separation of parents	69		
Death of a brother or sister	68		
Change in acceptance by peers	67		
Pregnancy of unwed sister	64		
Discovery of being an adopted child	63		
Marriage of a parent to a step-parent	63		
Death of a close friend	63		
Having a visible congenital deformity	62		
Serious illness requiring hospitalization	58		
Failure in school	56		
Not participating in extracurricular activity	55		
Hospitalization of a parent	55		
Jail sentence to parent for over 30 days	53		
Breaking up with boyfriend or girlfriend	53		
Beginning to date	51		
Suspension from school	50		
Birth of a brother or sister	50		
Increase in arguments between parents	47		

Loss of job by parent	46		
Outstanding personal achievement	46		
Change in parents' financial status	45		
Accepted at college of choice	43		
Being a senior in high school	42		
Hospitalization of a sibling	41		
Increased absence of parent from home	38		
Brother or sister leaving home	37		
Addition of third adult to family	34		
Becoming a full-fledged member of a temple, mosque or church	31		
Decrease in arguments between parents	27		
Decrease in arguments with parents	26		
Mother or father beginning to work	26	.	
Total number of Life Change Units (This is your overall stress score)	XXXXXX	XXXXXXX	

After you add-up the Life Change Units in the right-hand column to come up with your overall stress score, compare your score with the figures in the following chart:

Score	Stress Rating	Risk of Illness
300 or higher	High	Maximum – practically a guarantee of stress-related illness in your future
150 to 299	Moderate	Risk of illness due to stress is 30% less than the maximum risk category
Less than 150	Low	Low to moderate risk of illness due to stress

So how does your score stack up against your pre-test expectation? Most people's pre-test assessment is off by an entire level: if they thought their stress was moderate for example, it turns out to be high. Most readers will find they are much more stressed than they thought, and that their health is at significant risk because of it.

Did some of the events on the Holmes-Rahe scale surprise you? It is hard to imagine that positive events like graduating from college or getting married are stressful but they are. To understand how this could be so, recall that stress is triggered in the conscious mind anytime there is an unacceptable disparity between our expectations and our actual experience. This disparity can work both ways however. This means that stress will assault you if your expectations are too high (I expect that my parents will never argue with each other) or too low (I do not expect to win the National Science Scholarship Award). Any major achievement can lead to some degree of fear and apprehension about the future and therefore has the potential to trigger the stress response.

The Holmes-Rahe Scale was developed and tested in cultural settings that were relatively secure and free of internal and external conflict or threat. If you or a family member have been directly victimized by civil unrest, crime, terrorism or war in the last year, you should take the stress of such events into account. If this is you, your overall stress score is significantly higher than the one you just calculated. In the absence of specific research and related data, it is impossible to quantify just how much stress and susceptibility to stress-related illness you carry now because of your recent exposure to such events. You will have to scale it for yourself. If you lost your family home or if a loved one was killed or severely injured for example, you can be rest assured that your overall stress score is higher by at least 50 Life Change Units.

The biggest benefit of the Holmes-Rahe Scale is that it has proven to be a solid predictor of your susceptibility to stress-related illness. If your self-rating was High or Moderate and you do nothing to ameliorate your stress, you are at serious risk of illness.

Signs and Symptoms of Stress

In this section, I provide a checklist of the common signs and symptoms of stress. To evaluate just how much stress you carry, check any symptoms that apply to you.

Psychological Symptoms:

___Poor memory/forgetfulness

___Inability to concentrate

___Confusion

___Excessive worry

___Irritability

___Impatience

___Poor judgment

___Seeing only the negative

___Racing thoughts

___Moodiness

___Anger

___Feeling overwhelmed

___Feeling lonely and isolated

___Sadness

___Feeling insecure or fearful

___Anxiety (see description below)

___Depression (see description below)

Physical Symptoms:

___Dry mouth

___Enlarged pupils

___Sweating

___Motor agitation/inability to relax/restlessness

___Jaw clenching

___Frequent headaches, backaches, neck aches or body aches

___Diarrhea, constipation, heartburn or stomach ache

___Nausea

___Sleeplessness

___Heart palpitations

___Rapid heartbeat

___Pain in your chest

___High blood pressure

___Dizziness

___Loss of sex drive/no interest in sex

___Frequent colds and flu

___Sleeping way too much or way too little

Behavioral Symptoms:

___Under-eating or over-eating

___Isolating yourself from others

___Angry or irrational outbursts

___Crying or feeling like you want to cry

___Procrastinating

___Neglecting your responsibilities

___Conflict in relationships

___Relying on alcohol or cigarettes

___Nervous habits (nail biting, fidgeting and pacing)

___Uncharacteristically poor performance

___Excessive work

How Serious Are Your Symptoms?

If you checked *any* of the items on the checklist you need to ask yourself how serious your symptoms are. People don't take their stress seriously enough. In particular, they tend to discount the psychological symptoms. This is true despite the fact that studies show psychological risk factors are the strongest determinant of future health and productivity. One recent study involved 47,000 individuals representing 22 companies and governments who were followed over time. According to this study the top two risk factors for poor health and high consumption of costly health care services over time were: 1) depression, and 2) stress in general. These two factors swamped all other causes of poor health, even things like diabetes, obesity, high blood pressure and smoking.

All this is to say, if you have any symptoms on the checklist then you should take your symptoms seriously. You also need to consider how frequent and intense your symptoms are. If you can't remember the last time you slept through the night then "Sleeplessness" is more than a symptom for you – it's an absolute nightmare. Serious symptoms will be those which are fairly frequent and noticeable, impair your work and relationships with others, hold you back from realizing your goals and keep you from feeling healthy, happy and self-confident.

Nearly every reader will find that they carry too many of these symptoms and the fiercely honest among you may conclude you need to take action right away. Not to worry. If you want to take action, you have the needful tools in this book.

How Stress Leads to Illness

It is important to understand why unresolved distress is so lethal. If you are already ailing in some way, this information will be invaluable to you. If you are not presently ill but suffer from high levels of stress, you should know the risks involved. If you know a loved one who is ill, you will be able to help them with the information in this chapter.

The most immediate harm done to the body by chronic distress is done to the brain and Sympathetic Nervous System (SNS). Using advanced brain imaging (magneto-enhanced electroencephalogram and functional magnetic resonance imaging), scientists have shown that chronic distress alters brain biochemistry and physiology in very harmful ways. A reduction of grey matter density (neuron death) in the prefrontal cortex is one serious result. This is the area of the brain behind your forehead that houses executive functions like reasoning, decision making and short-term memory. People in a chronic "fight or flight" mode experience insufficient and erratic energy flow to this part of the brain. Over time this causes brain cell death and dampened flow of chemical and electrical signals from neuron to neuron. This explains why distressed people can't think straight and can't remember things.

Parts of the brain involved in emotion and nervous system regulation – the hypothalamus and pituitary I mentioned in Chapter One plus the amygdala and hippocampus – are also hyperactive during the "fight or flight" response. Not surprisingly, chronically distressed people show definite changes in grey matter density (number and type of neurons) and biochemistry in these areas of the brain too. The hippocampus shrinks, the amygdala becomes inflamed and the entire HPA Axis is constantly on red alert. With chronic activation these parts of the brain and nervous system lose their ability to "turn off." The result is you can't relax or stop feeling terrified and angry, even when life is calm and non-threatening, because these segments of your brain can't stop producing stress chemicals.

Chronic distress has the same effect on the brain's default mode network, a region of the brain associated with introspection and self-referential thought and feeling. With chronic activation, this network also loses grey matter density and becomes biochemically dysregulated. The mind then becomes prone to negative, ruminative "me" thinking: *"How could this be happening to me? What is wrong with me? What will happen to me if I can't regain my strength?"* If your default mode network has been impaired by chronic distress, you will find this type of anxious, repetitive, negative thinking invading your mind often, no matter how you try to control it.

Sadly, without successful intervention these harmful brain changes become permanent or worsen, leading to significant mental and physical illness. Distressed people who do not take action to reverse these changes are very likely to develop clinical levels of anxiety, depression or both, as well as serious physical illness.

Chronic distress is the main reason why people succumb to depression and anxiety. These problems can be caused by other issues (for example, undiagnosed hypothyroidism), but nearly 85 percent of all cases of depression and anxiety are due to acute and chronic distress. Owing to the increasing magnitude of stress in society the incidence of depression and anxiety are steeply rising. In the U.S., one in every three persons will suffer from these conditions at some point in their lives. In India, the lifetime prevalence of depression is about 36 percent and at any one point in time, more than one out of five persons suffer from a diagnosable anxiety disorder. The World Health Organization estimates that depression will be the leading cause of disease in the world by 2030 – a greater cause of illness than hypertension, diabetes, heart disease, cancer or any other problem.

In India where the social stigma associated with mental illness is strong, people needlessly suffer in silence from depression, anxiety and other mental illnesses. Don't let this be you. These problems are common and they can be successfully treated. To help you discern whether you might have anxiety or depression, I've listed their symptoms in the table below. Only a mental health professional can accurately diagnose and treat anxiety and depression. If you have any of the following symptoms, please be wise and consult a licensed clinical psychologist or psychiatrist.

Anxiety	Depression
Five or more of these symptoms that persist for at least 2 weeks:	Five or more of these symptoms that persist for at least 2 weeks:
• Excessive, ongoing worry • Restlessness or motor agitation • Exaggerated view of problems • Irritability • Anger • Muscle tension • Headache, backache, or neck ache • Sweating • Difficulty focusing or concentrating • Nausea or heartburn • Sleep disturbance • Bouts of tiredness • Frequent urination • Trembling • Being easily startled	• Feelings of worthlessness • Sadness all day, nearly every day • Loss of interest in favorite activities • Loss of interest in sex • Excessive feelings of guilt • Difficulty focusing or concentrating • Feelings of restlessness • Thoughts of death or suicide • Trouble making decisions • Fatigue or lack of energy • Sleeping too much or too little • Change in appetite or weight • Bodily pain, usually muscular

You can see that on the surface, anxiety and depression appear to be opposites. Anxiety is usually accompanied by excessive, exaggerated worry about everyday events and hyper-activity. Depression tends to be dominated by feelings of sadness, guilt, lack of self-worth, in-activity and withdrawal. However, the truth is not so simple. Anxiety and depression often go together. More than half the people who have depression also have anxiety. This is known as "agitated depression." If you have it, you will have symptoms from both columns in the table.

As you can observe, the symptoms listed for anxiety and depression are almost identical to the symptoms of stress. The difference between the symptoms of stress versus those for anxiety and depression lies primarily in their intensity and how chronic or persistent they are over time. The reader should also be aware that there are different types of anxiety and depression – all the more reason to see a properly credentialed mental health professional if you have any of the symptoms listed in the preceding table.

Distress, depression and anxiety activate the Hypothalamic-Pituitary-Adrenal (HPA) axis, causing sustained arousal of the SNS and high levels of circulating cortisol, epinephrine and norepinephrine. These stress chemicals have been shown to redistribute body fat, increase heart rate, increase blood pressure, cause plaques in the arteries, weaken arterial walls, weaken the heart muscle, increase inflammation throughout the body and suppress immunological function. SNS dominance (the medical term for chronic biological distress) also harms basic cellular metabolism, which directly contributes to the development of diabetes, cancer and many other illnesses.

The biochemistry of stress I just outlined goes a long way to explain why distress makes us sick. The strain placed on the brain, mind and body by a chronic long-term "fight or flight" response is more than they can bear over time. Any physician will be quick to assure you that chronic stress will make you ill. Almost 80 percent of all visits to a family physician in the U.S. are for stress-related symptoms.

Basic biochemistry however, does not explain why one person develops heart disease while another person develops breast cancer and yet another develops early Alzheimer's in response to chronic distress. The explanation for this phenomenon – the differential presentation of stress-related disease – has chiefly to do with what is going on in the mind of the individual.

Because of my expertise people come to me from all over the world looking for a cure for every type of mental and physical illness. In many cases their physicians have told them that chronic pain, depression, anxiety, dysfunction, disability or even the specter of death are unavoidable. Most of these people come to me in a state of despair   for understandable reasons, certain that their illness has caused their despair. That is usually when I introduce them to the most basic rule of mind-body science. "If that's what you think," I say, "you've put the cart before the horse." Most people who are emotionally or physically ill got that way because, whether they knew it or not, they were unhappy with their lives to begin with.

You might not believe this is true. You might point to a family history of diabetes, a congenital heart disorder, or the degradations of twenty years of smoking. You could insist "These are the reasons I'm sick." True, there may be hereditary and lifestyle factors that are relevant to the onset of your suffering, but they are not the original cause of illness. More importantly they are not the best keys to a cure. The key comes in a simple but powerful revelation from the field of mind-body science: any chronic health issue you might have – mental or physical – corresponds directly to some level of distortion in your thinking and the unresolved inner conflict and distress that are resulting from it. Recall Ann's problem with degenerative disc disease, or Ed's problem with uncontrollable diabetes? In both cases, unresolved distress was fueling the onset of their problems and making them more severe with the passage of time. When the historical distress was removed, they both healed quite nicely.

Once distress arises, there are three stages at which we can intervene effectively to heal from its effects. The first stage is "in the moment," when distress first arises in response to a specific stressor – the loss of one's job for example, or physical abuse from a family member. Ideally, we can talk out our fears and concerns and receive the help we need at the very point the stressor occurs. However, this is not always possible. Sometimes, unaware, intolerant or abusive family members, teachers, employers or others prevent or prohibit us from working out our thoughts and feelings. Sometimes trauma comes at us so fast and furiously we only have time for crisis management. If a flood destroyed your family home, all your effort would go toward survival, with little or no time devoted to handling the traumatic stress. Or perhaps you've had the experience of purposely setting aside your own emotional needs in order to care for those you love – like the teenager who quits school after his father dies, so he can work to support his family. For these and other valid reasons, we tend *not* to deal fully with distress at the point it first occurs.

If we are unable to deal with our distress when it occurs, the thoughts and feelings associated with it do not go away. They haunt us in the form of unrelenting fear, worry, anger, grief, shame, guilt, resentment and other powerful negative emotions. If we carry these emotions long enough without release, they end up getting pushed down into the subconscious mind where they fuel a continual "hidden" distress syndrome. The thing to understand about this process is that the original conflict stays alive in the subconscious. At a conscious level, you may think the worst of the crisis is behind you. However, in the subconscious mind where your memories reside it is happening *now* – every minute of every day. You are simply unaware of it. What you do become aware of is a baseline level of anxiety or depression, the single most obvious and prevalent symptom of chronic distress. This is your subconscious mind's way of telling you that something is wrong that deserves your attention.

The second stage of intervention we have at our disposal involves dealing with the effects of a historical stressor after-the-fact using psychological or spiritual means. A good part of my clinical practice is involved with this very thing: liberating people from the effects of past conflicts and distress. It doesn't matter what the issue is or how long ago it happened: the woman who comes into forgiveness and understanding four years after a difficult divorce from an unfaithful husband; the man who comes into self love and acceptance after being raised by a shrewish unhappy mother who berated him often when he was a child; the soldier who comes into peace after being dogged for years by the vivid recollection of battlefield trauma. There is nothing in your past that can harm you, define you or confine you if you make up your mind to be free of it. There are good psychological and spiritual tools you can use to free yourself from it entirely (for example, the tools in this book).

When the subconscious mind is liberated from the burden of old conflict and distress, life starts getting truly fantastic. The first thing that happens is you become free of anxiety and depression, a huge gift in itself. The second thing that happens is you end up with much more power at your disposal – power you can use to realize your noble ambitions. This happens because the power that had been utilized by your subconscious mind to deal with old conflict and distress is no longer needed for that purpose and is now available to you for any purpose of your choice. It's like making the last payment on a long-term loan. All of a sudden you have that money to use however you see fit.

Even more important, once you find liberation from unresolved subconscious distress, your "soul force" will become more available to you. This is true because, in order to come into your conscious awareness, your individual super-conscious mind (soul-consciousness) must *pass through* your subconscious mind. If your subconscious mind is loaded with conflict and distress, your soul-consciousness has trouble punching through it. When the subconscious is free and clear of distress, soul-consciousness will more naturally arise in your mind. At this point you will feel as if you've been *reborn*.

Let's say however, that for some reason you do **not** intervene after-the-fact to free yourself from the burden of unresolved conflict and distress. In this case, you will remain handicapped by depression, anxiety and distorted thinking. What happens next is that your subconscious mind will take matters into its own hands. It will take the negative energy associated with your unresolved distress and place it in your body in the form of illness. In doing so, your subconscious is making a desperate attempt to convey to you that something is seriously wrong and you can no longer afford to ignore it.

The subconscious mind is much smarter than you think. It is aware that you cannot pursue your *Story Behind the Story* for so long as you continue to ignore unresolved conflict and distress. The subconscious is also aware that this inner conflict is keeping you alienated from your own soul awareness and therefore alienated from God. To your subconscious mind, this is an intolerable state of affairs that is directly opposed to your reason for being here. So it takes action and it does it in a very predictable way.

When the subconscious mind places the energy associated with your distress in your body as illness, it does it in a way that *symbolizes* the distorted thinking at the heart of your conflict. This is the way the subconscious mind communicates. Recall from Chapter Three that the subconscious mind "speaks" using symbol, metaphor and imagery. The subconscious mind's symbolic way of placing illness in the body as an attempt to communicate the nature of the underlying problem is fairly obvious. For example:

- People who develop diabetes tend to be those who are driven to perform and won't slow down long enough to "enjoy the sweetness of life."

- People who develop heart disease tend to be people who've suffered too much love loss – hence they suffer from "a broken heart."

- People who develop arthritis tend to be people who block their emotions, in which case their emotional "rigidity" ends up getting transferred to their joints which then become inflamed.

- People with lower back problems tend to be people who feel as though they are always in a state of confrontation with the world and have to gird their lower back in order to "heft the demands of life."

This action of the subconscious mind – its tendency to symbolically embody the mental or spiritual cause of unresolved distress in the cells of your body – is called "symbolic somatization." Somatization is a term derived from the Greek word *somaticos* which means *cells of the body*.

If you suffer from illness in the mind or body then you have arrived at the third stage of intervention. It is still not too late for you to discover and liberate yourself from the mental conflict and distress that are fueling your health problems. Do this and you will find that healing will proceed much more quickly and completely. For your benefit and for the benefit of those you love, I have summarized the most typical underlying mental and spiritual causes for each of 48 common physical and mental ailments in the Appendix. If you are already ill and if you have a bonafide diagnosis from a medical doctor, you should take a moment to look up your diagnosis in this Appendix before you move on.

Eustress Versus Distress

It's a good idea to have a better feel for the two types of stress. Remember, stress can fall into one of two camps. It is either:

* *Distress* - a harmful and intense emotional, cognitive and biological reaction, or

* *Eustress* - a sense of being challenged, maybe agitated or fearful, but in control of the situation.

Remember the frog in the pot of boiling water? It's a slippery, fast slope to move from eustress to distress and fail to realize it until it's too late. The difference between the two types of stress is not so much a matter of how many symptoms you have. It is more about how intense and long-lasting your symptoms are. By definition severe and long-lasting symptoms constitute distress while symptoms that get resolved readily with intervention are eustress. Anxiety and depression that are stress-induced are, by definition, extreme forms of distress. All forms of distress have disastrous consequences for health and wellbeing however.

To get a better feel for the distinction between the two types, let's take a closer look at the cognitive process that triggers stress in the first place. Recall that your cognitive process – your thoughts, perceptions, attitudes, beliefs and expectations – will determine whether you experience distress or eustress, not the stressor itself. This process begins with a stressor of some sort – your boss doesn't like your work on an important project, you are abused by someone you love, you don't have the money to send your children to school or you have a parent who is dying. In response, your cognitive process comes into play to determine the stressor's impact on you, your loved ones and your future. Part of this cognitive process takes place in the subconscious, so some of your "logic" is hidden from your awareness. You may not even know all the thoughts, perceptions, attitudes, beliefs and expectations that are involved in your analysis. What you do become immediately aware of is your emotional response. Your emotional response will chiefly determine whether you experience distress or eustress.

If your cognitive analysis indicates that the stressor constitutes a high risk of harm and you are powerless to do anything about it, your emotional response will be intensely negative. Fear, anger, guilt, shame, frustration, self-loathing, hatred, resentment and other harmful emotions will arise in direct response to your analysis. When negative emotion is intense and unrelenting, the "fight or flight" response is also intense and unrelenting. Distress is the usual result. One chief characteristic of distress is that you must work very hard to overcome it once it is initiated. That's why it is better to prevent it from happening in the first place. Don't worry. I'll show you how to do both: prevent it and intervene effectively when it occurs.

For now I just want you to understand the mental process that gives rise to distress in the first place and something about what it feels like. With distress, emotion is strongly negative, persistent and overpowering. Ruminative, destructive "me" thinking occupies the mind and won't stop no matter what you do. It becomes increasingly difficult to control your emotions and behavior. You have several symptoms from the stress checklist and they are frequent and intense. Positive attitudes like courage, determination, faith, love, hope and optimism, are absent or nearly absent. This gives rise to a biological stress response that is similarly intense and chronic. The two then "feed" off of one-another in a vicious cycle: the biological response contributes to further distortion in thought and feeling, which continues to fuel the "fight or flight" impulse. Distress runs rampant.

Eustress feels different from distress. Eustress will arise in one of two cases. The first case applies to situations where your cognitive analysis promotes less acute, less negatively charged emotion. While the biological stress response gets initiated, it is less intense and with intervention it resolves more quickly. While you are experiencing it, you feel challenged but confident you can manage the stressor, perhaps even work it to your advantage. You might feel a little fear or anger but you also have a sense of faith, hope, trust, optimism, determination, courage and love – the heroic attitudes and feelings you need to surmount your challenge.

Eustress will also arise in a case where your cognitive analysis promotes intensely negative emotion but your heroic attitudes are of such great magnitude and force that you are able to master your negative feelings. The biological "fight or flight" reaction gets initiated and it may be strong, but your heroic attitudes have the effect of dismantling the negative emotions that are fueling it and it resolves quickly. This type of eustress typifies the experience of successful career soldiers on the battlefield. While their stressors are among the most intense imaginable, they manage the resulting negative emotion with extravagant amounts of faith, hope, courage and love – in this case, love of country, love for their fellow soldiers, love of family or even love of honor itself.

Eustress therefore may or may not be accompanied by the intense negative emotion that characterizes distress. With eustress, if strong negative emotion arises it is mastered then dismantled by heroic attitudes like courage, faith, hope and love. Without the negative emotion to fuel it, the biological stress response cools down more readily. Eustress is usually shorter in duration than distress and easier to resolve with intervention.

While there are a host of negative emotions that come into play during the mental calculus that precedes the onset of stress, fear is always somewhere in the mix, but it may not be the most prevalent emotion that rises in your awareness. Let's take anger as an example because anger can also initiate the biological "fight or flight" response. Anger is a secondary emotion, which means it is a response to another feeling. The most frequent cause of anger by far, is fear. Shame can also give rise to anger. Or to be more precise: a "fear of being shamed" gives rise to anger. Guilt can work both ways too, which is to say that guilt can cause both fear or anger.

Often fear and anger are both present in the emotional response to a perceived stressor. It's just that one emotion expresses more strongly than the other. Whether a person responds to a stressor chiefly with anger or with fear will depend mostly on their degree of self-esteem. If you have strong self-esteem you will most likely get angry in response to a perceived stressor and you'll have a strong "fight" response. If you have poor self-esteem your prevailing emotion will likely be fear and you will want to flee from the stressor. Either emotion – anger or fear – will trigger the biological "fight or flight" response.

The precise "mix" of emotions you experience and their intensity, including whether you tend more toward anger or toward fear, will be a function of your early-life exposure to stressors and the conditioned habits of thought you've acquired because of them. The conditioned habits of belief, attitude and expectation you brought forward from your past incarnations will also factor in your emotional response to a stressor.

61

The thing you should take away from this discussion is the process itself: 1) a stressor triggers a cognitive analysis; 2) the cognitive analysis triggers an emotional response, and; 3) the nature and intensity of the emotional response will determine whether you experience distress or eustress.

Before You Move Ahead

If you checked any of the items on the symptom list you should ask yourself how long you've had your symptoms and whether you can tie them to specific stressors. If your symptoms are stress-related you should be able to identify at least one stressor responsible for the onset of your symptoms. It is always wise to consult a medical doctor for a physical exam. The signs and symptoms of stress can be caused by other physical problems, certain medications or even toxic chemicals in your environment.

In any case always keep in mind that stress makes people ill and if it goes unchecked it will become lethal. Please be wise. If you are already unwell, be sure to seek conventional medical treatment in response to your needs. Use the methods in this book to greatly magnify your health and happiness but be sure to also use good conventional medical care if you need it. Use *all* the tools available to you, and be well.

5

Your Historical Stress Rating

Your Holmes-Rahe score gives you an objective understanding of how stressed you are at a conscious level right now based on your recent exposure to stressors. However, it does not reflect the extent to which your own thoughts (perceptions, beliefs, feelings and expectations) are keeping you stressed out and unhappy on a day-to-day basis. There are a host of distorted thoughts that will keep you distressed and sabotage your efforts to find happiness, even in the absence of current stressors. Distorted thinking drives stress-building behaviors or tendencies. In the scientific literature these tendencies align themselves according to specific typologies. For example:

The Perfectionist

Do you feel a constant pressure to achieve?

Do you criticize yourself often?

Do you feel you haven't accomplished enough, no matter how hard you try?

Do you give up important things (like eating) in order to be the best at what you do?

Do you set unrealistically high goals and fret when you can't achieve them?

The Control Freak

Do you have to be perfectly in control at all times?

Do you worry about how you appear to others when you're disheveled or nervous?

Do you feel that any lack of control is a sign of weakness or failure?

Do you fail to delegate work to others because they won't do it right?

Do you think there is only one right way to get something done?

The People Pleaser (also known as The Martyr)

Does your self-esteem rise and fall based on everyone else's opinion of you?

Are you better at caring for others than caring for yourself?

Do you keep most negative feelings inside to avoid displeasing others?

Do you do things for others even when it involves inappropriate levels of self-sacrifice?

The Shrinking Violet (also known as The Incompetent)

Do you feel you can never do as good a job as other people?

Do you feel like an impostor when told your work is good?

Do you wait for other people to make things happen?

Do you pretend you know what someone is talking about even when you don't?

Do you compare yourself to others all the time and find yourself lacking?

The Worry Wart

Do you always see the glass as half empty rather than half full?

Do you constantly gnaw on problems throughout the day?

Do you spend a lot of time ruminating about the past?

Do you worry even when things appear to be going smoothly?

Do you always anticipate another problem on your horizon?

The Con Artist

Do you tell little white lies that make it appear you're more capable than you are?

Do you often put difficult tasks off until the last minute?

Do you blame your mistakes on other people, or claim credit that isn't yours?

Do you gossip about other people to make yourself feel important?

The Speed Freak

Do you race through the day as if you are on fire?

Do you fail to take time to relax every day?

Do you get terribly impatient when events arise that slow you down?

Do you fail to pay attention to what's going on around you?

Do you fail to see the humor in situations others find funny?

The Narcissist

Do you get angry and blow your top when things don't go your way?

Do you always look to other people for the source of your problems?

Do little things irritate you badly?

Do you feel justified being rude to other people?

Do you think, by and large, that other people are stupid?

Can you see tendencies on these lists that apply to you? You may not fit one of these typologies. For example, you may have one or two tendencies of **The Perfectionist** and some inclination toward being **A People Pleaser**. Whatever your tendencies may be, it is important for your wellbeing that you do not dismiss them as mere human frailties or entrenched personality characteristics. These tendencies, and others like them, are driven by distorted beliefs, assumptions and expectations that are secreted away in your mind as a function of your exposure to stressors early in life. This includes the mental conditioning imposed on you by your family and culture. These tendencies do not define who you are or your possibilities. While it seems like they are permanent, they are not.

In fact they are all signs of unresolved inner conflict and distress from your past that still reside in your subconscious mind.

There is no objective scale for subconscious stress, no Holmes-Rahe equivalent for assessing the amount of stress you carry today that is a result of unresolved conflict from your past. Such matters are usually discerned as a function of private discussions with a licensed psychologist or enlightened teacher. However, you can scale how much stress you carry at the subconscious level – low, moderate or high – using the information I provide in this chapter.

How to Rate Your Subconscious Stress

To scale the stress you carry in your subconscious mind, you only need to do two things: recall how many stressful events you've experienced in your past, then ask yourself in all honesty whether you fully resolved them or whether they are still haunting you.

To do this, start with the obvious. Go back to the Holmes-Rahe Scales in the last chapter, and ask yourself if any of the stressors on either list have happened to you at any time in your past. Make a little notation next to any event that applies. Then ask yourself if you've had to endure any obvious stressors in the past that are **not** on these lists. If you are elderly, perhaps you were exposed to the civil unrest that occurred during and after Partition when you were a child. Perhaps you or a member of your family has been the victim of violent crime, terrorism, civil unrest or forced relocation. Maybe you were in an auto accident or your best friend died when you were young. Whatever these historical stressors may be, for now just write them down.

Now it's time to give some thought to the conditioning factors imposed on you by your family of origin and culture – conditioning factors that may have caused you to adopt limiting ideas about who you are and what you can do, making it difficult for you to live out your *Story Behind the Story*. These conditioning factors are more subtle than obvious trauma – sometimes very subtle indeed – but they are equally stressful. Many years ago a lovely woman in her mid-forties came to me with an interesting problem. She suffered from hypertension (high blood pressure), was carrying more than fifty pounds of excess weight and wanted to do something about it. Under her doctor's supervision, she had been following a stringent weight-loss plan of only 1,200 calories a day for three months. She had not cheated on her diet and engaged regularly in moderate exercise, but she actually *gained* three pounds. Her doctor was stupefied because her situation defied the laws of biochemistry. Her unusual circumstances had a benefit however: they persuaded her that her weight problem had a mental component, which made her open to the idea of working with me to find a solution.

Significant weight gain is almost always a function of distress due to internal emotional conflict that hasn't been resolved. Even in cases where there is a biological cause for weight gain – hypothyroidism for example – unresolved distress is usually the causal agent for the biological problem. The same is true of hypertension: the original cause is most often unresolved conflict and related distress that is associated with too much love loss. To be sure, my client had all the earmarks of chronic distress. She was depressed and anxious, socially isolated, had trouble sleeping at night and had difficulty concentrating at work. Like many people, she was unaware of her excessive distress but (at the prompting of her doctor) very concerned about her weight and blood pressure.

Using the technique I provide in Chapter Eleven she went back in time to unravel the cause of her problems. Very quickly the source of her difficulty became transparent to her. It turned out that her father had been very reserved while she was growing up and she became a people pleaser in an effort to gain his love and attention. In fact, she came to define her own self-worth based on the degree to which she could satisfy her father's whims – a trait she carried into adulthood. As an attractive people pleaser, she had no trouble gaining the attention of men. Not surprisingly, she found herself falling in love with men who were emotionally closed-off and unable to give her the love she needed, just like her father.

The result was that, over the course of her adult life until the age of 40, she'd been through a string of painful, failed relationships with men. Her experience led her to conclude that love relationships simply weren't ever going to work for her. Her subconscious mind then fixed on the distortion "If I am attractive men will like me, I'll get involved and I'll get hurt again. I am better off alone." This distortion was keeping her overweight and unattractive, despite her ultra-low calorie intake. It was also keeping her in a state of forlorn lovelessness, which in turn was driving her hypertension.

When she found this distortion at work in her subconscious mind, she freed herself from it by realizing there was nothing wrong with her – she was a lovable person who could find healthy love with a man. She was able to take control of her life after that, achieve her ideal weight, regain a healthy sense of self-esteem and move forward into a bright future, free of distress. Her blood pressure fell into the normal range.

I share this example to demonstrate just how unique each person's response is to their past. My client's experience with her father was hardly traumatic. But she was a very sensitive, loving woman who wanted badly to be loved in return. This was her archetype: she was a lover, something she carried into this life as a function of her past incarnations. Had she been born with the archetype of a warrior, she might have been relatively unmoved by her father's disregard. In fact she might have been quite a handful as a child and given her father a good bit of grief! But that was not her *Story Behind the Story*. Her soul chose to locate her in a family where she would have to learn a very sophisticated lesson: she was lovable just the way she was. She needed to learn to take her cues about her identity from her own soul and deny the personality of *"People Pleaser"* that had been imposed on her by her conditioning.

After you come up with your list of stressors from the past you need to ask yourself whether you've fully resolved them. Even distress relating to horribly tragic events can be resolved completely if you have the right resources and knowledge at your disposal. Everyone should consider their historical stressors in stages. Stage one is the stressful experience itself – let's say your father died when you were eight years old, an acutely stressful event.

The second stage involves how you reacted to it. If your mother and extended family were lovingly supportive, they would have helped you understand the loss had nothing to do with you and given you a great deal of nurturing. Your mother would have remained a rock-solid symbol of love in your life. If all these things were true, you'd probably be able to heal from the distress created by your father's death and you'd develop good emotional resilience too – you would probably become a pro at dealing with stressful circumstances later in life.

However, what if life were a lot less loving and a little more complicated after your father died? Perhaps your mother was too wrapped up in her own suffering to pay attention to your needs and left you alone to figure out what to do. In this vacuum, you may have reacted to the distress with any number of likely distortions in your thinking: "I must've done something wrong for this to happen … I'm going to fry in hell for the argument I had with Dad before he died … I deserved this … Mother is never going to rally … I'm screwed." You'd feel swamped by shame, guilt, confusion, powerlessness and a sense of abandonment, as if life were over. Those patterns would sink into your subconscious and haunt you through life. Every time you encountered a new stressor – like your boss telling you that your work on an important project was awful – you'd respond with shame, guilt, confusion, powerlessness and a sense of abandonment.

You'd be haunted in this fashion until such time as you sought to heal yourself through psychological or spiritual means later in life.

If you've endured stressful circumstances in the past and you never had the opportunity to heal from them, you can be sure there is distortion in your thinking and feeling that is keeping you prone to distress in the here and now.

Your Subconscious Stress Rating

Now sit back and ponder the unresolved stressors from your past: the obvious traumas as well as the subtle stressors you endured as a function of your conditioning. Also consider whether you have any of the subconscious stress-building tendencies I listed at the beginning of the chapter. To the extent you possess these tendencies, realize they are an indication of the degree to which your subconscious mind may be holding onto distorted, negative beliefs, self-concepts and expectations. Now rate yourself by circling the number that best reflects your subconscious distress as it exists today, according to the following scale.

Subconscious Stress

1 ------ 2 ------ 3 ------ 4 ------ 5 ------ 6 ------ 7

A one on this scale indicates you are entirely free of subconscious distress and conflict that has carried forward from your past – a highly unusual rating that would apply only to a few very enlightened individuals. A rating of seven indicates that you're swamped with unresolved grief, fear, anger, shame, guilt, poor self-esteem or other negative emotions and you have the stress-enhancing tendencies to show for it.

Once you have scaled your response to this question convert it to the same rating scheme we used for Holmes-Rahe. If you scaled yourself as 1 or 2, your subconscious stress is *Low*. If you scaled yourself at 3 to 5, your subconscious stress is *Moderate*. If you scaled yourself as a 6 or 7, your subconscious stress is *High*. Whichever rating applies to you based on your self-scaling, place it in the table below under Stress Rating.

Level of Mind	Stress Rating (High, Moderate or Low)
Subconscious Mind	

Whatever your rating, realize it is well within your means to liberate yourself entirely from unresolved historical distress. Make it your goal to be free of it, realizing it's part of your *Story Behind the Story* to be rid of it once and for all. Only if you jettison it will you know what it's like to live your life as an epic, heroic adventure. I'll show you how to do it in the pages that follow.

6

Your Spiritual Stress Rating

So far you've used the Holmes-Rahe scale to rate your stress at the level of the conscious mind based on your recent exposure to obvious stressors. You've also rated the subconscious stress you carry as a function of exposure to stressful events in the past.

Now I'll help you take a look at the level of stress you carry at the super-conscious level.

Recall that stress at the individual super-conscious level (your soul) arises if you are unable to pursue your *Story Behind the Story* and stress at the universal super-conscious level (God) arises if you feel alienated from the Universal Mind. I designed the questions and self-rating scales in this chapter to let you assess your level of stress – high, moderate or low – at both levels of mind. Your answers to these questions will give you an understanding of:

- The major twists and turns of your life, how they've affected you, how you've reacted to them and the extent to which they've confined or liberated you.

- How well you've fared so far relative to your expectations, dreams and desires.

- The major themes threading through your experience and what they imply about who you are and where you're going.

As you move through this self-assessment you might also gain more clarity with regard to how much stress you still carry in your subconscious. If this happens you can always revise your subconscious stress rating when you're finished with this chapter.

The self-assessment in this chapter requires a little time and thought. You can choose to complete the entire assessment now or just read over the questions, move on through the book and come back to this assessment later. Either way the degree of self-knowledge you gain from this assessment will open your eyes. It will allow you to see your life as an adventure featuring you as its hero or heroine – something you must do in order to access your power.

All you'll need for this self-evaluation is a pad of paper or a computer and some time set aside to consider the texture of your life and what you've learned from it. Then answer the following questions with as much honesty as you can muster, at a pace you find comfortable.

1.   **Who are the five people who've had the biggest influence on you?**

Go back as far as you can remember. List each name and write a sentence or two explaining why you've chosen this person. Keep going beyond five if you want to. Be sure to list people who've been a bad influence, not just the mentors and saviors.

2.   **What are the five major events that have shaped your life?**

The key here is to identify the events that have had the greatest impact on you, for the good and for the bad. Again, go back in time as far as you can remember. Write down each event and a sentence about why it was important. Remember powerful personal events like marriage or the birth of a child. Be sure to consider events that have had an impact on you from a cultural perspective (Partition, the wars with Pakistan, the economic reforms of the 1990s, emergence of the Internet and so on). If you can think of more than five life-changing events, write them down.

3.   **What really jazzes you in life?**

Give this careful thought and write detailed answers. Has a particular passion had an important place in your world for as long as you can remember? Do you love dancing, sports, travel or community service? Is there a cause that moves you or a specific philosophical, political or religious theme that underscores your outlook? How might your interests have changed over time, and

71

why? For example, you may have had a long-standing love of medicine and entered medical school, but dropped out to support your family and never went back.

When you're finished thinking about this question, try to synthesize all aspects of your history as they relate to "what really jazzes you in life" and then sum them up as a metaphor(s) for who you really are. For example, at heart are you a healer, warrior, lover, sage, statesman, mother/nurturer, caregiver, musician, artist, writer, public servant, entrepreneur, saint or something else? Your answer to this question will help you gain clarity with regard to your archetype. You may have more than one. Write them down.

4.   Write down your life script.

Write down your history in two or three pages as if you were writing a synopsis to the Bollywood screenplay of your life. Do it in chronological order: birthplace, family of origin, schools, moves, jobs, important relationships, memorable accomplishments, major setbacks, lost loves and so on. Chronicle the five major people and five major events at the point they occurred, along with important events relating to the things that jazz you. Also write down major turning points in your attitudes about life – the big "AH HAH" moments. If you suffer from illness or infirmity of any kind, write down approximate dates for the onset of these conditions, whether you received treatment and anything else that comes to mind regarding your health over time.

5.   Rate yourself according to each of the following scales.

What follows is a series of highly personal self-rating scales I designed to provide you with a snapshot of where you are. These will help you understand yourself more deeply and provide a baseline against which you can measure your future progress. These scales are not quantitative, scientifically validated psychometric testing methods, and this is intentional. This means *I'm not* scoring you, *you are*. You won't be able to compare your scores with anyone else's.

Now score yourself using the following twelve scales. Rate yourself based on your own attitudes, expectations, thoughts and feelings. These are seven-point scales – a rating of one is the best outcome and a seven the worst. Rate yourself by circling the number that best represents your self-assessment. Be sure to read the guidelines for each scale.

5a.   How aware are you?

1 ------ 2 ------ 3 ------ 4 ------ 5 ------ 6 ------ 7

How present are you to what is going on in your environment, your body and mind? A rating of one indicates you are immediately aware of changes in your health, mental state and the world around you. A rating of seven indicates a profound lack of awareness regarding all three.

5b.   How serious are your health concerns?

1 ------ 2 ------ 3 ------ 4 ------ 5 ------ 6 ------ 7

If you are presently unwell, rate how serious your problem is. A rating of one represents a condition that is irritating and slightly debilitating. A rating of seven would represent a major life-threatening condition like heart disease, cancer or severe depression.

5c.   How mobile and functional is your body?

1 ------ 2 ------ 3 ------ 4 ------ 5 ------ 6 ------ 7

Rate your body's overall level of mobility and functioning. A one indicates outstanding mobility and functioning (you are a track star) and a seven indicates little or no mobility and/ or functionality. Rate yourself with the use of physical aids if you need them (a wheelchair, cane or orthotic device for example).

5d.   Rate your physical pain.

1 ------ 2 ------ 3 ------ 4 ------ 5 ------ 6 ------ 7

Rate your pain on a scale of one to seven, with one being no pain at all and seven being the worst pain you can imagine.

5e.   How happy and joyful do you feel?

1 ------ 2 ------ 3 ------ 4 ------ 5 ------ 6 ------ 7

A rating of one on this scale means you're happy and joyful all the time and a seven means you are unhappy almost all the time.

5f. **How successful are you in your major life role?**

1 ------ 2 ------ 3 ------ 4 ------ 5 ------ 6 ------ 7

Measure your success relative to your most important role in life as you define it. The question is equally applicable to the CEO of a major corporation as for a stay-at-home mom. If you feel strongly you have two equally important roles in life (say that of being a great husband and that of being a successful entrepreneur) then scale your success in both roles. A rating of one means you're highly successful and a seven just the contrary.

5g. **How much meaning and purpose do you get out of life?**

1 ------ 2 ------ 3 ------ 4 ------ 5 ------ 6 ------ 7

Define meaning and purpose in whatever way works best for you, then scale your status. A rating of one means your life is richly abundant with meaning and purpose and a seven means you feel a total vacuum in this regard – questions like "Why am I here?" never cross your mind.

5h. **How good are your most important relationships?**

1 ------ 2 ------ 3 ------ 4 ------ 5 ------ 6 ------ 7

Consider the strength of your relationships with family, friends, colleagues and lovers. A rating of one indicates your relationships are mutually supportive and highly rewarding, while a seven indicates your relationships are, by and large, harmful.

5i. **How well do you like yourself?**

1 ------ 2 ------ 3 ------ 4 ------ 5 ------ 6 ------ 7

This is a self-acceptance scale. A rating of one indicates you respect yourself and you're very happy with who you are. A rating of seven indicates you have no self-acceptance whatsoever (you can't stand yourself).

5j. **How good is the love in your life?**

1 ------ 2 ------ 3 ------ 4 ------ 5 ------ 6 ------ 7

A rating of one indicates a life rich in love from any number of sources: a girl or boy friend, spouse, family members, friends, a family of faith, business associates. You can be single and still feel richly loved. A rating of seven means you have no love in your life whatsoever.

5k.   How would you rate your overall personal growth?

1 ------ 2 ------ 3 ------ 4 ------ 5 ------ 6 ------ 7

A rating of one indicates that you're extremely satisfied with your rate of personal growth (you've been continually making progress despite obstacles) and a rating of seven indicates you are extremely dissatisfied (no personal growth at all).

5l.   How difficult do you think your life has been so far?

1 ------ 2 ------ 3 ------ 4 ------ 5 ------ 6 ------ 7

A rating of one indicates you've had a great life (no complaints). A rating of seven indicates you've had the worst possible life story – the only luck you've ever had is bad luck.

5m.   How heroic are you?

1 ------ 2 ------ 3 ------ 4 ------ 5 ------ 6 ------ 7

A rating of one indicates you are undaunted by any obstacle, have never shied away from a challenge and have many times stuck your neck out to achieve a goal, despite your fears and insecurities. A rating of seven indicates you've never really put yourself on the line for something you believe in, never stretched yourself to overcome your fear and never accomplished much of anything. Your tendency is always to hang back.

6.   Develop a list of strengths and challenges

Now go back to questions one through five and review your assessment so far. Be sure to look at the big picture as well as the trends and details. Then, using a piece of paper or your computer, create two columns on a page. At the top of the left column write "Strengths" and at the top of the right column write "Challenges."

Start with your strengths. Keep going until you've identified at least five. They should leap out of your assessment. For example, perhaps your life has been very difficult (scale 5l) and your physical pain high (scale 5d) but you consider yourself happy (scale 5e), are making good personal progress despite your difficulties (scale 5k) and you're heroic (scale 5m). That's extraordinary and you need to explain why that is. Perhaps you are strong-willed, courageous and innately optimistic or maybe you are a person of deep, abiding faith in God. Whatever it is, write it down in the Strengths column. Even if your assessment paints a despairing picture you will still be able to identify at least five strengths. You are a survivor. Ask yourself why you think this is so and write it down.

After you've finished your list of strengths move on to your challenges. These should also leap off the pages of your assessment. Has lack of awareness or an inability to trust others complicated your life? Have these or other challenges caused you to lose in love or otherwise miss opportunities to fulfill your dreams? If so write it down. Perhaps you are alone and overly alienated from other people? Why? Or perhaps you need to develop more self-acceptance. If so you'll want to identify what stands between you and better self-love and respect. Write down at least five challenges you can identify. Do the best you can. You can return to this list later after you've made gains in self-understanding.

7.   **How well have you lived out your story so far?**

1 ------ 2 ------ 3 ------ 4 ------ 5 ------ 6 ------ 7

Given the results of your self-assessment, how would you rate your performance as the lead character in the story of your life? A rating of one signifies you think you've done a great job moving through your life given what you've had to endure. A rating of seven means you'd give anything to have the chance to go back and do it differently.

Time to Look Deeply in the Mirror

Before you continue, take a few minutes to appreciate the uniqueness of your story and its beauty. No matter how you answered question seven, I assure you that if you had to go back and live your life again using only the knowledge you had at the time, you'd live it out precisely the way you have. There's nobility in that – regardless of how you feel about your life. You've learned things you would not have learned otherwise and accomplished things that were important to you and those you love. There is greatness in you and in your history and there's a good chance this greatness has escaped your attention. Physical or emotional pain or past trauma might be obscuring it for you, but it is there if you know how to see it.

It is possible to find beauty or ugliness in anything you look at or anything you experience. If you look closely at a painting by a great master you'll find some of the brush strokes aren't quite right. If you focus on what's negative, that's what you'll see. If instead you think of your life as an epic adventure in self-discovery with you as its hero, you'll see something else entirely – something inspirational and affirming. Why not start right now?

I invite you to step entirely outside your life now and look at it as though you are reading a novel or watching a movie. Find the audience appeal in your story. See the triumphs and losses, the joys and betrayals, the great breaks and the missed opportunities as part of a heroic saga that has an underlying purpose. Ask yourself:

• What are the major themes in this saga?

• What is the central mission of the hero (you)?

• What are your strengths and how has the "screenplay" hidden them or brought them to light?

• What are your flaws and how does the "action" challenge you to overcome them?

• Who are the "bad guys" and other antagonists that confront you on your mission and how do you deal with them?

• What constitutes justice for you and how do you try to get it?

• When and how are you aided on your quest – can you see the hidden hand of God at work in your story so far?

If you have any form of illness in your body or mind, look very closely for metaphorical and symbolic meaning in your story. Did the hero break his back after he tried to carry the weight of the world on his shoulders by working two jobs to support his family? Did the heroine develop congestive heart failure after a string of lost loves?

Now write down the most essential things you can appreciate about your life as an epic journey in self-discovery, about you as hero or heroine. You are beginning to see your *Story Behind the Story*.

Your Complete Stress Profile

After you conduct the self-assessment you will be able to complete your stress profile: a snapshot of how stressed you are at all four levels of mind. You've already rated your stress as high, moderate or low at the conscious and subconscious levels. Go ahead and move these ratings forward from the last two chapters to the table below.

Level of Mind	Stress Rating (High, Moderate or Low)
Conscious Mind	
Subconscious Mind	
Individual Super-conscious Mind (Soul)	
Universal Super-conscious Mind (God)	

Now you can rate yourself for the remaining two levels of mind. If you completed the self-assessment in this chapter you'll be able to do it effortlessly.

To scale your stress at the level of the individual super-conscious mind (soul), review your self-assessment with particular attention to scales 5a through 5k. Also look at your answer to question 7 and be sure to look at your list of strengths. These indicators will reveal how well you feel, how much love and happiness you have in your life and the degree to which you've pursued your dreams and aspirations. When you're finished reviewing this material, rate yourself by circling the number that best reflects your individual super-conscious stress as it exists today, using the following scale.

Individual Super-conscious Stress

1 ------ 2 ------ 3 ------ 4 ------ 5 ------ 6 ------ 7

A one on this scale means you are a rock star when it comes to fulfilling your highest personal destiny: you are happy, well-loved and loving, doing what you enjoy and making great progress toward pursuing your dreams. A rating of seven indicates you are unhappy and unwell, feel alienated and alone, take little or no pleasure in life and haven't really accomplished much – the concept of a heroic destiny is the farthest thing from your mind.

After you scale your response to this question convert it to the same rating scheme we used before: low, moderate or high. If you scaled yourself as 1 or 2, your individual super-conscious stress is *Low*. If you scaled yourself as a 3 to 5, your stress is *Moderate*. If you scaled yourself as 6 or 7, your stress is *High*. Whichever rating applies, place it in the preceding table under Stress Rating for the Individual Super-conscious Mind.

Now you're ready to look at your stress at the level of universal super-conscious mind (God-awareness). To do this, simply rate yourself according to the following scale.

How well do you know God?

1 ------ 2 ------ 3 ------ 4 ------ 5 ------ 6 ------ 7

This question is not designed to assess your religious practices or philosophical understanding but whether you actually experience God. A rating of one would indicate you have all the fruits of enlightened awareness: you directly perceive God's presence in yourself and the world around you, you feel an essential oneness with other people and nature, you have keen intuitive awareness, a peaceful mind and a loving heart that are almost impervious to distress, and you live in a constant state of joy. A rating of seven indicates you have no awareness of God or The Universal Mind whatsoever or you do not believe God exists.

Now convert your answer. If you scaled yourself as 1 or 2, your universal super-conscious stress is Low. If you scaled yourself as a 3 to 5, your stress is Moderate. If you scaled yourself as a 6 or 7, your stress is High. Whichever rating applies, place it in the table under Stress Rating for the Universal Super-conscious Mind.

Time to Move on

Whether you chose to complete your stress profile now or finish it later, when it's done you will have a baseline measure of your stress at all four levels of mind. The vast majority of readers will find they are carrying too much stress at all levels – a serious issue that deserves attention. Other readers will find their profile highlights very specific areas that merit further attention and focus.

Whatever the results of your profile, you have learned a great deal about stress and its impact on the brain, mind and body. You have also learned that you contain tremendous power at deeper levels of your mind. Beginning with the next chapter you will have the tools you need to free yourself from distress completely and claim your power.

Part II
The Methods

This section of the book contains simple yet powerful methods you can employ to free yourself from distress and live out your highest destiny. They will allow you to achieve enlightened awareness, create a lifestyle that assures your health and happiness, free yourself from the past, find your *Story Behind the Story*, heal yourself and others, and influence the course of events – all the necessary ingredients for a fearless, heroic life lived in joy.

7

A Gift from the Gods—Scientific Meditation

Both my parents were scientists who greatly valued learning. My father was an internationally prominent biochemist who spent his life finding a cure for brain cancer. Science and public service were his mantra and he brought me up to think the same way. My fond childhood memories are of countless hours spent in my father's chemistry lab, working under his tutelage. Back then if you asked me about my religious beliefs, I would have said I had none. I wasn't the most likely person to embrace meditation.

I went off to Brandeis University in 1966, determined to get an M.D. and a Ph.D. and follow in my father's footsteps. Brandeis was a crucible for radical thought at that time. The U.S. was in turmoil over the war in Vietnam and the scourge of racism was ripping apart the cultural fabric. Enthralled by the climate for social change at Brandeis, I quickly traded my white shirt and tie for fatigues and long hair and spearheaded a number of anti-war and anti-discrimination campaigns. I'm afraid I vexed my poor mother sorely during those years.

In 1969 Dr. Richard Alpert, now known as Baba Ram Dass, returned to the United States from a long stay in India. His father was one of the founders of Brandeis and when Ram Dass returned he lectured a class I was taking. His personal charisma was overwhelming. He spoke of the infinite power of the mind and of his experiences in India, where his guru regularly demonstrated the ability to foresee the future, heal the sick, change events and otherwise defy the limits of time and space. He taught a simple meditative technique as a means to access this power – a power that exists in everyone.

That first seminar with Ram Dass stirred my soul and awoke a sleeping giant within me. I'd never experienced anything like the peace and joy of meditation. In the blink of an eye, the rigorous scientist and social reformer had discovered the liberating qualities of Spirit.

Meditation Is for Everyone

Meditation is the single most effective means you have at your disposal to conquer distress, fulfill your dreams, and live-out your highest personal destiny. Researchers in the field of mind-body medicine have documented a huge array of specific benefits that derive from meditation. Here is a brief summary of its clinically proven benefits:

- Invokes the human relaxation response (the opposite of stress)
- Improves immune system function
- Lowers blood pressure
- Improves circulation
- Lowers heart rate
- Reduces plaque in the arteries
- Increases energy and stamina
- Shortens recovery time from surgery and medical procedures
- Releases endorphins and other "feel good" chemicals in the brain
- Reduces dependency on medication
- Provides freedom from chronic pain
- Reduces the frequency of illness
- Vastly improves rates of recovery from illness
- Increases grey matter density and improves neurological function in 8 brain regions:
    - Prefrontal cortex – executive functions
    - Frontopolar cortex – meta-awareness
    - Sensory cortices and insula – interior body and exterior relational awareness
    - Hippocampus – memory consolidation and reconsolidation
    - Anterior and mid cingulate; orbitofrontal cortex – self and emotional regulation
    - Superior longitudinal fasciculus; corpus callosum – intra- and inter-hemispheric communication

- Alleviates depression

- Lowers anxiety

- Promotes clear thinking, happiness and peace of mind

- Prolongs life

This is a **very** impressive list. If you could develop a pill that delivered these benefits, everyone in the world would want it and you would end up very rich indeed!

The first item on the list deserves special mention. Dr. Herbert Benson at Harvard, the father of mind-body medicine in the West, was the first to show that meditation invokes the relaxation response – the biological opposite of stress. During meditation, heart rate and breathing slow and circulation normalizes so blood flow is restored to the brain, kidneys, digestive system and other vital organs. The muscles, tendons and ligaments of the body – taut like bowstrings during the "fight or flight" response – relax completely. The heart muscle, which is in overdrive when we're stressed, regains its ability to pump blood through the body without strain or deterioration. Pulse and blood pressure go down. The fragmented and erratic thinking brought on by stress are replaced with a calm, serene mental clarity. Dr. Benson proved that the human relaxation response can be achieved with as little as 20 minutes of meditation each morning.

Meditation is also a panacea for the prevention and treatment of physical ailments. Its ability to stop stress, improve circulation, amplify disease resistance, reduce plaque in the arteries and lower blood pressure make it the ideal health insurance strategy. It has been shown to improve rates of recovery from a variety of illnesses, especially heart disease, hypertension, cancer, stroke, ulcers, asthma, arthritis and immune problems like fibromyalgia. It is instrumental in the management of physical pain. Indeed, it can wipe out pain altogether. It also reduces dependency on medication and reduces the toxic side-effects of pharmaceutical regimens like chemotherapy.

Meditation has an especially wondrous effect on the brain. Recall the harmful effects of distress on critical brain structures from last chapter? Regular meditation has been shown to reverse these effects and even go beyond restoration to build new brain capacity.

Meditation has been proven to increase the production of new brain cells and speed neurological processing in 8 key brain structures, beginning with the pre-frontal cortex. Recall this is where we conduct our executive functions: planning, problem solving, verbal reasoning, multi-tasking, use of working memory and ability to pay attention. This part of your brain also governs your ability to initiate, control and monitor your behavior. Everyone can use more strength in these areas. Meditation also grows new neurons and restores neurological activity in brain regions involved in the production of stress hormones (the HPA Axis), memory and memory consolidation (the hippocampus), emotion regulation and self-control (the amygdala) and self-referential thought and feeling (the default mode network).

Try to imagine what you could do if your brain worked more efficiently, accurately and faster than it does now. Studies indicate the average person only uses about 10 percent of their existing brain capacity. Meditation can increase this percentage, to give you a substantial edge over others when it comes to your ability to perceive, understand and problem-solve quickly.

Meditation also has a number of mental benefits which have substantial impact on our quality of life and (because distress in the mind ultimately causes illness in the brain and body) our physical health. It substantially reduces fear, anger, anxiety and depression. It delivers mental clarity, peace of mind, joy and optimism. It increases energy in the mind and body and thereby delivers greater mental and physical stamina.

The spiritual benefits of meditation have been documented and understood by enlightened teachers and their followers for millennia. In fact all the physical and mental benefits of meditation I've mentioned in this chapter so far actually derive from its spiritual effects. These are essentially threefold. First, during meditation the mind and body are saturated with extravagant levels of healing quantum energy from the cosmic mind. Second, meditation expands the intuitive insight of your individual super-conscious mind (soul). Third and most importantly, it is the only sure means by which you can access the infinite power of the universal super-conscious mind (God). Guru Nanak said, "One cannot get to Him (God) through reason, even if one reasoned for ages." Reason won't get you to God but meditation will.

Regular meditation will bring you profound insights and vast amounts of power. You can use this power to master your health and wellbeing, your day-to-day pursuits, your most deeply held dreams and ambitions – any and all goals critical to understanding and living out your destiny. Regular meditation will help you perform faster and better. It will also move you into expansive states of spiritual awareness, and ultimately, full merging with the universal super-conscious mind (God). It is the only sure path to enlightenment, the only sure means of discovering you are a god.

Why People Don't Meditate

Clearly, meditation is a gift. Its benefits to mind, body and spirit are vast, well-documented and well-publicized. Besides, it's so easy a child can do it. So why isn't everyone meditating? There are five main reasons.

1.   *I don't have the time.*

Everything in society urges us to "go out there and conquer the world," and we're all busy trying to make that happen. Taking time out to go inward in silence seems counter-productive. However it works. I've converted many hard-working rationalists to the ease and potency of meditation – among them some of the busiest and most powerful people in the world, who subsequently have become less busy and more powerful. The fact is daily meditation will save you much more time than it costs you. Tasks are made simpler and get done with less time and effort. The opportunities you seek and the things you need start to come your way a bit more easily. The physical benefits of meditation let you do more with less mental and physical fatigue. Your decision-making improves at home and work. Plus regular meditation will add an average of 8 healthy years to your lifespan. You can't afford **not** to meditate!

2.   *Meditation is for swamis, gurus and sadhus, but not for me.*

In India meditation is often associated with the ascetic lifestyle: study, discipline and a willingness to forsake worldly enjoyments. Despite this belief, it was never true that the ascetic life was a pre-condition for enlightenment, and it's especially not true today. In the West, traditional Eastern meditation has been supplemented by Western science to create methods that anyone can use to attain super-conscious states of awareness virtually overnight (the very methods contained in this book). Using these methods, you can have it all: a worldly life, enlightenment and all the benefits associated with living out your noblest dreams and aspirations.

3.   *If I meditate, I'll lose my zeal for worldly achievement.*

I hear this from people the world over but especially from the youth of India, perhaps because of their strong feelings relating to Objection 2. In fact, nothing could be further from the truth. If you meditate you will gain more zeal for expanded states of awareness but you will also gain more inspiration for being in the world and living out your dreams. For example, if you came to be a statesman and you meditate regularly, your achievements are likely to be remarkable and your rise up through the political ranks meteoric, with perhaps even a nomination for the Nobel Peace Prize in your future.

4. *I tried meditation and it didn't do anything at all for me.*

This complaint usually arises in cases where the meditation method itself doesn't deliver results. Not all meditation methods are effective. There are a lot of methods in popular use that pass for meditation which in fact are not. If you want to get the benefits of meditation, you have to use a proven method. The method I teach in this book has been scientifically validated for effectiveness. In general, the methods taught by a bona fide teacher from any religious tradition founded by a fully enlightened being can also be trusted.

5. *I tried meditation, found it frustrating and gave up.*

A calm mind and body are necessary for effective meditation and early attempts to meditate can be frustrating for people who find it difficult to relax. The method I provide at the end of this chapter has been scientifically formulated to take care of this problem. It will allow you to relax, go deep into meditation and enjoy the benefits right away.

What Meditation Does

Meditation is simply a means for calming and focusing the searchlight of your awareness so you can directly perceive the super-conscious mind and tap its infinite power. A good meditation method accomplishes three things that are absolutely necessary for gaining this perception. First, it limits the distractions that are captivating your attention and blinding you to the presence of your own super-conscious awareness. Second, it provides your mind with the energy it needs to expand into higher levels of consciousness. Third, it strengthens your mind and body so you can handle the high levels of energy that will come pouring into you once you open the portal to super-consciousness.

As I described in the last chapter, you are already unified with the universal super-conscious mind. You and God are one. You are simply unaware of it. You are like a corked bottle filled with seawater floating in the ocean. What's keeping the water in the bottle from merging with the ocean? The cork. If you pop it, the bottle sinks and you flow out to merge with the sea of infinite awareness that surrounds you.

You pop the cork by getting rid of the distractions that confine your awareness to the bottle. When you stop devoting all your mental energy to the sensory world around you and to the thoughts and feelings "bottled up" in your head, you free up your mental energy to focus instead on the ocean of intelligent energy that is hidden behind your day-to-day experience. At that point you will naturally merge with the ocean and obtain the power you need to fulfill your destiny.

There are three levels of distraction that keep our awareness "stopped up" in the bottle. The first level consists of outer distractions: traffic congestion, a crying baby, music, TV, the copier machine at the office or the construction project next door. The second level consists of bodily distractions: your backache, your stiff neck, your indigestion and so forth. The third level is composed of the thoughts and feelings that occupy our own minds: that important meeting, the embarrassing situation at work, remembering to call the doctor and so on. Subconscious fear, sadness, anger and anxiety also distract and preoccupy our minds.

Meditation silences the first two levels of distraction by cutting off the sensory nerves to the outside world and the body. To accomplish this it pulls the energy in your peripheral nervous system inward to the base of the spine, then channels it up the spine and through the crown of your head (where your portal to the infinite is located). This is an essential function of good meditative practice called "magnetic pull."

The magnetic pull of meditation has two invaluable benefits. First, as I observed in Chapter Three, if you have no energy in your nerves, you have no sensory awareness (no electric impulses can reach the brain). You may feel as if you do not have a body in a deep meditative state. It's a delightful relief, especially if you suffer from chronic pain or illness in your body. Another benefit is that the energy flowing to the crown of your head is now at your disposal to utilize for vast levels of expansion in awareness and power. If you want to fly to the moon, you need rocket fuel. If you want to launch into super-conscious awareness, you need some energy to help propel you there.

Meditation silences the third level of distraction – the thoughts, feelings and other forms of mental chatter that plague our minds – by training the mind to focus exclusively on one thing. Depending on the meditation method you use, this "thing" might be your breath, a sound, a word, a symbol, an idea or a combination of these.

There is an old saying from the East that trying to calm the mental chatter of the mind is like trying to tame a wild, drunken monkey. The meditation method I'm about to teach you will gradually calm this chatter until you're left with only pure awareness and profound peace. This is not to say you will enter an unfocused, diffuse state of mind. Meditation will help you achieve perfect mental focus and clarity as well as absolute stillness.

How still can stillness get? Several years ago I came out of meditation to see a close friend of mine standing in front of me, staring at me wide-eyed. As was the case with some of my colleagues, it was her habit to join me for morning meditation. I asked her what was wrong and she said, "I know I shouldn't have done it Rick, but I opened my eyes while you were meditating and it looked like you weren't breathing. So I got my compact mirror and put it under your nose. You didn't breathe for twenty-two minutes." I laughed and said, "Yeah, but the important thing is I'm breathing now." I had learned to meditate so deeply, to become so still, that I had no need to burn energy, hence no need for breath. The heart rate and circulation also slow down measurably during meditation. Your body doesn't use energy while you're meditating, so it doesn't need to draw it in (as oxygen) or cycle it through the body (via the bloodstream).

Another reason the body doesn't need energy during meditation is that it is receiving much higher-than-usual levels of energy directly from the cosmic mind (the universal field for those of you with a scientific orientation). In fact, some of what goes on in the initial stages of meditation has to do exclusively with training your mind and body so it can handle ever-increasing levels of energy. The untrained mind cannot stand the billion megawatts of power that would pipe through a fully open door to super-consciousness. We get what we can handle. As you meditate and as you go deeper into the process you're learning in this book, you'll gain greater and greater access to super-conscious power because your mind and body will become incredibly strong.

The Method

Here is a simple meditation method that has good magnetic pull and has been well-researched for effectiveness. To begin, do what you can to limit distractions. Check your bladder, turn off your phone, dim bright lights and turn off the music. Some people think it's better to meditate with music. Music may make you feel better but it is also a distraction that limits your awareness. You want to have as much silence around you as you reasonably can. If you want to chant before you meditate, then by all means do it. Chanting works rapidly and effectively to calm the body and mind in preparation for meditation. Total silence during meditation however, is preferable and necessary.

Choose a comfortable chair or recliner that allows you to keep your back, neck and head reasonably aligned and straight. You don't want to contort your spine or neck because this will impede energy flow. Sitting down is preferable to lying down because the latter invites sleep, but if you have too much discomfort sitting up, by all means lie down.

Now close your eyes and let your awareness go inward.

Next lift your eyes up comfortably behind closed lids as if you are looking at a faraway mountain peak. The scientific reason for this is based on neurological studies which show that keeping your eyes lifted will foster a calm, focused mind. If your eyes are looking straight ahead you will likely engage in a stream of analytical thought ("don't forget that report that's due tomorrow") and if your eyes are lowered, you will likely fall asleep. The spiritual reason for keeping your eyes focused in this way is that your portal to super-conscious awareness – the Third Eye – is in the middle of your forehead. In India the existence of the Third Eye is well understood and well documented. In western Christianity this reality is less widely accepted, though when Jesus said "If thine eye be single, thy whole body be full of light," he was referring to the Third Eye or single eye of soul perception in the forehead. It is an energy portal.

If you are a person of faith, this is the time for a brief prayer or invocation for Divine guidance. Even if you are more of the scientific humanist type and skeptical about the existence of God, you should still take a moment to express a level of respect for the majesty and magnitude of intelligence that undergirds the universe. Remember the discussion in the last chapter about the degree to which science and religion are converging to prove the existence of universal, cosmic intelligence? The greatest scientific minds down through the ages have been certain of its existence. Albert Einstein said "My religion consists of a humble admiration of the illimitable superior Spirit who reveals himself in the slight details we are able to perceive with our frail and feeble minds."

Start the meditative process by monitoring your breathing. Don't time or control it. You are not trying to harness your breath in any way. Just let it go in and out on its own. Breathe in at the point you find the body breathing in. Breathe out at the point you find the body breathing out. It doesn't matter if it's slow and deep or rapid and shallow. Let the breath do whatever it wants but observe it closely. If you're a beginner do this for about two minutes while not allowing any other thought to distract you. If something does distract you – a sound, a feeling in your body or a concern for example – gently return your attention to watching your breath flow in and out.

Next, for the length of the out-breath only, mentally say to yourself the sound *"Om."* It is pronounced as *aum* or like the word "home" without the "h." Om is a remarkable sound. Electroencephalograph (brainwave imaging) studies show that silent repetition of Om causes brain waves to become very relaxed and smooth out while increasing mental clarity. The silent chanting of Om on the out-breath will significantly calm and focus your mind by removing those pesky distractions. Om is actually the sound of super-conscious thought, literally the "hum" of super-conscious intelligence (God) at work creating and sustaining reality. It is a sound that is heard in deep states of meditation by advanced meditators the world over. Silent repetition of this sound in meditation will not only calm your mind but will invite the actual experience of hearing the cosmic Om.

Please be aware that the sound of *Om* to the Hindu is the same as *Amen* to the Jew, Christian or Egyptian, *Amin* to the Muslim, *Aum* to the Tibetan and *Hum* to the Buddhists of Southeast Asia. The founders of all world religions are in accord regarding the cosmic Om and its significance. Choose whichever word is appropriate for you based on your religious tradition. The goal here is to achieve the right sound, so try to mimic it as closely as possible (i.e. Amen would be chanted as Aummm-en).

If you are a beginner, try observing the breath and silently chanting Om on the out-breath for at least five minutes. In all likelihood you're going to drift off into a thought, a feeling, a daydream or an anticipation of some sort. At first you may not even realize you've drifted off. After all it's perfectly normal for one's thoughts to wander. As soon as you realize it however, let go of what you're thinking, feeling or imagining and come back to the method: Om on the out-breath.

That is the method, start to finish. Here is a short-cut summary:

1. Relax, with head, neck and spine reasonably aligned, then close your eyes, let your awareness go inward and keep your physical eyes lifted comfortably up to focus on your Third Eye.

2. Observe your breathing - don't time or control it, just let it go in and out on its own (if you're a beginner, do this for about two minutes).

3. Next, for the length of the out-breath only, mentally say to yourself the sound Om (if you're a beginner, do this for at least five minutes).

4. In all likelihood, you're going to drift off into a thought or a daydream while you're practicing the method – as soon as this happens, let go of what you're thinking and come back to the method: Om on the out-breath.

With practice of this method you will gradually drift off less and less. Think of a glass jar filled with mud and water. If you shake it and put it on a table, at first you see a million specks whirling about. Those specks are like the everyday thoughts and feelings of your conscious mind. As you let the jar sit still on the table however, you'll see the specks settle down until the water above the mud becomes crystal clear. Similarly, if you meditate every day for several minutes you'll soon find that conscious thought and reactive emotion settle down and stop completely. At that point your mind becomes like the clear water in the jar. You will then naturally experience your own individual super-conscious awareness (your soul).

You cannot stop "thinking" as an act of will. That will just keep you busy thinking about not thinking. The method is the key here – silent chanting of Om with the out-breath. By returning to the method each time you drift off, you start locating your consciousness in a place that is "outside" of the everyday thought and feeling you're trying to quell.

When you are ready to conclude the formal part of meditation, stop the method (no focus on the breath; no Om on the outbreath). Now just sit in the stillness with your focus on the Third Eye, dwelling in the extravagant joy, peace and power of soul-consciousness. As you sit in this stillness your "thinking" is very powerful. This is an outstanding time to pray to God or commune spiritually with other people. In later chapters I provide you with highly specific, powerful techniques that can be applied at this point in the process.

Very early in your attempts to meditate you will begin to reap the benefits. The first symptom of your success will be a feeling of peace that keeps deepening into joy (a gift you will carry with you throughout the day). The more often you meditate and the lengthier your meditations, the more your awareness will expand. The Third Eye may begin to manifest as high intensity white light or color in your forehead (a sign that this energy portal is opening). When you come out of meditation you will actually feel larger because meditation super-charges your body's electromagnetic energy field and causes it to expand in size. Because of this increase in your energy field you will notice you have a great deal more stamina and sensitivity to things in your environment. Intuitive insights will start coming your way because of the increased size and power of your field. Keep up the good work. These are all definite signs that you're on your way to enlightened awareness.

Hypnotic Meditation

You can meditate on your own using the simple method I just described or you can allow me to assist you. When you first start meditating, you may find you cannot relax or that your thoughts drift off with such frequency you have trouble getting anywhere near a meditative state. I have removed this problem by using tools from the field of clinical hypnosis to calm the mind and body in preparation for meditation.

Clinical hypnosis is a mainstream medical discipline that is used to rapidly calm and focus the mind. In the U.S. and Europe it is used very effectively to achieve a wide variety of outcomes – everything from curing cancer to enhancing sports performance for professional athletes to smoking cessation. I use it often in my clinical work and I am board-certified in this clinical specialty. Clinical hypnosis is *not* to be confused with "stage hypnotism," an entertainment medium that uses authoritarian methods of mind control. Authoritarian hypnosis is unhealthy for the mind. You should never allow anyone to gain control of your mind.

The methods I use are called *permissive* hypnosis. This means you are in control the whole time, you'll be aware of everything that's happening and you'll remember everything. You will be directing yourself through the entire process. The guidance I provide is merely designed to help you free your body from stress and rid your mind of mental chatter so you can quickly relax and focus your mind. This will let you go deep into meditation and enjoy its benefits right away. If you have trouble meditating or if you have never tried meditation, this is the method to use: it will let you glide into a calm meditative state with ease.

For a hypnotic assist with your meditation, set aside some time and prepare yourself just as if you were going to meditate on your own (check your bladder, limit the distractions, dim bright lights and situate yourself comfortably with spine and head aligned). Now put the CD that accompanies this book into a CD player and play Track 3: *Hypnotic Meditation*. In it, I will use a simple progressive relaxation method and guided imagery to help you calm your mind and body. I will then leave you to meditate as long as you can in the silence that follows. During the silent interval on the CD you'll be meditating entirely on your own. You can use the method I just described or one of your own choosing.

Your Plan for Developing Skill in Meditation

Whether you choose to meditate on your own or rely on a hypnotic assist, start meditating now. Meditate each day, early in the morning if you can. If you can't just try to find a time each day to meditate. God loves routine and so does the mind. You'll get better results if you meditate at or about the same time each day.

The first day you meditate and for a few days after, try meditating for just seven or eight minutes. If you find you've drifted off onto a thought or feeling (this happens to everyone), simply come back to the method.

Some beginning meditators have trouble with intrusive thoughts and feelings and believe they can't meditate. This is absolutely not true. Just stick with the method and you'll be delighted with the results.

After the first few days decide to expand the time you spend meditating, but do it in small increments. Many of us are so problem-focused and achievement-oriented that we'll turn anything into a job. It is neither necessary nor helpful to make meditation another job. Try for eight minutes initially, then move up to ten, then twelve and so on. The experience should grow naturally and in a pleasant way. When you reach 30 minutes per day, you should begin experiencing the awesome benefits of meditation.

You may have a "dry" meditation once in a while, where you feel as if you didn't accomplish much of anything. This is typical too. Just stick with the process. You'll soon find yourself spending an hour or more in daily meditation just because you enjoy it so much and are reaping its rewards, which grow with each passing day. Stay with it and meditation will open a wondrous world to you, a world of endless increase in power, joy and insight – a world you will delight in.

Note to the Reader: ————————————————————

Ram Dass introduced me to meditation but he was not the first teacher of Hindu philosophy in America. Sri Ramakrishna's disciple, Swami Vivekananda, came to the U.S. in 1893 to address the Congress of World Religions in Chicago. For two years he lectured widely on Vedanta and Yoga. So popular were his teachings and so enthralled were his audiences that he was offered the Chair of Eastern Philosophy at Harvard and a similar post at Columbia University (widely regarded as two of the finest universities in the world). Thereafter his mission took him to Europe, but he returned to the U.S. in 1899 to found Vedanta Societies in San Francisco and New York.

During Vivekananda's stay in America he foretold of another guru from India who was to come. Paramahansa Yogananda arrived in the U.S. in 1920 as India's delegate to the International Congress of Religious Liberals. He then embarked on a cross-continental speaking tour. Tens of thousands came to his lectures. Before he came to the U.S. he founded the Yogoda Satsanga Society of India to disseminate his teachings on the Subcontinent. Once in the U.S. he founded the Self-Realization Fellowship to disseminate his teachings worldwide. He became the first Hindu Swami to live in America. Yoganandaji has been my beloved Gurudeva since 1975. He is the guiding force behind my research and methods.

8

Lifestyle Matters

To ensure freedom from distress and success in pursuit of your dreams, you need to structure your lifestyle so it sustains harmony at all levels: spiritual, psychological, physical and social. Mind, body and spirit thrive on regular nurture. When they don't get it disharmony sets in and disharmony fuels distress.

Despite all the good information available, too many intelligent people let go of "little things" like sleep, healthy food and the company of loved ones in order to meet the demands of day-to-day living. People who do this usually think they're making a necessary trade-off, that they can handle the loss or that they will "catch up" with their personal needs later. This is the very kind of thinking that will keep you locked in a cycle of chronic distress. You cannot overlook your most essential needs without paying a penalty and life almost never affords us the opportunity to "catch-up" until it's too late. A harmonious lifestyle is therefore not a luxury to be set aside until you have more time, it's an absolute necessity. In this chapter I provide a series of simple guidelines that will help you create it.

Organize Your Time for Harmony

Start by looking at "the big picture." Ask yourself how you spend your time over the course of an average workday. There are 24 precious hours in a day and each one counts. Too many people allocate their time unconsciously, which means they don't plan their daily activities – they let other people and circumstances dictate how they spend their time. Don't let this be you. Decide how your ideal day should look, then do what you can to make it happen. There will be plenty of occasions when you have to forsake your daily schedule because of some opportunity or emergency, but by-and-large you want to stick to the same daily schedule. This is the best way to ensure your harmony, amplify your personal power and ensure your success.

Now let's look at an ideal 24-hour workday. You'll want to take 8 hours right off the top for sleep. Studies indicate the average person requires 7 to 9 hours of sleep each day. You don't want to short-change yourself on sleep because chronic sleep deprivation is bad for you. Even if it is minimal – maybe you get 6.5 hours of sleep each night – its cumulative effects on the body are insidious. Sleep deprivation will tax your thyroid and adrenal glands, which will increase the biological stress response and its consequences: neuronal death and neurological impairment, fragmented thinking, anxiety and depression, exhaustion, sleeplessness, a depressed immune system, no interest in sex, a higher frequency of illness and more. The skyrocketing incidence of sleep disorders in post-industrial countries is being fueled by rising rates of chronic distress, anxiety and depression. To avoid these problems, plan for 8 hours of sleep each night on a regular basis and do whatever you need to do to pare your stress levels down.

After sleep you'll want to allocate one hour exclusively to meditation. It is the most powerful tool you have to ensure your health, harmony and success – the only tool that will make you immortal. It will vastly improve the quality of your day, amplify your success in all you do, keep you healthy and draw to you the things you need and desire in order to pursue your *Story Behind the Story.* It will save you much more time than it costs you, as well as prolong your life. For all these reasons you definitely don't want to skip daily meditation.

Perhaps you haven't yet developed the ability to meditate for an hour. Make it your goal. Until you reach it, meditate for as long as you can and spend the remainder of the hour reading and contemplating the writings of an enlightened teacher of religion, philosophy or science. Meditation is more restful and beneficial to the body than sleep, so you can feel quite comfortable exchanging one hour of sleep time for meditation.

You are left with 15 hours in your day. Look next to your essential physical needs. You'll want to allocate about 2 hours each day to preparing and consuming wholesome food to fuel your mind and body, 30 minutes to some form of exercise and at least 30 minutes to cleansing and pampering your body (an hour for the ladies). These activities are essential to human wellbeing and you should do them on a daily basis. Remember, your soul is sojourning on earth in a body, so for as long as you live your body is a temple of God. If you treat your body with the respect and reverence it deserves as a holy shrine it will serve you well. Also be aware that your body's wellbeing and the wellbeing of your mind are closely intertwined. Stress in the body fuels mental distress, so you can't afford to ignore your body's essential needs without suffering some level of mental impairment. What's good for the body is good for the mind and vice versa.

You still have about 12 hours left in your day. Next consider how much time you spend working, however you define it. You may run your own company, work for someone else, are currently a full time student, or perhaps you maintain a household and raise children. Whatever your "work" is allocate a maximum of 10 hours to it. Do not make the mistake of assuming you can or should work for more than 10 hours per day as a steady diet. This is a set-up for distress, fatigue and failure. You may occasionally have to work for more than 10 hours in a single day, but if you do, shorten your working hours on the following day (or days) to compensate.

Readers who must do all three – work full time *and* have full time family and household responsibilities – need to be aware this pattern is not sustainable healthwise. The burden too many Indian mothers bear – working full time while raising children, cooking and maintaining a household – shows up in the alarming rates of increase for cardiovascular disease and stroke among middle-aged Indian women. If this is you, do everything you can to get help with your responsibilities. Whatever your highest destiny may be for this lifetime it does not include working yourself to death. If your soul thought you could benefit from being a beast of burden you would have been born a donkey. Everyone is born a son or daughter of God and has the innate power to fulfill their noble dreams without compromising their health. This is even true for the powerless servant who is facing an oppressive, tyrannical dictator. Ask Gandhiji.

You still have 2 hours or more left in your workday. This is time you should spend nurturing your happiness, your sense of connection with people you love and your devotion to God. Hold hands with your spouse or partner, listen to music, get on your mobile and connect with a friend. Do a little gardening, work a favorite hobby, create something or read a book on a topic that is not work-related. You might do some writing, or in some other way reflect on your own thoughts about your day and its implications for your *Story Behind the Story*. You might do some yoga – a scientifically-proven means for amplifying mind-body-spirit health. If you are so inclined you might use this time to attend services at your temple, mosque or church. If you are disinclined toward worship, you should know there are more than 100 research studies showing that people who regularly attend worship services are happier, more successful in life, make more money and get sick less often than people who don't worship regularly.

Once you've structured your workdays to ensure work-life balance, turn your attention to whether there is balance and harmony in your average week. No matter what your responsibilities, you should try to set aside one entire day each week when you do not work – one whole day that is exclusively devoted to your harmony. This would be the day for an extended meditation or participation in religious services, a major event or outing with friends or family, or a trip to a place you've never been. Take a nap or sleep in late to catch up on needed rest. Go out to a restaurant for your major meal of the day if you can afford it. Apart from taking care of your family's most essential needs, don't work. You need and deserve one whole day each week that's devoted to your own nurture, however you define it.

Once you've structured your weeks, consider how you will "schedule" time for harmony in the year ahead. You need to take regular vacations. It's a good idea to plan for several short breaks and at least one long vacation from work and responsibility each year. It takes three days of rest and relaxation to de-activate the stress response once it has been active for an extended period of time, so vacations of three or four days every two months are a good strategy for de-stressing.

Plan also for at least 9 days of continuous, uninterrupted vacation each year – time you use for relaxation, adventure, renewing your closeness with loved ones or deepening your devotion to God. Vacations do not have to be expensive to deliver a benefit. The important thing is to stop doing the things that contribute to distress and exclusively do things that nurture you, your relationships and your unity with God. A change of venue is a good idea if you can afford it however. It is sometimes very helpful to put some geographic distance between yourself and your stressful, work-a-day world.

Once you've given thought to allocating your time you'll want to consider precisely how to use it to your advantage. The remainder of this chapter is devoted to the science of harmonious living and a variety of options you have at your disposal to ensure your wellbeing. As you read through the chapter, don't make the mistake of thinking that your health is doomed if you cannot afford to implement the suggested strategies. You don't want to look at the implementation of a healthy lifestyle as yet another job that needs to be done and worry if you should fail at achieving it. This attitude will only increase your stress! The important thing is to start thinking in a focused, consistent way about what you need in order to be healthy and happy. Then do what you can to achieve it with the attitude "I need this and it's good for me. Because that's true, I know I shall have it." This is the type of winning attitude that will ensure your success.

Food for Harmony

The right kind of diet will help prevent stress, counteract its impact once it occurs, keep your body and mind functioning at peak levels and prevent you from becoming sick. A nutritious, well-rounded diet has powerful stress-reducing benefits. It will shore up your immune system, lower your blood pressure, improve your circulation, take the pressure off your heart, reduce toxins in the body, improve your brain functioning, give you more energy and make you feel a lot happier and calmer. There are also specific foods that reduce levels of cortisol and adrenaline, the stress chemicals that activate the "fight or flight" response.

Before I describe "what" to eat let's look at "when" to eat. To minimize stress and maximize wellbeing it's best to eat at regular intervals during the day. Eating three small meals with wholesome snacks in-between is the best way to accomplish this goal. Whatever you do, don't skip breakfast – studies show the brain functions better all day if it has fuel first thing in the morning. Eating breakfast will also boost your energy levels throughout the day, as well as increase your metabolism, which is great for people who could stand to lose a few pounds. Excess weight causes high blood pressure, high blood sugar and way too much stress on the heart and arteries of the type that leads to heart attack, stroke and peripheral artery disease.

Now let's look at "what" to eat. We're going to keep it simple by using a short list of guidelines that are easy to remember. These are:

If it grows in the sun, it's good for you

As a general rule a low-fat diet rich in vegetables, fruits and nuts is best. These are all things that grow naturally as a function of sunlight, soil and water – they are loaded with valuable nutrients and chemicals. Complex carbohydrates – vegetables and fruits, nuts and whole grains, whole grain cereals, whole grain bread and whole grain pasta – will boost levels of serotonin, a chemical in the brain that makes us calm. They are also rich in nutrients and especially good for your circulation and heart health. Green, orange and yellow fruits and vegetables are rich in vitamins, minerals and phytochemicals which fuel healthy cellular construction and boost immune health to help you fight disease. Dark-colored fruits and vegetables are especially rich in anti-oxidants which lower blood pressure, de-toxify the body, improve immune system functioning and prevent cellular damage of the sort that leads to disease, especially cancer. Garlic, a frequent ingredient in Indian cuisine, is one of the most potent antioxidants in existence. Eat as much of it as you like – just be sure to carry some sugar-free gum or breath mints.

Fruits, vegetables and whole grains are also excellent sources of fiber. You want to be sure to consume enough fiber each day, because stress has a very bad effect on the stomach and bowels, resulting in heartburn, cramps, diarrhea and constipation. Eating more fiber will also help you lose weight. Aim for at least 25 grams of fiber each day – that's about 6 small servings of vegetables, fruits, nuts or whole grains. For breakfast, or at anytime during the day, eat whole fruits instead of fruit juice to maximize your fiber intake.

Of the many food choices available consider making oranges, spinach, bananas, avocados, potatoes, pistachios and almonds a regular part of your diet. Oranges and spinach are both rich in Vitamin C, which helps to reduce stress hormones while strengthening the immune system. Spinach also contains high levels of magnesium, which helps to regulate cortisol and adrenaline levels, thereby retarding the "fight or flight" response. Too little magnesium can trigger headaches and fatigue. If you don't like spinach try eating cooked soybeans, also high in magnesium. Bananas and avocados are both rich in potassium, which reduces high blood pressure. The lowly potato is also a good source of potassium and Vitamin C.

Nuts are an essential component of a stress-free diet. Eating a handful of pistachios every day will lower your blood pressure so it won't spike as high when the "fight or flight" response is activated and your heart won't race so fast. If you snack on a quarter cup of almonds daily you will benefit from their high levels of Vitamin E, which bolsters the immune system. Almonds also contain a range of B vitamins that make the body more resilient when it is stressed. One simple, effective stress management strategy is to keep pistachios and almonds in your pocket or purse to snack on throughout the day. I use this strategy to keep my body and mind well-fueled, no matter how hectic my day is.

Consider eating more raw vegetables too. Eating a handful of raw carrots or broccoli will not only provide you with essential nutrients, it will help you fight the effects of stress in a purely mechanistic way: the act of "crunching" helps release pent-up stress in your jaw and can ward-off tension headaches.

If it's white, eat it sparingly

Medical research cautions against the use of simple carbohydrates like white sugar, white flour and white bread. It is best to stay away from anything "white" if you can. White sugar, bread and rice contain little or no nutrition and they are all high on the glycemic index, which

99

means they cause a rapid rise in blood sugar. High blood sugar will give you a short-term burst of energy but relying on simple carbs for your energy supply will harm your health in the long run. High blood sugar taxes the adrenal glands, which can result in irritability, poor concentration and even depression. It also puts a lot of strain on the pancreas, which means an increased risk of developing diabetes. High blood sugar also hurts your chances of controlling your appetite, because as soon as your "sugar high" starts to abate, your body will crave more simple carbs to drive its sugar level back up again. The body literally becomes addicted to sugar in order to maintain its energy plateau, resulting in excess weight gain. So strive to consume "white" foods in small amounts. Try to substitute brown rice for white rice if you can. Use only unrefined (brown) sugar and use it sparingly. Go for whole grain bread instead of white bread if you can afford it.

Omega-3 fatty acids – nature's stress-buster

Omega-3 fatty acids have been shown to prevent cardiac disease and cancer, improve immune system functioning, bolster brain and nervous system health, improve mobility and ease joint pain. Foods rich in Omega-3 fatty acids include yogurt and cheese from grass-fed cows, fatty fish (like tuna), flaxseeds and flaxseed oil, mustard oil, eggs, broccoli and milk. Mustard oil is not only high in Omega-3 fatty acids it's also low in saturated fat, which makes it ideal for cooking. Just try not to heat it until it smokes because high temperatures will destroy the valuable Omega-3s in the oil.

Try milk

Not only do dairy products contain Omega-3 fatty acids, they are rich in calcium, which helps to soothe tension and ease anxiety and mood swings. Dairy products are therefore an important part of a stress-free diet, provided they are low in saturated fat. Try drinking a glass of low-fat milk daily to obtain the benefits without the fat and consider a glass of warm low-fat milk before bedtime. It really does relax and soothe you in preparation for a good night's rest. In fact, any bedtime snack that is high in complex carbohydrates will speed the release of serotonin and help you sleep. If you have trouble sleeping and you don't like milk, try eating a slice of whole-grain bread before bedtime.

Tea time keeps stress at bay

Tea – black or green – is rich in antioxidants, which ensure cellular health, detoxify the body and help prevent disease, especially cancer. Research also suggests that black tea can help you recover from stressful events more quickly. Try not to drink more than three cups a day of black tea because it contains caffeine. Green tea is equally rich in antioxidants but contains only trace amounts of caffeine. If you are the type who can't go for more than 30 minutes without a cup of tea, try relying on green tea for half of your tea consumption.

Hydrate for health

You should try to drink 6 glasses of filtered water each day, more if you spend a lot of time out in the sun or if you are exercising. The body needs to be sufficiently hydrated so it can carry out its myriad critical functions. Even mild dehydration will cause sleepiness or tiredness, muscle weakness, headaches, low blood pressure, dizziness, lightheadedness, confused thinking, sadness and even depression. Severe dehydration constitutes a medical emergency that requires hospitalization before it leads to fever, delirium and unconsciousness. Be aware that thirst is not the most reliable gauge of whether your body is in need of water, especially in children and older adults. The color of your urine is a much better gauge: clear or light-colored urine means you are well hydrated whereas a dark yellow or amber color usually signals dehydration.

Supplements

To avoid the effects of stress, it's a good idea to take a basic multi-vitamin and mineral supplement each day if you can afford it. There are many herbal supplements and spices on the market which also claim to be beneficial for reducing stress. The most studied of these is Saint John's Wort, which has been proven effective in the treatment of mild-to-moderate depression. It also reduces anxiety and calms mood swings associated with pre-menstrual syndrome. If you want to try herbal supplements be sure to do your homework to discover whether they are effective or not. Rely on the worldwide web for the information you need and if you can, seek the advice of a medical doctor.

You may also wish to explore the science of Ayurveda for guidance on herbal supplements and spices. If so, be sure to deal with an organization or individual practitioner who is properly credentialed in Ayurvedic medicine. It is a bad idea to obtain herbal supplements from a non-credentialed vendor because these can contain arsenic, lead and heavy metals (all of which are poisonous). You can find a properly credentialed practitioner of Ayurveda by contacting The Central Council for Research in Ayurveda and Siddha, or CCRAS, in New Delhi.

Stay away from stress-enhancing foods

- **Saturated Fats** – When preparing and eating your food, you want to limit saturated fats. These come mainly from animal sources – fatty beef, lamb, pork, poultry skin, beef fat, lard, cream, butter (ghee), cheese and other dairy products made from whole milk. Animal-based fats also contain cholesterol. Science believes these fats contribute to the build-up of bad cholesterol in your blood stream, poor circulation, artery disease and stroke. Research also indicates that saturated fats contribute to the onset of many breast, colon and prostate cancers. Worst of all, too much saturated fat in your diet will make you sluggish and overweight. Many ready-made baked and fried foods, especially fast food, contain high levels of saturated fat (and salt) and they should be avoided. Your body needs the fatty acids and other compounds in these fats so you do not want to cut them out of your diet entirely. Just use them sparingly.

- **Caffeine** – Caffeine in high doses will boost levels of cortisol and adrenaline, which will enhance the stress response and make you feel jittery. Coffee or any foods that are high in caffeine like chocolate or Coke are stress-inducers when consumed in large amounts. Try to consume them in very small doses, when in fact they can be beneficial. You can feel free to have a cup of coffee each day and a few bites of chocolate now and then, just don't overdo it.

- **Alcohol** – Alcohol in very small doses has been shown to benefit the cardiovascular system, but overall, it's bad for your health and a major source of stress. Alcohol stimulates the secretion of adrenaline, which results in nervous tension, irritability and insomnia. Excess alcohol will increase fat deposits in the heart, decrease immune function and increase risk of cancer. It also limits the liver's ability to remove toxins from the body – toxins which increase during the "fight or flight" response. Without efficient liver functioning, these toxins continue to circulate throughout the body, prolonging the stress response and doing harm to your vital organs and circulatory system.

- **Salt** – You also want to avoid too much salt. Salt increases blood pressure, depletes the adrenal glands and causes emotional instability. You'll want to use it in moderation and avoid foods rich in salt, especially junk foods like potato chips.

- **Meat** – You'll want to minimize the use of meat in your diet. Eating meat elevates brain levels of dopamine and norepinephrine, both of which are associated with higher levels of anxiety and stress.

Some beef suppliers feed their cattle steroids to make them larger – eat this beef and you're eating steroids, which are well-known to cause agitation. Beef also tends to be rich in saturated fat. Chicken is a better source of animal protein than meat. Fish is even better than chicken, and the best source of animal protein is eggs, cheese, yogurt and milk.

These dietary guidelines are designed to ensure your overall health and safeguard you from stress. They are simple, backed by solid research and effective. However, some people want and need very detailed dietary guidance because they have a pre-existing condition like diabetes or heart disease. If this is you, you will need to speak with a physician before starting any dietary regimen. There are also a number of highly specialized diets available for managing stress. Ayurveda offers distinct dietary guidelines, including herbal supplements and spices, appropriate for individuals based on their *doshas* (energy patterns or humors). If you wish to explore Ayurveda in this regard, be sure to work with a person or organization that is properly credentialed in Ayurveda.

Regular Exercise

One of the most effective things you can do to manage stress and avoid distress is to exercise regularly. Aerobic exercise is the most effective type. The word aerobic means "with oxygen." It refers to exercise that improves oxygen flow in the body and the body's energy-generating process (known as *metabolism*). By definition, aerobic exercise is exercise you perform at moderate levels of intensity for extended periods of time like jogging, swimming, biking or walking at a brisk pace. To get the maximum benefit you need to get your heart rate up to 110 to 120 beats per minute for 30 minutes, three to four times per week.

Aerobic exercise will improve your health and harmony in several important ways. It produces endorphins – the feel-good chemicals in your brain – so it will make you feel happier. It also improves brain functioning by increasing blood and oxygen flow to the brain, helping to create new nerve cells and increasing chemicals in the brain that help cognition. In other words, regular aerobic exercise helps you think and perceive things more clearly. In fact, studies show that aerobic exercise is as effective in treating moderate depression as prescription anti-depressive medication. Regular aerobic exercise will also help ensure your cardio-vascular health, which is most susceptible to failure due to chronic stress.

Catharsis is the term used by modern psychology to describe the act of expressing deep emotion, and regular exercise is extremely cathartic.

It works quickly to release the negative energy associated with pent-up emotion, a major trigger for the "fight or flight" response. Remember, your feelings exist as subtle electromagnetic energy. When you exercise you burn energy, including the harmful emotional energy that might be fueling your distress. For this reason, many people effectively manage chronic stress with a regular morning jog, workouts on the stair-climber at the gym, swimming, tennis or a stint on the football field. A good aerobic workout will bleed-off accumulated stress, relax your body, clear your thinking, and help you feel more optimistic. It has the potential to help you turn a distressing "gloom and doom" scenario into eustress – a means for finding inner strength, insight and optimism.

You don't have to be a marathon runner to enjoy the cathartic benefits of physical exercise. Perhaps you have heart disease, respiratory disease, arthritis or some other condition that creates mobility and flexibility issues. Perhaps you are undergoing chemotherapy. If this is you, you'll need to exercise less rigorously and to consult with your doctor before embarking on any exercise regimen. If your doctor tells you it's OK, consider slow walking, light bicycling, mild forms of yoga, flexibility exercises or therapeutic stretching. All of these can suffice for cathartic release in folks with limited mobility and/or bodily pain. You can also turn ordinary household chores into an exercise in cathartic release. I treated a woman many years ago who helped heal herself of severe arthritis by ritualizing ordinary housework. She imagined every cobweb or smudge to be some aspect of her own frustration that she was "sweeping out." This woman lived with unrelenting levels of stress – a high powered job, a chronically ill child, financial difficulties from too much medical debt – but she arrested and reversed her arthritis through regular meditation, a better diet and her own form of "broom therapy."

The stress-busting benefits of yoga are innumerable. Yoga is a Sanskrit word that means "union" and it refers to any one of six schools of Hindu philosophy that describe the path to enlightenment. Hindu texts establishing the basis for yoga include the Upanishads, the Bhagavad-Gita, the Yoga Sutras of Patanjali, the Hatha Yoga Pradipika and many others. The main branches of yoga have been classified as Hatha Yoga (attaining enlightenment through postures and breath control), Karma Yoga (attaining enlightenment through good works), Jnana Yoga (attaining enlightenment through wisdom), Bhakti Yoga (attaining enlightenment through devotion), and Raja Yoga (attaining enlightenment through a balanced spiritual life that has meditation as its hub). All forms of yoga are designed to help you attain the physiological, mental and spiritual balance needed to attain enlightened awareness.

Outside India, yoga is almost exclusively associated with Hatha Yoga, which has been shown to increase and balance the flow of energy through the body and mind. In research conducted by Dr. Jon Kabat-Zinn in the U.S., mild forms of Hatha Yoga in combination with meditation demonstrated significant levels of stress-reduction, positive changes in brain activity, improved emotional processing, better immune functioning, better circulation and symptom reduction in people who suffer from stress-related illnesses, including heart disease and breast cancer. Over 200 medical centers and clinics in the U.S. and Europe now use Dr. Kabat-Zinn's approach for their patients who suffer from stress-related illnesses. According to Dr. Kabat-Zinn's research, 15 or 20 minutes of mild yoga followed by meditation every day will make you almost impervious to distress, as well as improve your health. A daily program of this type is also a sure path to enlightened awareness, provided you use a proven meditation method.

Time for Love

Human beings are social by nature. Strong bonds of love with family and friends are essential to our health and happiness. Love is a precious gift. It should never be taken for granted and must be nurtured over time with regular attention and devotion. If you are a full-time employee with a family it's easy to let your time and energy get hijacked by work and be too tired when you get home to devote attention to your family. If this is you, try building family time into your daily routine. My wife and I are both busy health professionals with family responsibilities. Every night we put it all aside and give each other our uninterrupted attention. During this time we share the events of our day, chat about current events, make plans, hold hands, kiss, tease each other and tell jokes. Every day we call one another to say "I love you." Our love has grown deeper and more passionate with time in large part because we have "ritualized" mutual affection as part of our daily routine. We have also ritualized time for affectionate connection with our children.

Love doesn't just happen. You have to invest the time and effort to nurture it on a regular basis. Otherwise you will wake up one day to find yourself alienated from the people you love, and lonely.

The same thing holds for friendships. They're an important part of a passionate, joyful life and a huge comfort when things get tough. A true friend is someone who believes in you, even when you have lost the ability to believe in yourself – something none of us should live without. So take the time at regular intervals to nurture positive friendships. If you don't have any friends, you should recognize the shortfall as a symptom of your own disharmony and take necessary action to rectify whatever is wrong. Too much unresolved distress is the chief reason why people become friendless "loners." These are typically people who received no unconditional love as children or who were traumatized by another person early in life. Through their experience, they developed the idea that it is dangerous or unwise to trust others. If this is you, the methods in this book will help you make a peace with your past so you can experience, perhaps for the first time, what it feels like to open your heart to another person in true friendship.

Have Fun

Your soul chose to incarnate on earth to find happiness. That's true for everyone. Happiness is actually something you are – it is the very nature of your own soul. Once you find communion with your soul and the cosmic universal mind that lays beyond it, you will find lasting and profound happiness. In the meantime, you should be aware of two important universal truths. The first of these is that the cosmic mind designed the world as a playground for our enjoyment. The second is closely related to the first: the journey toward soul awareness is supposed to be fun. If you are on this journey, then the earth and all that is in it will rise up to provide you with joy.

The upshot of these two principles is this: as long as you are pursuing your *Story Behind the Story*, you're entitled to have as much fun as you can stand, and the universe will help you have it. Recognizing this fact is an important part of the journey. So don't hesitate to take advantage of a gift that God has made available to any seeker of Truth: make time to have fun. Go out with friends and act a little crazy, dance in the moonlight, create something, play games, stretch yourself to try something new, visit a place you've never been to before, or watch a funny movie. Whatever brings you joy, the universe is happy for you to have it as long as it's legal and doesn't hurt anyone.

Pamper Yourself

It feels good to be pampered now and then. Some of us are fortunate enough to have people in our lives who pamper us, but when we don't, we should pamper ourselves. In saying this I am not proposing you plunge yourself into debt with a major shopping spree or a weekend at the spa. However, it is good to gift yourself with things that help you feel relaxed, happy and sensual. This could be a new suit or kurta or pair of shoes, a massage or facial, a new haircut, new cologne or a new bangle. Maybe you've always wanted to have your chipped tooth fixed by a dentist for purely cosmetic reasons. Make a wish list of things like this for yourself and every so often, gift yourself with something from the list that is within your financial means. All the items I just mentioned have beneficial effects on self-esteem and some of the items – like massages and facials – are proven stress-busters. Anything that positively stimulates the five senses will make you feel happier, calmer, more confident and less stressed.

See a Health Professional

Be sure to see a doctor for your health care needs. Do it sooner rather than later if you suspect something is wrong. Doctors know that the chances of effective treatment for any health problem are higher with early diagnosis. Actually it's best to prevent problems before they start, so it's a great idea to see a physician for an annual physical, especially as you get older. Your physician will be able to assess your health status, gauge your distress based on your symptoms and provide you with sound medical advice.

People in India sometimes consider it a sign of weakness to see a psychologist. Only people who are mentally ill need to see a psychologist right? Actually that's not true. In the U.S. most people who see psychologists are simply suffering from the effects of chronic distress. There is nothing wrong with them, they're just massively stressed. A good psychologist can help you get on top of your distress in a tiny fraction of the time you can do it on your own. They can also help you resolve ongoing conflicts with other people, increase your performance, improve your love life and in many other ways, help you find harmony when it is elusive. Psychologists are the gurus of stress-free living. If you wanted to learn to fly a plane, you would hire a pilot to teach you. If you want to quickly navigate your way out of distress, you should consider seeing a psychologist.

Things You Should Not Do

There are a number of "quick fixes" people turn to in their efforts to cope with stress which turn out to be toxic. Smoking cigarettes for example, relieves stress in the very short run: nicotine is a stimulant that helps alleviate depression and the carbon monoxide in the smoke tends to lessen anxiety. Despite its short-term benefits however, smoking is absolutely lethal. It causes high blood pressure, respiratory illness, heart disease, vascular disease, stroke and a variety of cancers. It is also a social turn-off. Nothing will alienate a potential friend or romantic interest like the smell of tobacco smoke and smoker's breath. If you smoke and you have not already done so, you should resolve to quit. There are many good smoking cessation methods available and a doctor will know which one might work best for you.

The same caution holds for non-prescription drug use. People go for this quick fix because it provides short-term relief, but then chemical dependency sets in and life becomes a sordid, sometimes horrifying affair with terrible consequences for the individual, their family and loved ones. If you are involved with non-prescription drug use, consider seeing a medical doctor or a doctor of psychology for a consultation. There are medications and therapies that can help.

Lifestyle Harmony Checklist

This chapter covers a wide range of information. To keep it simple I've summarized the entire chapter in the following checklist. You can use this list for a reference. I suggest you return to it at intervals to assess how well you're faring in your efforts to create and maintain a harmonious lifestyle.

Organize Your Time for Harmony

___Eight hours sleep per night

___No more than 10 hours of work per day

___Daily meditation (or mild yoga followed by meditation)

___Time in each day for love and fun

___One entire day off of work each week

___Regular worship

___Regular mini-vacations and an annual vacation

Food for Harmony

___Eat regularly (breakfast, lunch and dinner with small snacks in-between)

___Eat foods close to the sun (veggies, fruit and whole grains)

___Eggs and yogurt (low-fat preferable)

___If it's white, eat it sparingly

___Omega-3 fatty acids

___Try milk (low-fat)

___Tea time

___Stay hydrated

___Daily vitamin & mineral supplement

___Only small amounts of saturated fats, caffeine, alcohol, salt, beef

Exercise Regularly

___30 minutes of aerobic exercise 3 to 4 times weekly (if health allows)

___Hatha Yoga, stretching, walking or other mild exercise every day

Take Time for Love

___Ritualize time with loved ones as part of your daily routine

___Stay connected with friends whose company you enjoy

___Make new friends

___Rely on friends for support

___Don't allow yourself to become socially isolated

Have Fun Regularly

___Dance, sing, cook, paint, weave, sculpt, garden, play games, build things

___Go out with friends

___Take a day trip to a place you've never been before

___See a funny movie

___Read literature that is unrelated to work

Pamper Yourself

___Get a massage, facial or pedicure (works for gents as well as the ladies)

___Buy something to wear that makes you feel handsome or beautiful

___Do little things that are gratifying to your senses, like listening to music

Rely on a Health Care Professional

___Annual check-ups

___Medical care when necessary

___See a psychologist when needed

Try Never to

___Smoke cigarettes

___Engage in non-prescription drug use

Before You Move on

If you wanted to build a new house, you would first be concerned with building a rock-solid foundation to support the structure above ground. Similarly, a harmonious lifestyle that includes daily meditation provides the foundation for a healthy happy life, lived without limits. It's a must. Beginning with the next chapter, I provide you with a set of powerful tools you can use to ensure the integrity of your foundation and build the house of your dreams.

9

Moving Energy with Your Mind

In this chapter I provide a simple method you can use to heal yourself, powerfully influence the welfare of others, and shape the course of future events. Nothing is more distressing than feeling powerless in the face of unrelenting problems that pose a threat to your harmony and the welfare of those you love. Become proficient in the use of this method and you will never feel powerless again. It will allow you to demonstrate beyond a shadow of a doubt that you have the power to master your own wellbeing and directly influence the wellbeing of people and circumstances around you. In short, it will prove to you that you are a god.

You can use this method to de-stress yourself, heal your body and mind of illness or pain, enhance your performance, radically increase your knowledge and awareness, or to achieve any goal. You can use it to de-stress and heal another person or group of people – your spouse and children, your classmates or your colleagues at work for example. You can also use it to shape the destiny of your business, your community or nation, or the world we all share.

The method I describe in this chapter involves "conscious life force control," or *pranayama*, a term that is derived from two Sanskrit words – *prana* (life force) and *ayama* (containment). Anyone can learn *pranayama* and use it effectively to have an immediate, measurable effect on their own wellbeing and the wellbeing of others.

Pranayama has its roots in Eastern philosophy, but in the West, it is now established scientific fact. The Rishis of India taught that the universe is a manifestation of energy derived from the Infinite Spirit of God which permeates and sustains everything in existence. Within the universal energy field, *prana* exists as a subtle energetic force responsible for sustaining life, peace and harmony. The Rishis taught a specific method by which *prana* could be harnessed and directed for any purpose associated with achieving enlightenment, and they called it

110

pranayama: conscious life force control. In China this energy is called *Qi* (pronounced chi) and the art of controlling it is called *Qigong*. In Japan the energy is called *ki* and the art of controlling it is *Reiki*. In the West the existence of subtle energy and our ability to use it for healing has been proven using advanced instrumentation and controlled scientific studies. There, the force is called *biofield energy* or *subtle energy*, and the methods used to control it are called *biofield therapies* and *subtle energy medicine* respectively.

Subtle energy *(prana, Qi, ki, or biofield energy)* is readily available in abundant supply from the universal energy field. Our ability to use "thought" to direct it to heal ourselves, or to effect healing in another person, group or situation, has been proven through scientific study. I cited two top sources for these studies in Chapter Three: the National Center for Complementary and Integrative Health in the National Institutes of Health in the U.S. and the International Society for the Study of Subtle Energy and Energy Medicine. Readers might also be interested in the *Journal of Alternative and Complementary Medicine* (online, open source) or in Richard Gerber, MD's book titled **Vibrational Medicine**. Dr. Gerber's book is an encyclopedia of hundreds of research studies showing the efficacy of subtle energy. Among these sources there is sufficient research proving it is possible to use your mind to move energy into a person, place or situation to effect change, even at a distance.

In 1998 I presented at a medical conference in Washington, D.C. After my seminar on how to manipulate subtle energy to heal physical problems I invited volunteers to come to the stage from the audience. Up walked a woman laboring badly with the aid of a tripod cane. She had been a dancer in her youth. Her knees had worn down completely and multiple knee surgeries had done little to help. For about fifteen minutes I used biofield therapy to channel subtle energy directly into her injured knees. What happened next did not surprise me, but it certainly surprised her. She stood up, smiled broadly and began to dance about on the stage, ecstatic with her newfound health. She left the auditorium without the use of her cane, to huge applause.

Five years later I was sitting in the front row at another conference, waiting for my turn as speaker. This same woman took the seat next to me. "You don't remember me do you?" she said smiling. Terribly abashed, I had to confess that I recognized her but couldn't remember her name – a professional hazard when you see so many people for brief encounters. She reintroduced herself and told me she registered for this conference because she knew I'd be speaking and she wanted to thank me. She went on to explain that after I healed her knees, she embarked on a

111

three-month tour of Europe, followed by three weeks in Australia. Her life had been one great adventure since she regained the use of her legs.

Two years ago a good friend of mine came to me for help with a most distressing problem. His son, a soldier stationed in Iraq, had just been put in charge of a unit responsible for finding and dismantling Improvised Explosive Devices, or IEDs – one of the most dangerous jobs in the military. His unit was known for its exceedingly high rate of combat losses. My friend feared for his son's life so I taught him the method I teach in this chapter, which he used during his son's tour of duty. From time to time my friend and I worked the method together to ensure his son's welfare. A year went by. One day I came out of my office to see my friend standing there with his son, who was still wearing his army fatigues and combat boots. His son had insisted on coming to see me straight away after he landed at the airport. The son then explained he had been profoundly aware that some force was protecting him during his combat maneuvers. Day in and day out he was surrounded by death and destruction. Yet miraculously, he made it home alive. He'd come to thank me.

These are the kinds of things that are possible to do when you learn how to move subtle energy with your mind. You can do these things yourself – and much, much more – if you take a little time to learn and practice the method I teach here.

The Nature of Subtle Energy

Subtle energy has several predictable characteristics. The first of these is its sheer power. In fact the term *subtle* is a misnomer. Used in this context *subtle* simply means "hard to measure." Subtle energy consists of extremely fine waves of quantum (subatomic) energy. This is a level of energy below Planck's Constant, named after the famous Nobel Laureate in Physics Max Planck, a mass of energy (a "quantum of action") so miniscule that science only evolved the technology to measure it about two decades ago. It is far from subtle in its effects however. It is the essential subatomic force that sustains all matter and life as we know it. Some people find this hard to believe, but there are many examples of unseen, subtle energetic forces that possess awesome power. The quantum energies released from a scant few atoms of uranium generate enough electricity to power the city of Hong Kong for six months. In the not-too-distant future humanity will discover how to harness these energies safely and effectively to fuel every energy need on earth with clean, green power.

The second important characteristic of subtle energy is that it is governed by thought. The universal subtle energy field is created and sustained by the cosmic universal mind (God). As God "thinks" God's intelligence acts on the subtle energy field to create life and sustain it. You and I are "made in the image of God" – a metaphor meaning that our thoughts are also capable of directing subtle energy to achieve specific outcomes for ourselves, other people, organizations, nations, even the world we all share. As you sit reading this text your thoughts are governing the flow of energy through your own mind and body to determine the degree of your physical, mental and spiritual health. Your thoughts are also radiating out into the world to impact the energy fields associated with other people, places and things. This is established scientific fact, not some hopeful religious fantasy. Thought governs energy and energy governs reality as we know it.

This leads me to the third important characteristic of subtle energy – it will invariably act to heal, nurture and evolve anything it infuses. Let's take a look at human beings as a case in point. Subtle energy enters the body through the medulla oblongata – the brainstem located at the base of your brain, at the back of your head. From there, it flows down the spinal cord to the base of the spine. Then it flows upward, and as it goes, it channels outward into your body to power your organs, circulatory system, immune system, peripheral nervous system and other bodily processes. If you have a robust, positive, unimpeded flow of subtle energy throughout your body, you have a virtual guarantee of physical and mental health. However, if the flow of subtle energy through your body is sluggish, or if it is blocked, then your mental and physical health will be poor.

It will not surprise you to know the single biggest barrier to a robust unimpeded flow of subtle energy throughout your body is distorted thinking and the distress it causes. This, more than any other factor, will dampen or stop the flow of positive energy through your body. If you do nothing to ameliorate your distress and if your thinking remains distorted, it will eventually subvert the subtle energy in your body into a negative energetic force of the type that causes illness.

The Method

The method I teach here is one I use in my own work: effective and easy. It works by using focused, directed thought to move subtle energy from the universal quantum field into your own body and mind or into another person, place, thing (a business for example), or situation (i.e. your financial prosperity or women's rights).

The method can and should be used anytime, but by far and away it is most powerful if you use it in meditation. There are three reasons why. First, your super-conscious mind (soul) comes to the forefront of your awareness in meditation, and super-conscious "thinking" is exponentially more powerful than the thought of the conscious mind. Hence any noble desire you express in the stillness of meditation will come into being if you get enough energy and willpower behind it. Second, meditation will help you achieve the mental focus and concentration you need for success. Third, the amount of subtle energy flowing through you during meditation is far greater than when you are in a non-meditative state. This is because in meditation your soul-consciousness – your energy portal to the infinite power of the universal cosmic mind – is open. You become like a living nuclear energy plant capable of directing vast levels of energy into any target anywhere, for any noble purpose.

If you practice the method in meditation you will naturally develop the skill required to use it successfully in a non-meditative state. I'm going to teach you how to use the method both ways: in and out of meditation.

Using the Method to Heal Yourself

We'll begin with self-healing, because it takes precedence over every other worldly goal. All good things in life begin with our own internal health and harmony. It is from the wellspring of internal harmony that we gain harmony with God and with the world around us. Without it, we fall easy prey to the destructive, negative forces that permeate society. For everyone, the pursuit of their own internal harmony is a most essential part of fulfilling their highest destiny for the incarnation. Furthermore, if you don't have internal harmony, you cannot effectively influence any other person, place or thing for the good. For all these reasons, your internal harmony must come first and foremost. In fact, it is a good idea for you to use this method regularly on the heels of your daily meditation or anytime you feel the slightest internal distress. It is that effective and it's so easy a child can do it.

To use the method you must know how to meditate. Use your own method, or if you don't have one that works for you, use the method I provided in Chapter Four. Using either method, meditate until your mind is very calm and you feel the first-fruits of soul contact: profound peace. Next draw in a long deep breath. As you do so, put your awareness at the base of your head (in the back, where your neck meets your head) and imagine energy flowing inward. At the point where the indrawn breath pauses, focus your attention on yourself. Then as the breath goes out, imagine the captured energy flowing into your illness, injury or psychological issue.

114

That's the method, start to finish. To apply it successfully, simply repeat this process with every breath (draw in energy with the in-breath, then send the energy into yourself with the out-breath) for at least 5 minutes, longer if you can. If you become distracted by a thought, a feeling or a daydream, simply let go of it and return to the method. Focused concentration on the method without allowing your attention to become diverted, will deliver measurable results. When you are finished, simply close your meditation with a prayer of thanks and open your eyes. You should feel a strong sense of euphoria and peace because of all the energy you just pumped through your mind and body. You'll feel better physically and mentally right away and carry this sense of wellbeing throughout your day. You should feel much stronger, more peaceful, aware and happy.

The method really is this simple and effective. You can easily tailor it to suit your learning style and goals for self-healing. For example, imagine energy flowing into the back of your head with the indrawn breath, in any way that works for you. The indrawn breath creates a vacuum or "pull" inward. When you feel that pull, all you have to do is "think" energy is flowing into the back of your head, and it will. Visual, creative people often prefer to imagine a cloud of white healing light flowing into the base of the head as they draw in their breath. Any combination of these or similar techniques will allow you to take in vast amounts of energy for healing (more than you need actually).

The same holds true for the exhaled breath and how you focus it. If your issue is a physical illness or injury, focus the energy specifically on the affected body parts – for example, your heart, kidneys or a bad knee you inherited from playing rugby. If you have a system-wide problem (like diabetes or leukemia) send the energy throughout your entire body. If your issue is psychological, focus the energy on your head and down the length of your spine, filling your torso with energy as you go. If you hold too much fear, anger, guilt or shame, focus some energy on your sternum, stomach and bowels (where we tend to hold the negative emotions that fuel chronic distress). If you suffer from too much grief and love loss, be sure to concentrate energy on your heart. If you need a clearer sense of meaning and purpose in life, or you feel alienated from God, concentrate the energy in your Third Eye (the point between the eyebrows – your portal to the infinite) and just above the crown of your head.

As you exhale, as long as you are concentrating on your issue, you will get the job done. When you breathe out just "think" that energy is flowing into your problem and it will. Or you can "imagine" energy flowing into your problem in the form of white, healing light. You can send the energy "through" your body to its destination or you can stream it "laser-like" from your medulla directly into your affliction. Some people "place" the energy in their issue instantaneously – one moment it is residing at the medulla, and with the out-breath it immediately manifests at its destination with no sense of a path it followed to get there. Any one or a combination of these techniques will work. As long as you are concentrating your attention on your illness, injury, psychological or spiritual issue, the energy will flow into it. Remember, quantum energy follows thought. Recall the experiments at the Stanford Accelerator Laboratory. Science has proven that quantum energy follows thought. Your ability to concentrate your thought and attention on your target issue is all that's required to send quantum energy where it needs to go.

When you come out of this meditative exercise you will feel strongly energized. After a little practice of this technique, you will be able to move extraordinary amounts of energy for healing, and actually begin to perceive or "feel" the energy flowing into and through your body.

Once you've practiced this technique in meditation, you can use it anytime. Perhaps you have a few minutes while you're standing in line at the store, at the airport waiting for a flight, or sitting in a very boring meeting – use the method (energy flowing in with the in-breath, energy flowing into your body with the out-breath). Be sure to use it if you find yourself in a stressful situation – a heated discussion with your boss, classmate or spouse for example. It will provide immediate measurable relief from fear, anxiety, shame, guilt or anger, keep you calm, and help you maintain a clear perspective on what's happening.

How to Heal Another Person, Group or Thing

The same basic method can be used to heal another individual or groups of people, such as a family, business, organization or branch of government. You can use it to heal an entire population in need. You can also use the method to heal a place – a location where the energy field has been polluted by an act of war, civil strife or toxic waste. You can also use it to heal a situation – your marriage, your annual income, the profitability of your business or even something very large and complex like poverty in India or the Indian economy. Anything you can conceive of in your mind – in other words, anything you can make into an object of thought or imagination – you can send energy into it to effect change.

Within the universal energy field, subtle energy travels through any obstacle, does not lose power over distance traveled, and moves at super-luminal speed (faster than the speed of light from point A to point

B with no time lost at all). Scientific studies prove that it can be moved instantly over great distances to effect healing. So you can send subtle energy to a person, group, event or situation that is half way across the globe, with no loss of time and no loss of healing effect.

Before you begin use of the method consider exactly what you want to accomplish. You can use the method for any noble purpose that's consistent with your *Story Behind the Story* – your highest personal destiny. Just be sure to have a clear, focused idea of what you want to achieve before you begin using the method. If you try to pursue multiple or ill-defined objectives you will not be able to achieve the one-pointed concentration you need for success. You can have multiple goals but you'll want to focus on just one discreet goal each time you use the method.

Just as importantly, don't think "small" with regard to your goals. Your soul and the cosmic universal mind are happy to provide you with what you need and desire as long as it is consistent with your own highest purpose for the incarnation. Think really big with regard to what you can achieve, then don't be too attached to the outcome. Be sure in the knowledge that your soul and the cosmic mind will deliver the best possible results. There is an old saying that applies to this kind of even-mindedness: "Shoot for the sun and be satisfied with the moon."

Once you have a clear idea of what you want to accomplish, you're ready to use the method. Begin with meditation. To move energy to heal a target outside yourself, you need to be able to meditate very deeply. If you are an advanced meditator, use your own meditation method. If not, you should use the hypnotic meditation method I provided in Chapter Seven: Scientific Meditation (track 3 on the CD that accompanies this book, or the track titled *Hypnotic Meditation* for online readers). It will get you into a very deep meditative state with little effort on your part, and ensure your success.

Using your own technique or mine, meditate for at least 15 minutes or until your mind is very calm and you feel the proof of soul-contact (a deep peace). This is the time to invoke Divine assistance on your behalf. Then, with your eyelids still closed focus your eyes comfortably on the point between your eyebrows – the Third Eye. It is through the energy portal of the Third Eye that you gain access to the power of the universal energy field. As you use this method you are channeling your thoughts through the portal of the Third Eye into the universal energy field, where they act to move vast amounts of healing energy into any target, regardless of location, anywhere on the planet.

While keeping your attention on your Third Eye, consider your target. You can do this by imagining what he/she/it looks like or just by "thinking" about the name and characteristics of the person, group or thing. Either or both of these approaches will work. All you have to do is maintain your mental focus on your target while concentrating on the location of the Third Eye.

Then, for at least 10 minutes apply the same technique I described for self-healing. As you draw in each breath, imagine energy flowing inward through the medulla oblongata at the base of your head. As you breathe out imagine the captured energy flowing into your target. If you are an artistic type you may want to visualize healing energy as white light flowing into your target until it is radiant like the sun. If you are a highly cognitive type who doesn't visualize things easily, just "think" of the person, group or thing filling with energy and becoming healthy, high-functioning and happy. Both of these approaches work.

You can "shape" future outcomes based on how you focus your mind during this phase. The more focused your conception, the more successful you will be. Let's say you need a new job. You could imagine yourself employed, working productively in a vocation of your choosing, going to work each day, earning a good wage, able to support yourself and your family and even how good it will feel and how happy you'll be – all while you are super-charging your imagery with white healing light. Likewise you could just "think" about yourself going to work each day, about being productive, receiving your salary, living life to its fullest with the money you earn and putting money away for savings each week. Either or both of these approaches will work well. Just remember to think big.

Even if your target is large and complex you will be able to apply the tools of imagination and thought to effect the change you desire. If you wanted to improve the economy of India for example, you could imagine every citizen in every corner of the country being filled with white healing light. As you continue to super-charge the citizenry with light, you imagine everyone working productively and happily, having all the abundance they need, with no one lacking for anything. The air is clean, people are bustling about in cars on new roads or efficient mass transit, every youngster safely going to school each day and so on. You could equally get the job done by "thinking" about the gross domestic product skyrocketing, a hugely burgeoning middle class, a zero percent unemployment rate, and vast increases in annual income for everyone in the country. Just remember to imagine or think about your goal in very large terms.

When you are finished moving energy, conclude your meditation with a prayer of gratitude and open your eyes. You will notice a profound sense of peace and wellbeing.

That's the method, start to finish. To apply it successfully strive for good concentration and a calm, compassionate mind. If you become distracted by a thought, feeling or daydream simply let go of it and return to the method. As often as you do this, you will quickly train your mind to achieve the one-pointed, focused concentration needed for success.

To get results you must also be able to focus on your target with virtuous thought and feeling. Peace, compassion and love will direct vast amounts of healing energy. By contrast, negative thought and emotion (grief, resentment, fear, anger or shame) generate destructive energies that can potentially cause harm. A good meditation method, rightly employed, will help you achieve *both* one-pointed concentration and the virtuous mind-set you need to get rapid, positive results.

Once you've practiced this method in a meditative state, you will be able to use it to great effect outside of meditation on targets that are in close proximity to you. With very little effort you can use the method with no loss of participation in your activities as you move through your day. For example, let's say your wife is severely distressed over the recent death of her dearest friend and you want to help her. Simply use the method (energy flowing in with the in-breath, energy flowing out through your Third Eye into your wife with the out-breath) when she is nearby at intervals throughout the day. Use it on your colleagues at the office, on a homeless child you pass on the street, or on the people who congregate at your temple, mosque or church.

With continued practice you will be able to use the method effectively outside of meditation on a complex problem (the Indian economy) or a target that is geographically distant (your son who is in college in Great Britain). Effectiveness using the method outside of meditation on complex or distant targets is based on your ability to concentrate and how often you meditate. If you are meditating daily and if you practice the method outside of meditation, you will develop the skill to do this. In my line of work we call it "holding a space in your mind" – the ability to focus on another person, place or thing with unbroken concentration as you move through your day fulfilling the tasks of daily living. A mind that has been expanded through regular meditation has no problem "holding a space" for several people, places and things in need of healing.

119

Important Considerations

As you become proficient in the use of this method you will find that the things you need start coming your way with less effort, in much less time than you expected. As a result, you'll have more time and resources to accomplish what you want to do in life, to refine your aspirations and live out a destiny that is more elevated than the one you are living right now. Consider the man who is an entry-level employee in a manufacturing plant, where the average time required to become a supervisor is 10 to 12 years. He wants to become a supervisor so he can support his growing family – a noble goal – so he employs the method and becomes a supervisor in 10 to 12 months. Having satisfied his need to earn money, he now has the freedom to turn his attention and effort to attaining loftier goals and he has 10 additional years to pursue them. Having fulfilled the primal need to support his family he can turn his attention to spiritual matters – to finding more enlightened awareness. He has become a master of his own destiny.

If you intend to apply the method there are some important considerations to keep in mind. First of all be aware that a dose-response relationship applies to energy healing, which means that regular small doses of energy will deliver results even if the problem is severe. So use it with consistency. If your target's issues are complex (an economic recession) or acute (you have a sister who is near death from cancer) you will need to use the technique in meditation several times a week over time to make a difference.

A second consideration to keep in mind is that subtle energy is endowed with universal intelligence (God's own wisdom). It knows precisely how to heal and evolve people or situations in the most virtuous and efficient way. You do not have the same degree of knowledge at your disposal. So if you employ the method you must trust the cosmic mind to effect the best outcome, with the understanding that it may not be precisely the outcome you hoped for. Using the example in the last paragraph, if your sister is ready to leave her body and continue her journey in the heavens, you may not be able to prolong her life. However, the energy you send will ease her symptoms, move her into peace and raise her level of enlightenment prior to her passing – an eternal gift of extraordinary magnitude.

Let's consider a corporate example of this same principle at work. Imagine that your business, which sells new computers, is failing: sales are plummeting and you've had to fire employees. So you use the method to make your firm more profitable. Meanwhile, the cosmic mind is aware that the manufacturer of your product line will be purchased next year by a big transnational corporation that intends to produce junk computers just to make fast money at the consumer's expense – a move that will give the transnational giant a monopoly over your market and cause endless frustration to the consumer.

The cosmic mind knows the only virtuous and efficient way for your firm to become highly profitable is for it to stop selling your current product line and manufacture its own inexpensive but reliable line of new computers. So the energy you send goes into motion to effect this outcome. You end up re-tooling your business, which means a lot of sacrifice and hard work – not the outcome you hoped for. However, the energy you put into the effort assures your corporate vision is stellar, your transition is well-capitalized and you attract the talent you need. In two years your firm is one of the fastest growing businesses in Asia because you offer a reliable product that serves an unmet need at a fair price. You end up rich while ensuring justice for the consumer and financial stability for a growing number of employees. Everybody wins.

A third consideration in the use of this method consists of a somewhat ironic caution: you might get **precisely** what you want using the method, but the reality of it is not what you hoped for. For example, take a man I've been working with over the last few years. He could never win his father's love, his mother was harsh with him while he was growing up, and he never felt like he amounted to anything. He didn't have much culture, income or education. Then he married a woman who belittled him all the time, just like his mother. His children didn't respect him either. Even so he loved his family very much. The distress he carried because of lost love and lack of self-esteem had caused significant depression, along with weight gain, circulatory problems and bowel disease.

As we worked together, this man came to understand that his *Story Behind the Story* was compelling him to learn how to love and respect himself. His depression cleared and his health improved remarkably. As part of his quest to make justice for himself, he decided he really wanted to have a nice big house to enjoy with his family. His desire was not entirely superficial. After having too little in life he wanted "the American dream" and the ability to give it to his family.

When he started working with me, he was making a paltry annual income doing work that he despised. I taught him how to work this method. Now he's clearing more than a million U.S. dollars annually doing work that he loves and he uses his wealth to help other people. He's a good man, a hero in his own way. However, his financial success has come at a great cost. He is always on the go. He has the beautiful house but he is seldom home to enjoy it, and remains alienated from his family.

The fourth consideration concerns the existence of two caveats on the use of the method. You cannot use it to create harm and you cannot use it to override another person's free will. These two caveats are consistent with how the cosmic mind (God) operates: it always acts to evolve and nurture, and it always respects our free will. If you are going to use this method to behave like a god, you have to be mindful of what God requires.

Let's look at a specific example of these two caveats in action. Let's say that you are totally committed to your marriage but you don't have a loving, joyful, intimate relationship with your spouse and you want to change that – a noble goal. So you use the method to focus healing energy on your relationship, imagining or thinking of yourself and your spouse having a perfect union characterized by extravagant levels of love, joy and intimacy. If your spouse's will is diametrically opposed to change, what you will find is that *you* are the one who ends up changing. You will become much more patient, aware, honest, supportive, attentive, unconditionally loving, joyful and romantic. Most likely your spouse will end up changing because he or she is inspired by the change in you. If your spouse steadfastly refuses to change however (which happens only rarely), the energy you focus on healing the relationship will do two things. It will stay in your spouse's energy field and be available for healing as soon as they change their mind in any positive direction. It will also act to create virtuous opportunities by which you can acquire the love you need – a stronger relationship with God for example.

A fifth consideration to be aware of is that the energetic healing effects of this method are powerfully multiplied when many minds focus on the same problem. If your target's issues are extremely complex or acute (like poverty in India) you may want to invite friends, family or colleagues to join you in using the method. You will get faster results. You do not have to agree to meditate at the same time every day or even to meditate in the same place. A number of minds focusing their thought and energy on the same target with regularity is sufficient to get the job done.

In a group experiment conducted in Washington, D.C. in 1993, researchers collaborated with the Washington D.C. Police Department in an attempt to reduce violent crime using subtle energy. Four thousand people agreed to meditate on the problem – that's four thousand people directing subtle energy onto a large, highly complex set of energies associated with criminal tendencies, social and economic oppression, illiteracy and so forth. The result: violent crime in Washington, D.C. dropped by an unprecedented 25 percent on the targeted day, as attested to in the press by the D.C. police chief.

A sixth consideration to keep in mind is that consistent practice of the method will bring demonstrable success. The human mind is a kinesthetic learning instrument: it learns by doing. As you become proficient with the method your intuitive awareness (soul-consciousness) will become strong and accurate. You will find yourself gifted with an immediate, accurate sense of knowing how and why things are out of harmony within yourself, other people and situations. This insight will allow you to fine-tune your thinking and therefore improve your ability to direct healing energy with increasing levels of accuracy. Further, the amount of energy you can move will keep increasing. For this reason, anyone who regularly practices energy healing can become a powerful force for change in their own life and the lives of others.

Indeed, through use of this method you have the ability to gift many thousands of people, even millions, with justice and healing. If people worldwide were to use the power of directed super-conscious thought to focus on those in need, the world would be redeemed from disease, strife and oppression in no time. If you use the method often you will become a key player in the redemption of your community, nation and world.

This leads me to the last and most important issue for consideration. I raised it near the beginning of the chapter, but it is so important it deserves another mention: the single most critical criterion for success using this method is whether you are moving in tandem with your *Story Behind the Story* – your own highest purpose for the incarnation. Whatever your destiny may be, your own internal harmony and your harmony with the cosmic universal mind (God) are central to your mission. If you are ignoring your own disharmony and try to use the method on other people, places or things, you will not get very far. The reason is that your soul will slow you down in order to get you to focus on your own issues. Even if it is your chosen destiny to become a healer, you will find that you cannot become proficient at healing others if you aren't also focused on healing yourself.

You cannot teach others what you do not know. You do not have to be perfect to employ this method to great effect, but you do have to be willing to grapple with your own distortions of thought and feeling – the very things that keep you locked in a cycle of distress, the very things that keep you convinced you are not a god.

If you practice this method you will directly observe your ability to change things. This experience will convince you beyond a shadow of a doubt that you are not a mere mortal. It will let you lead a truly heroic, adventurous life.

123

10

Think Straight, Feel Great

In this chapter we jump into a quick, practical method that delivers freedom from distress. It's brief. After you learn how to do it you can use it anytime, anywhere, and if you use it correctly, you'll feel dramatically better in just three weeks. Use of this method will quickly make it obvious to you just how much power you can exert over your own wellbeing.

Before you start the method, remember a very important principle from earlier chapters: your thinking (perceptions, beliefs, attitudes and expectations) is driving your distress, not your circumstances. The method in this chapter will let you master your thinking, at which point you will be able to convert your *distress* (a harmful, intense biological and emotional stress reaction) into *eustress* (a manageable challenge that will help you become stronger and happier).

As You Think, So Shall You Be

The method I teach here comes from Cognitive Therapy, a branch of traditional psychotherapy that is responsible for most of the advances in the field of psychology over the last thirty years. Aaron Beck, M.D., first introduced cognitive therapy to the field of psychology in the 1960s. Beck discovered that the way people perceive and interpret their experiences (known as *cognition*) will determine their emotional states. Their emotional states, in turn, will determine whether they feel distress or eustress.

We discussed the mental process that gives rise to stress in Chapters One and Four. The thrust of those discussions is summarized in the following table. The important thing to remember is the order of the mental events that lead to stress: on encounter with a stressor, you conduct a cognitive analysis to determine whether the stressor constitutes great risk of harm, is a challenge you can manage and overcome, contains opportunity, or is simply a non-issue. This analysis usually takes place in a matter of moments, and part of it is hidden from your awareness, secreted away in your subconscious mind. The cognitive analysis then triggers an emotional response, and the nature of the emotional response will determine whether we experience distress or eustress.

Step	Event			
1 Stressor Occurs	A disparity between your expectations and your actual experience occurs.			
2 Cognitive Analysis	Your subconscious and conscious minds analyze the situation to see if it constitutes a threat of harm, is a challenge you can undertake and overcome, if you can benefit from it, or whether it is simply a non-issue. *Note: Distorted thoughts, perceptions, beliefs and expectations in the subconscious and conscious minds come into play during this step*			
3 Decision	It's a threat of great harm and I am powerless to do anything about it	It's a challenge, maybe even life-threatening, but I can overcome it	It's an opportunity	It's a non-issue
4 Resulting Emotions	Fear, terror, shame, guilt, grief, anger, rage, resentment, frustration, self-loathing, without heroic attitudes present	Challenged by negative emotion, but also faithful, hopeful, determined, and courageous	Intrigued and excited	Relief
5 Biological & Mental Response	Distress	Eustress	Eustress	None

Distress occurs when your cognitive analysis indicates you are at risk of great harm and powerless to do anything about it. The emotions that result are intensely negative and the heroic attitudes you need to surmount the stressor (courage, faith, hope and love) are absent or nearly absent. This scenario will typically trigger maximal distress: an acute biological "fight or flight" response accompanied by significant mental anguish.

Conversely, eustress will result under one of two alternative scenarios. In the first case, your cognitive analysis results in an assumption of harm and strong negative emotions arise but the heroic attitudes and feelings needed to surmount the stressor are strong too. You end up with a sense of being challenged, anxious and fearful, but willing to endure and confident everything will be alright in the end. Eustress will also result in cases where we determine that the stressor, while challenging, constitutes an opportunity. In such cases, negative emotion is milder and the heroic qualities needed to surmount the challenge are powerfully present.

The bottom line here is simple: what you think about the stressor will determine your emotional response, and your emotional response will determine the type of stress you experience. So, if your thinking is distorted in some way, you may conclude that the stressor constitutes a real and immediate threat to your wellbeing, one you are powerless to do anything about, when in fact this is simply not true. Distorted thinking drives unrelenting, strongly negative emotion – the thing that leads to distress. Distorted thinking will also prevent you from maintaining the heroic attitudes you need to triumph over negative emotion – triumph over negative emotion and you will effectively convert your distress to eustress.

It is unfortunate but true that *everyone* suffers from distortions in their thinking. Errors in thought arise from numerous sources: unresolved stressful experiences you had in your family of origin, social milieu, school and personal relationships. The attitudes and expectations of your family and culture have also introduced some level of distortion in your perceptions, beliefs, attitudes and expectations. There are also distorted tendencies of thought that you brought with you into this world as a function of your experience in past incarnations.

Dr. Beck developed cognitive therapy as a means to discover the distorted, or "unrealistic," thinking that drives a person's negative emotions. Discover the distortions in your thinking and remove them, and negative emotion cannot rise to the level required to trigger and maintain distress in your mind and body. Remove distortions in your thinking, and the heroic attitudes of courage, faith, hope and love will come to the forefront of your awareness. Free yourself from distorted thoughts and the vicious cycle of negative emotion they create, and you can free yourself from repetitive, stress-building tendencies of behavior. The key to finding freedom from distress is therefore to discover and re-program the distortions in your thinking. It's that simple.

Hear me loud and clear: if your thinking is accurate at all levels of mind there is no stressor on earth that can throw you into a state of distress or keep you locked in despair. Every stressor, no matter what its nature or magnitude, has limitless potential for growth and understanding.

Cognitive therapy has evolved a lot over the four decades since Beck's groundbreaking research. The core notion behind it remains the same however: stress follows feeling, and feeling follows thought. People who suffer from chronic distress suffer from chronically negative emotions (fear, anger, shame, resentment, guilt, powerlessness, poor self-esteem, etc.) driven by a distorted thought process. The good news is, if you can discover and correct the distortions in your thinking, the negative emotions (and the distress they cause) will disappear.

This concept is liberating and should inspire a great deal of optimism about yourself and the human species. If you think accurately in any situation you find yourself, even if it's a difficult situation, strong negative emotions will not overwhelm you. Your heroic qualities will prevail and you will not experience distress.

When I introduce my clients to this concept, many agree with it. However some say, "No way, Doc. When I'm swamped by bad feelings, I'm not thinking at all – the feelings just rise up out of nowhere. I'm not thinking, I'm just feeling." Certainly that's how it seems when powerful emotion arises, but the research is abundantly clear: thought is the governor of your emotions. Remember that you are always "thinking" at multiple levels: most of what you are "thinking" is hidden from your awareness, secreted away in the subconscious mind. When you feel smothered by powerful emotion, it's usually because distorted thinking in the subconscious has been churning away in secret. You are only aware of the negative emotion that follows and the degree to which it is stressing you out.

There are many cognitive therapy methods, several of which are quite helpful. The method I teach here differs from the majority of approaches in one important way: it allows you to *drill down into the subconscious mind* to reprogram the distorted thought process there. In other words, this method will allow you to free yourself from the effects of historical stress.

The healing effects of this approach are rapid and extraordinary. A few years ago a successful middle-aged businessman came to see me for help. This man constantly suffered from colds, flu and viral infections of every sort. No sooner would he recover from one when another would assail him. His doctor could find no physical cause for it and referred him to me on the hunch that a psychological problem was fueling his chronic illness. When I met with the man I found him to be extremely anxious and driven. For his entire adult life he had worked a 70-hour workweek. When most people would be on the brink of exhaustion, my client would find a burst of energy and complete his task no matter what it took out of him. He didn't realize it but he was literally working himself to death.

This man's father, a colonel in the army, had raised him under the strictest military expectations for performance in the face of adversity. His history made it clear that the focus of our work was to find and dismantle the distortions in his thought that compelled him to sacrifice his own essential need for rest. I taught him the cognitive reprogramming approach I describe in this chapter, which he used (not surprisingly) with military consistency.

Shortly after we began our work together he arrived one day in my office to say, "I've found the distortion in my thinking. The last time we were together I told you I thought the cause for my anxiety was my work ethic and too much responsibility. You said 'those thoughts are accurate' and told me to look a little deeper. So I applied the cognitive reprogramming method again and again last week. I found the distortion in my thinking that makes me feel like I'm going to explode if I don't keep working: I thought I would be punished if I didn't make the grade."

It turned out when my client was a boy his father placed high demands on him and punished him severely if he failed to perform. As a boy, my client's experience created a distortion in his thinking: "If I don't perform at the top-flight level *all* the time, I'll be punished." So he drove himself to be a superman. After he found this distortion and reprogrammed it, he eased back and moved into a phase of life that was self-loving, self-compassionate and a whole lot healthier and happier - interestingly with no loss in performance.

The Method

The following simple cognitive reprogramming method will change the way you think at both the conscious and subconscious levels. In doing so it will allow you to shift your negative feelings into peace and personal potency. It will also allow you to free yourself from stress-building beliefs and behaviors driven by unresolved conflict and distress from your past. The focus of this process is to target distortion in your thought process as it arises in response to specific events and challenges. You can and should use it any time you feel strong emotional distress.

The process has seven simple steps. As you gain familiarity with its use, you will be able to complete it in a couple of minutes. Near the end of this chapter, I summarize the steps in a seven-bullet "cheat sheet" you should carry in your pocket or purse for future reference.

Step 1: Be aware of what you're feeling in the moment

This method works best if you use it at the very point when you start to feel bad. If you have your antenna up, you'll catch negative emotion as it actually happens. A lot of us move through the day without realizing how we actually feel until someone or something draws our attention to it. The first crucial step in this process therefore is to stay aware and notice when you are starting to feel bad emotionally. If you aren't aware of it, you'll miss the opportunity to reprogram it altogether.

Step 2: Label the emotion(s) you're feeling

At the point when you realize you're feeling bad, take a few seconds to put a label on what you're feeling. Is it anger, fear, sadness, frustration, shame, guilt or some other emotion? At this point, you are only trying to understand what you're feeling, not what you're thinking. Some people have trouble distinguishing between the two and it is important for you to discern the difference. If your boss takes you down a peg in a meeting with your colleagues because you failed to get a job done, you might feel anxious, fearful, shamed, guilty or angry. You might *think*, "I don't deserve this" or "He's being an ass," but that's a thought, not how you feel. As best you can, take note of how you're feeling. Early on, you might even want to write this down. It will allow you to see that you possess patterns of emotional response to similar situations – as do we all. This will deepen your self-awareness and your success with the method.

Step 3: Look at the thoughts behind the feeling

Now ask yourself, "What are my thoughts related to this feeling?" This step is usually as simple as looking at the thoughts moving in the back of your mind at that moment. Let's say the boss *has* embarrassed you publicly and you're feeling very anxious, angry and fearful. You start looking at the "thoughts" related to these feelings and you find several. In addition to, "I don't deserve this" or "He's being an ass," you also may think, "My boss doesn't like me and wants to get rid of me." Whatever you think, make a mental note of it or if circumstances allow, write it down.

Step 4: Ask yourself "Where's the distortion?"

At this stage you're concerned with finding the distortion in your thinking. If you're feeling strong negative emotion moving through you *assume* your thinking is distorted. Sometimes you have to look hard for the distortion. Consider our example: your boss has publicly embarrassed you and you become very anxious, angry and fearful. You are immediately aware of three thoughts related to your feelings ("I don't deserve this," "My boss is an ass," and "My boss doesn't like me and wants to get rid of me"). Now you have to ask yourself, "Where is the distortion?" You may review your thoughts and conclude they are entirely accurate: you didn't deserve the harsh treatment (you are dedicated to your work and a productive employee overall), your boss is being an ass (only an angry, selfish boss takes down a subordinate in front of his or her colleagues), and based on your boss' historical pattern of antagonism toward you, you conclude your boss really *does* want to see you fired. All three of your initial thoughts on the matter appear to be accurate and free of distortion. In this case you have to look deeper. Only a distorted thought will drive chronic emotional distress. Accurate thoughts, even if they point to a significant challenge on your horizon ("My boss wants to fire me"), will not create chronic ill feeling.

Sometimes finding the thought distortion is a little tricky. I remember a man who came to me years ago. He was a brilliant young doctor and research scientist who was suffering from chronic depression. He'd gotten into trouble by standing up to a very powerful superior who had unfairly criticized him. After that he experienced continuous difficulty at work. When I asked him to identify the thought behind his depression he exclaimed, "I'm depressed because this powerful man is ruining my career!" I pushed him saying, "Well, that thought is accurate. To find the source of your depression you have to go deeper." He pushed and pushed and finally found it. Dropping his head into his hands and beginning to weep he said, "I've ruined my career just like my father ruined his."

It ended up that at a similar age his father had crossed his own boss and his father's boss went on a crusade to damage the father's reputation. The father's career eventually plummeted, leaving the family in bankruptcy. In the back of my client's mind was the distorted thought that his problems with his boss were going to ruin his future in the same way. When he realized the distortion he let it go. He came to understand he was a different person from his father – there was no basis in fact to assume his career was going to be ruined. The corrected distortion in his thinking freed him of his depression. He went on to make amends with his boss and subsequently achieved extraordinary levels of success in his field. Like my client, you may have to dig a little to discover the source of the distortion in your thinking.

Step 5: Correct the distortion

Once you've found the distortion, correct it with a simple "counter-claim" of undistorted truth. My client corrected his distortion by thinking, "I am not my father. I can make things right with my boss. My career will be fine." That correction freed him from depression and unleashed the mental power he needed to remake his destiny. As you get good with this process you will discover related patterns of distortion in your thinking and develop a series of "counter-claims," or "affirmations of truth" that directly reverse these patterns. You might want to write out these affirmations and use them whenever you discover a familiar distortion at work in your thinking.

Step 6: How would you feel if you believed the correction?

Now begin to imagine how you'd feel if you believed the correction in your distorted thinking. This step will facilitate a shift in your feelings. You may still feel challenged, but now hopeful, optimistic, confidant and open to other possibilities for your future. You might even be happy and become aware of precisely what you should do to move forward. Write down or make a mental note of these feelings and any details that arise in relation to them.

Some people have trouble with this step because they don't actually "believe" the corrected thought. The distorted thought might tug at you and you may want to cling to it out of habit. You are at a crossroads. If you find yourself in a tug-of-war between an old distortion in your thinking and a new distortion-free idea, throw some old-fashioned willpower into adopting the change. Realize you are attached to the old thought pattern because you've been brainwashed by the effects of memory. Do you really want to remain attached to your conditioned, distorted thoughts or would you rather adopt the new way of thinking and take control of your life? The old thought pattern needs to go if you are going to restore your freedom, dignity and self-efficacy. Remind yourself you deserve this newfound power and stick with the process. The benefits will far outweigh the effort required to jettison the old way of thinking.

Step 7: Imagine the new feelings for sixty seconds

Whatever these new more positive feelings might be (optimism, confidence, happiness and so on) repeat them in your imagination with a strong sense of conviction for sixty seconds. Revel in the release of the old emotions and the delight and freedom associated with the new distortion-free thought. Give it a full 60 seconds. You don't want to cut this step short. During this step you are broadcasting an advertisement to your subconscious mind – a new way of thinking and feeling that penetrates deeply into the subconscious and reprograms the distorted thought that is lurking there. Remember, the "language" of the subconscious mind is imagery, symbol and metaphor.

Some people have trouble with this step because they think imagination is for sissies. It is true that when imagination is delusional it isn't helpful and can sometimes be destructive. However, when we imagine something that is true, it has the effect of calling the imagined existence into being. So for this step, give everything you've got to imagining how you'd feel if you believed the corrected thought. You will in fact cause it to manifest.

Your Plan for Developing Skill with Cognitive Reprogramming

Here is a brief summary of the cognitive reprogramming method:

- Be aware of what you're feeling.
- Label your feelings.
- Look at the thoughts behind your feelings.

- Ask yourself, "Where's the distortion?"
- Correct the distortion.
- Ask yourself how you'd feel if you believed the correction.
- Run the new feeling in your imagination for sixty seconds.

This seven-step summary is your cheat-sheet for the cognitive reprogramming process. Copy it down and put it in your pocket or purse for future reference. If you follow this method you'll get amazing results. Implement it just one-third of the time you find yourself gripped by negative emotion and follow the method closely (no missed steps) and you will find that negative emotions and the stress associated with them are noticeably better in just three weeks. Stay aware of your emotional state and you'll get the results you're looking for.

When you're first starting to use the method, until you get good at it, you'll want to dwell on the steps in depth and write down your observations. Life doesn't always allow for an intermission of this sort but do what you can. If you're an attendant at your sister's wedding and feel intensely negative emotion in the middle of the ceremony, you aren't going to whip out a pad of paper and a pen. For situations like this I suggest you apply a simple, universal affirmation that will staunch most forms of emotional distress: repeat to yourself and imagine "I am infinite, eternal, ever-new joy." You will feel somewhat better immediately. However when you get home from the ceremony you might want to write down a few notes about the thoughts that were behind your distress at the wedding, and work the reprogramming process while the experience is fresh on your mind.

Working the cognitive reprogramming process is a little challenging for some people at first but if you stay with it, it will become second nature and it will work rapidly and powerfully. You will quickly be able to identify distortions in your thinking and readily employ a set of counter-claims (undistorted thoughts or affirmations) designed to reprogram them. In a matter of moments you will be able to identify how you feel, analyze your thinking, find the distortion, counteract it with an affirmation of truth, understand how the new idea would make you feel and imaginatively revel in the new feelings. People who get good at this method can work it in two or three minutes without creating any disruption in the flow of circumstances around them.

This hands-on method will deliver dramatic results that build your self-confidence. You'll be able to experience freedom from stressful emotion quickly and know you achieved it through your own will and effort. It will demonstrate to you beyond a shadow of a doubt that you have the power to control your mind, your distress and your future.

11

Freedom from the Past

Everyone reading this book has had to endure significant challenges in life and some readers will have endured great hardship. In this chapter I provide you with a method that allows you to go back in time to visit the challenges of the past, mine them for what they have to say about your *Story Behind the Story*, and totally free yourself from the mental legacy of painful experience early in life. Use of this method will have a profound effect on you, perhaps allowing you to move forward with your life in joy for the first time since you were a child. It can be that liberating.

To free yourself from the past you must be able to access your subconscious mind – our storehouse of memory. There is a psychological wall in the mind that stops most of our memories from passing into conscious awareness. If this were not so, you would hardly be able to function because everything you ever experienced – every thought or feeling, every song you ever sang – would flood your conscious awareness. The result would be mental chaos, making it impossible for you to concentrate on the here and now. In psychology this wall is known as a "gatekeeper."

In this chapter I use clinical hypnosis to let you bypass your gatekeeper so you can have access to the memories and wisdom that reside in your subconscious mind. Recall from Chapter Seven that clinical hypnosis is a mainstream medical discipline used to affect healing in the mind and body. I have used it for over three decades in my clinical work and I am board-certified in this medical specialty, which is very different from "stage hypnotism." Stage hypnotism is an entertainment medium that uses authoritarian methods of mind control and it is unhealthy for the mind. The methods I use are called *permissive* hypnosis. They are totally safe and clinically proven to improve a person's psychological, physical and spiritual health.

If you used *The Stressbuster* or the Hypnotically-guided Meditation method from previous chapters then you already know what permissive hypnosis feels like. It is very relaxing and peaceful. You are in control the whole time, aware of everything that's happening and you remember everything with great clarity. The real value of permissive hypnosis lies in its ability to relax the body and calm and focus the mind. When this happens, your gatekeeper simply relaxes and slides out of the way, allowing you to have access to the content of your conscious and subconscious minds at the same time. In the present case we're using permissive hypnosis to let you focus the searchlight of your awareness on memories that reside in the subconscious – a process that is called *hypnotic regression*.

Why Use Regression?

Eunice came to see me a few years ago for help to battle stage one breast cancer. She was in her mid 40s and had led a very low key private existence her whole life. She had never married and had not dated since college. She'd been working as an office administrator for the past 20 years without a single promotion, had no social life to speak of and had never done anything particularly extraordinary with her life. Overall her life had been rather dull and dreary up to the point she was diagnosed with cancer. She had undergone a lumpectomy and now the cancer had returned. She was undergoing chemotherapy when she walked into my office. She was anxious and depressed.

During our first interview it became obvious that Eunice suffered from a lifetime of lovelessness – a significant but often *overlooked* source of internal distress for many people. According to Eunice, her mother was cold toward her while she was growing up and her father simply ignored her. As an adult she found dating and socializing to be difficult and unrewarding, and eventually stopped trying to succeed with relationships. On the strength of her initial interview I suggested we use hypnotic regression as a means to discover and release the old emotional pain that Eunice was carrying. With breast cancer, the underlying mental root usually consists of distorted thoughts and negative feelings associated with poor nurturance early in life, which appeared to apply in Eunice's case.

Under hypnosis Eunice's mind took her on a tour of her childhood. In scene after scene her mother appeared as a disciplinarian who bossed Eunice around and was overly critical. Her mother never overtly abused her but she was never loving toward Eunice either. She never did anything to bolster Eunice's self-esteem. Eunice's father meanwhile lived life wholly unto his own, as if he had no family. He consistently ignored both his wife and daughter.

As Eunice relived her childhood she directly perceived just how little she'd been loved and the impact it had on her growing up. She had compassion for herself and began to cry tears of emotional release. She realized she didn't believe in herself because she was taught she wasn't worthy of being loved. All her adult life she had been dogged by poor self-esteem as a consequence. That's why she'd never really amounted to anything.

While under hypnosis Eunice decided to rally with a heroic effort to redeem her destiny. She realized she'd been defined by her parents' distorted attitudes toward her, that she was worthy of being loved and that she had the power to make it happen. On the heels of her experience in hypnosis she began to live a much larger life. She found new past-times that interested her and made some new friends while she explored her new interests. She started putting more gusto into her job, gained recognition at work and won a promotion. She started dating and found a man whose company she actually enjoyed. She became much happier. During this period her tumors shrank away. Within eight months of our first appointment her doctor pronounced she was in remission from breast cancer. All she needed to do was gain freedom from her past by jettisoning the small ideas of self that were imposed on her in her youth.

I share this true story because it illustrates how seemingly "normal" historical events can sabotage a person's health and happiness and blind them to the existence of a higher destiny. Eunice had not suffered any obvious trauma in her youth. Instead, she was brainwashed into thinking she didn't amount to anything. As a consequence, it never occurred to her she should be concerned about her past, and she never dealt with it. If she hadn't contracted breast cancer and come to see me for help, she would still be living an isolated, unproductive, lonely life, and she would be dying.

The vast majority of people alive today are in the same situation Eunice was: living lives of quiet desperation and unaware that life could or should be any better. That's where hypnotic regression comes in. It will let you explore long-buried memories, attitudes, beliefs and feelings from your past that are holding you back and free yourself from these delusions once and for all. At that point, you'll be able to take hold of your own destiny and live a much larger life than the one you're living now.

The same is true for people who've had major challenges in the past – challenges they're aware of that still haunt them in the present. If this is you, then hypnotic regression will provide you with a rapid, elegant way to find your freedom from old distress and mental anguish.

What to Expect Using This Method

When you use the hypnotic regression method at the end of this chapter, your mind will become very relaxed and focused at the same time. The gatekeeper will relax and slide out of the way and you'll have direct access to the content of your subconscious mind. Owing to the depth of your mental relaxation, the intuitive wisdom of your super-conscious mind (soul) will also become available to you. What this means is that you'll have access to three distinct levels of your mind at the same time. You'll be able to *re-experience* the past from three unique perspectives:

* **The subconscious perspective** – what you thought and felt about an event or series of events at the time they occurred, along with the ways in which they molded your self-perception, attitudes, beliefs and expectations.

* **The conscious perspective** – the life consequences of your experience and the degree to which you choose to exercise your free will to change yourself and your future.

* **The super-conscious (soul) perspective** – why things happened the way they did, what you were supposed to learn from your experience and how it relates to your *Story Behind the Story*, along with the power to re-design your future if you see fit.

The degree of knowledge, freedom and power you will obtain using this method will astound you. You will be thrilled with the adventure and freedom that comes from your exploration of the past under hypnosis. One of the greatest things about it is the ease with which you can release old pent-up negative emotion. All you have to do is access your hurtful memories and feelings. As soon as you do, you will find your subconscious mind is happy to jettison them. You may find yourself shedding a few tears or having a good hard cry, venting feelings of anger, shame or guilt out loud, pounding the chair where you sit or in some other way, letting go of harmful emotion that has dogged you for years. The feeling of freedom you enjoy on the heels of releasing old emotion will be life altering.

To start your regression session I will use the same progressive relaxation techniques I used for *The Stressbuster* to de-stress and relax your body and mind. Then I will help you focus your awareness away from the here and now onto a past time and place that will give you the freedom and insight you need. At this point you'll want to remain passive and let your mind guide you to your destination. You can trust your own subconscious and super-conscious wisdom to take you precisely where you should go in order to maximize your own healing. For example, you are probably aware of one or more difficult early life experiences and might naturally expect to go to one of these, but under hypnosis your inner wisdom might take you to an event you previously considered trifling. Only when you experience this event under hypnosis do you see that it holds deep significance you overlooked at the time it happened.

Similarly you might be hungry to revisit a specific trauma from childhood, one you've been trying to unravel for years, but your innate wisdom under hypnosis takes you instead to a time when life was pleasant. I had a patient who had serious problems with anxiety and anger, and as a result, battled a formidable case of Irritable Bowel Syndrome (IBS). When she was regressed, she did not go back to the source of her anger. Instead, she went to a time when she had been extremely courageous, peaceful and happy. This experience reminded her that she didn't need to be angry in the face of a threat. She embraced this feeling of courage and profound peace and was able to carry that feeling with her when she came out of hypnosis. Her IBS improved dramatically.

Under hypnosis you may find yourself reliving a single event in unusual detail with uncanny accuracy or you might take a whirlwind tour through a series of events with a shared theme. I remember one young man who went back to a difficult hospital stay when he was only two years old. During the regression, he saw a red-haired man standing nearby talking with his father. After he left my office he asked his parents about the man and they said, "Oh my goodness, we haven't seen that old friend in twenty years. How could you possibly remember him?" By contrast I recall a beautiful woman in her thirties who came to me for help with painful uterine fibroid tumors. She had tried medication and surgery to remove the tumors but they kept coming back. In her first hypnotic regression she surveyed her entire life: her father was overly critical, she learned to under-value herself as a child, then she underwent years of harsh treatment in important love relationships. Through these experiences she became convinced she didn't measure up as a woman, a distortion that lodged symbolically in her reproductive organs. When she found this distortion under hypnosis she released it. She went on to find the love she deserved with new optimism and her tumors shrank away.

Under hypnosis your history will present itself to you through a wide range of sensory and cognitive experiences. You may re-experience an event just as you lived it, seeing it through your eyes the way it happened at the time, accompanied by sensory awareness (sound, touch, smell, hearing, even taste). On the other hand, you may experience an event almost as though you were watching a movie, viewing it from outside yourself as a third-party observer. You could get extraordinary detail, or your experience might consist of somewhat indistinct images. Some people experience the past as thoughts about an event accompanied by mentally suggested imagery, with no actual visual impressions. All these types of experiences are valid and all will deliver a powerful healing effect.

It is also possible you'll see things with some level of distortion. You might experience a memory you're certain isn't completely accurate. Such a distortion would occur if your father appears looking young and fit, sporting a head of thick black hair when in real life your dad was older, overweight, balding and grey. A distortion of this type may be meaningless. On the other hand, sometimes the subconscious mind tries to make a point by changing history a little, adding features to the story or inserting symbols into a memory sequence. For example, if you were born to your father late in life and were ashamed of his advanced age and expanding waistline when you were a kid, the distortion above could have significance. Make note of these distortions if they arise. You can explore whether or not they have meaning during and after the regression session.

Occasionally, though it is rare, people experience an entire story that feels real but they know it never happened. Let's say there was a river near the house where you grew up and under hypnosis you experience yourself falling into the river – you might have drowned if your older brother hadn't jumped in to save you. You come out of hypnosis and think, "That didn't happen," but the experience seems so real you decide to call your brother and ask him about it. He says, "Are you nuts? Of course it never happened!" In this case your subconscious mind made up the entire story to communicate something important. It therefore has metaphorical significance and you should explore its meaning on this basis. A fantasy of this type might present itself if you felt as though you were always on the verge of "drowning" in distress when you were young and relied on your big brother for love and protection. Always remember that the subconscious mind loves to communicate through stories, symbols and metaphors.

Though it seldom happens, it is also possible to experience an obvious fantasy when you're regressed under hypnosis. A woman in her late 30s once came to me for help with moderate depression and anxiety. She was the oldest of eight children and had spent her entire youth taking care of her younger sisters and brothers. Even as an adult, she maintained the role of "parent" to her siblings and felt overly responsible for their welfare. In so doing she sacrificed too many opportunities to explore the meaning of her own life and to savor what the world had to offer. Under hypnosis, she had the experience of being the captain of a starship traveling to far galaxies, exploring new worlds and coming into contact with exotic alien beings. It was pure fantasy, but the effect of it was very empowering. It helped her understand that she was an explorer by nature, experience just how good it felt, and find a way to fulfill this innate archetype. She gained the confidence to insist her siblings take control of their own affairs. With her new-found freedom, she began to travel. As she did so, her depression and anxiety cleared up completely. Similarly, if you find yourself experiencing an obvious fantasy, let it play out, appreciate it for its metaphorical significance and try to follow where it leads you.

On extremely rare occasions you might experience a fantastic, imaginative dream-like sequence under hypnosis. Let's say you find yourself flying on the back of a giant eagle, cruising at top speed through the Ganga river basin. You land on a mountain top in the Himalayas where you are greeted by your dead grandfather dressed in the saffron robes of a swami with a serene smile on his face. This is an obvious fantasy but you can bet it has strong metaphorical significance. Perhaps life was *really* tough when you were a kid and your grandfather was your only ally. He made you feel on top of the world, taught you about the meaning of life and to have faith in yourself and in God. The subconscious might offer you a fantasy of this type to remind you how powerful you are, how good life can be and how much you loved your grandfather. You should anticipate profound levels of emotional release with this type of experience.

Regression is a thrilling and healing experience for the vast majority of people most of the time, but occasionally the subconscious will present a negative dream sequence. Frightening images could arise – you are running for your life through a forest being chased by evil spirits for example. Such images might arise if your subconscious is holding onto too much fear. This might be the case if you've been exposed to frightening events in real life or too many terrifying video images (including too many horror movies). If this type of experience arises for you under hypnosis, just *shut it down*. You can stop any hypnotic experience just by saying to yourself, "No, I'm out of here." You can then choose to go on to another event, or take yourself out of hypnosis simply by counting from one to five and opening your eyes. Working through negative subconscious imagery has the potential to provide deep levels of cathartic release from old fear, but you should *not* do it alone. To explore this type of experience under hypnosis, get help from a licensed therapist who is trained in hypnosis.

Past Life Regression

About 25 percent of the time, people using the method in this chapter will experience a story that appears to be an alternative life script – a completely different life that seems to have occurred in the distant past. This is the "past life" phenomenon, about which there has been a great deal written.

I have experienced hundreds of cases where a client of mine objectively verified a past life experience under hypnosis by comparing it with facts in a historical record. I have many times observed a client break into a fluent foreign language under hypnosis – one they have never been exposed to in this life. My friend and colleague Dr. Brian Weiss has spent the last three decades compiling scientific proof of past life phenomena accessed under hypnosis. Past lives are clearly a real phenomenon and they can be accessed rather easily under hypnosis by a board-certified professional.

In India reincarnation is fully accepted and understood. Even in the West, the idea of reincarnation is gaining acceptance. According to a 2007 poll about a third of all Americans believe in reincarnation, including more than 40 percent of people aged 24 to 45. There is however, another possible explanation for what appears to be a past life experience under hypnosis: the existence of subconscious archetypes, which I first discussed in Chapter Three. These are basic personality patterns like warrior, teacher, artist, caregiver, statesman, sage and so on. What seems to be a past life experience under hypnosis can sometimes be a subconscious archetypal pattern expressing itself as an alternative life script.

Whether you believe in reincarnation or not it is important to keep an open mind regarding past life experience under hypnosis because it has a potentially miraculous healing effect. Let me share a true story that brings home just how powerful it can be. Many years ago a social worker named Mark came to see me. He was an American Christian diagnosed with Bell's palsy – severe damage to the facial nerves, which causes facial paralysis. Three years earlier he'd been out on a lake in a boat. It got very cold and as the winds whipped up he became extremely chilled, particularly the left side of his face. While he was still out on the boat he felt as though that part of his face was frozen. From that day on he'd suffered partial paralysis and pain on that side of his face. It got progressively worse until the whole left side of his face and mouth drooped. His doctors had tried a variety of medications and therapies, but nothing worked.

During hypnotic regression Mark found himself in an unfamiliar place. At first he thought he was in a subway tunnel, but then realized he was on a concrete stairway in an underground military facility. He saw he was wearing a Nazi uniform (the warrior archetype) and became aware that he was working as a guard in a top-secret plant that was developing a nuclear bomb. He decided he couldn't be part of such a thing and made the decision to abandon his post. The facility was on an island in a cold northern sea. He caught a troop boat late at night and went back to the mainland, where he wandered lost and weary into the wilderness. He fell to the ground exhausted, went to sleep and froze to death just before dawn, with the left side of his face frozen to the ice and snow.

When I brought Mark out of hypnosis he touched his left cheek and discovered he could feel the touch. He smiled broadly and the smile extended to both sides of his face. The left side of his face no longer sagged. In fact his face had completely healed. He kept in touch with me for five years letting me know that his face was still fine.

Remember, Mark was an American Christian. He didn't believe in the possibility of past lives. Was he really a German soldier in a previous life, or was he just experiencing an archetypal, metaphorical drama playing out in his subconscious mind? In Mark's case we cannot know for certain. What we *can* know for certain is that he accessed this "past life" memory and was immediately and permanently healed of his disorder. I see this in my work all the time. A majority of people who experience a "past life" under hypnosis will experience profound healing effects – psychological, physical and spiritual. The healing occurs quite naturally once the historical or archetypal "drama" is passed into consciousness from the subconscious mind. So never waste a good past life experience under hypnosis – it may have the potential to heal you dramatically.

Super-conscious Experience under Hypnosis

There is one other type of experience you might have using hypnotic regression: the direct experience of your super-conscious mind. Super-conscious awareness is *not* fantasy. It is the actual experience of your own higher states of consciousness and it can vary from person to person. Common examples include the sense that you no longer have a physical body but instead a body of light or energy. You may experience vast expansion, as if your body of light has become large enough to embrace the earth and all that's in it. You may have conversations with enlightened beings. It is possible you will receive explicit insights regarding your purpose in life, why things have happened to you the way they have, what you should do and so on. You may gain the ability to penetrate some of the mysteries of the universe. About 15 percent of people will have a super-conscious experience early in their use of this method. You can expect the frequency of your super-conscious experience to grow however, both in and out of hypnosis, as you continue to use this method and the other techniques in this book.

Post-Traumatic Stress Disorder – A Special Case

People who suffer from post-traumatic stress disorder (PTSD) are typically those who have been over-exposed to trauma – things like natural disaster, civil war, terrorism, death of a parent or sexual, physical or psychological abuse. For many who are exposed to chronic trauma, the fear of being mortally harmed becomes so firmly embedded in the subconscious mind that it invades the conscious mind. These folks have the conscious expectation that everyday occurrences will be life-threatening. They are often hyper-vigilant in expectation of a new threat, prone to sleeplessness, irritability, impatience, anger, depression, high anxiety and flashbacks (vivid recollections of historical trauma). They are especially susceptible to stress-related illness, namely heart attack, pulmonary problems and stroke.

Studies with veterans indicate that 20 to 25 percent of active combatants will suffer from PTSD and that the majority of soldiers who acquire PTSD are those with a history of unresolved distress from trauma early in life. As I've noted in prior chapters, unresolved distress from the past will make you more prone to distress in response to current stressors and likely to suffer more extreme consequences. PTSD is an example of just how bad things can get.

I do a lot of work with veterans. About six years ago, a 55-year-old veteran of the Vietnam War came to my office seeking help with his symptoms associated with PTSD. Decorated for valor in the military, this man embarked on a successful career as vice president of a major electronics firm after the war. He fell in love, married and started a family, but the symptoms of PTSD haunted him throughout. For 30 years after the war he never slept through the night. He relived difficult battlefield experiences continuously, especially the day his buddy was blown up right beside him. He had never been able to expunge the guilt he felt for not being able to save his friend and other members of his unit. He was anxious and angry and anti-anxiety drugs had done little to help.

Try as he did to manage his symptoms, my client's erratic behavior was harmful to those he loved. His marriage and his relationship with his children literally became casualties of the Vietnam War. The pressure on his heart from chronically high levels of distress eventually manifested as a pulmonary embolism and major heart attack that forced him into early retirement. He had to take it easy after that, living on heart medication and suffering from chest pain, severe weakness and shortness of breath whenever he exerted himself.

He was a virtuous and courageous man and I had an oceanic compassion for him. Our work together involved the use of hypnosis to find and release the battlefield experiences that were continually playing out in his subconscious mind. As we did so, we dismantled the chronic stress-response syndrome that had been fueling his emotional and physical ill health. We also used hypnosis to help him move into super-conscious awareness. Here he found the peace and joy that had so long eluded him. He began to meditate regularly. He found his *Story Behind the Story* and began to live it out authentically – his quest was to move away from being a warrior and into peace. His heart improved to the point where he no longer felt pain or weakness. He began sleeping through the night and stopped relying on anti-anxiety medication. His PTSD symptoms went away entirely and he went on to find a new career and a new love in his life, free of the distress that had plagued him for decades.

Do you relate in any way to this story? Did you experience trauma as a child, adolescent or young adult? The battlefield of life snared many of us when we were young. If this is you then hypnotic regression can help you dismantle the legacy of your past trauma. However, if your trauma is significant you should not use this method without the aid of a properly credentialed mental health professional trained in clinical hypnosis. The resulting emotional release may be more than you can handle without assistance from a trained therapist. If you've experienced significant trauma, please contact a licensed mental health professional who is trained in clinical hypnosis and use this method only with their permission and guidance.

A Note of Caution

A very small number of people who use hypnotic regression will experience a traumatic event that seems utterly real but that cannot be verified through their own conscious recollection, a witness or other objective source. There is such a thing as recovering a fully repressed memory (an event you have no conscious recollection of whatsoever) under hypnosis. However, for reasons I outlined in this chapter, what appears to be a memory recovered under hypnosis may also be false. Except in cases where there is corroborating evidence that hypnotic recollections are accurate, there is no scientific way to prove that such events actually occurred.

Real or not, these recollections can be traumatic when they occur. If you use the hypnotic regression method in this chapter and experience what you believe to be a repressed memory of a traumatic event, you should work with a clinical psychologist or psychiatrist who is trained in

143

clinical hypnosis. You need clinical expertise to sort out whether what you experience is real or not and (in either case) deal with the consequences. If this happens to you *stop* working with this method immediately and seek professional help from a properly trained therapist.

Hypnotic regression is an extremely powerful tool that can liberate you once and for all from harmful emotion and distorted thinking buried in your subconscious mind. It is perfectly safe to use for the majority of readers but it is not for everyone. *Do not use it* if you are presently under the care of a mental health professional for a diagnosable mental illness. Check first with your therapist before you proceed and use it only with their permission. Also *do not use it* without the aid of a properly credentialed mental health professional if you have suffered major trauma in the past or if you are unable to control your emotions. The resulting emotional release may be more than you can handle safely without assistance. Please be wise, and be well.

Use of the Method

Hypnotic regression is an extremely powerful tool that usually evokes strong emotional release, penetrating self-insight and a sense of awe. You will want to give yourself some extra time with this method, plus some time to decompress afterward. Including time for a little reflection, you'll need to set aside about an hour to use this method.

To begin, set aside some time and prepare your surroundings. Check your bladder, limit the distractions and dim bright lights. Put the CD that accompanies this book into a CD player, then situate yourself very comfortably in a chair, bed or recliner. If you want to have a record of your experience you may also want to set up a tape recorder or digital recorder nearby. This will allow you to describe your experiences aloud while you are under hypnosis and reflect on the contents later. Speaking aloud during the process will actually serve to deepen the experience for you.

Now play Track 2 on the CD titled *Hypnotic Regression* (e-version readers simply queue-up the Hypnotic Regression audio file on your mobile or other device). In this recording I walk you through a simple progressive relaxation method (the same method you are now familiar with). Then I will gently guide your focus away from where you are right now into a different time and place. Remember to avoid steering yourself to anything in particular. Take a passive stance and let your mind lead you to your destination. Next you will hear me ask you a series of questions that help ground you in the new place and time. These will be questions like, "Is this place dark or light? Are you outside or inside?" As you move through these grounding questions, more and more of your attention will focus on the time and place you are visiting and it will become clearer. After I ground you in the new location I will remain silent while you follow your own internal guidance and revelations. During this time, if you've set up a recording device you will want to share your experience aloud for future reference.

During your use of this method you will remain totally aware of yourself and your surroundings in the present. I frequently teach this method in seminars. At the end of one such seminar that took place in a posh Washington D.C. restaurant a few years ago, I took the owner of the restaurant into hypnotic regression. She went to the experience of dancing in a gold silk ball gown covered with jewels and pearls at a palace ball in France in the 1700s. As she moved through the experience, she also deftly fielded questions from the patrons in the restaurant. As in her case, you'll go somewhere else but also stay home in the present.

Just before I conclude your experience I will ask you – while you're still in a hypnotic state – what your experience was designed to teach you. In all likelihood, given what you now know about the workings of your mind and your history, the answers will come easily. Finally I will ask you how, based on what you now know, you plan to be different because of the experience. How will you change your *Story Behind the Story* based on what you've discovered? Then I will count from one up to five and invite you to open your eyes.

When you come out of hypnosis you may want to spend some time writing about what you experienced and what you learned, even if you chose to record your observations during the session. You may want to return to these notes from time to time and compare your experience from one regression session to another.

Where to Take It from Here

Hypnotic regression can generate unbelievably powerful healing. More than two-thirds of the people who come to me with chronically debilitating, stress-related problems get dramatically better from hypnotic regression work. It has the power to knock out bodily illness and immediately liberate you from mental anguish that is fueling your distress and obscuring your *Story Behind the Story*. Once you start discovering who you have been in past lives and who you are trying to become in this one, your own nature becomes more intriguing and life starts to look much more like an adventure.

I suggest you try this method four times with one week between each session. The power of the method grows with each application and most people need a series of four sessions to attain sufficient depth of understanding. Our emotions are many-layered. One or two sessions will probably not allow you to penetrate deeply enough into your *Story Behind the Story*. For example let's say you have stress-induced migraines and in your first hypnotic session you connect with old anger as the source of your headaches. In the next session you probe deeper and discover there is great fear underneath your anger. In the session that follows, you uncover a well of sadness related to your fear and so on. A series of four sessions should help you break sufficient mental ground to achieve measurable, meaningful changes in your mental and physical health – enough to get you jazzed about your future – and in this example, enough to get rid of your migraines!

Owing to the power of this method, it's best to wait a week between uses so you can effectively take in the many revelations that are likely to come your way. More frequent use of the method could "swamp" you with new understanding and cause unnecessary confusion. After your "introductory series" you can return to it once a week until you feel you've made sufficient gains in understanding and freedom. In the final chapter I help you decide how to build this method into your personal plan for success.

12

Rapid De-Stressors

This chapter contains a wide range of scientifically proven, fast and easy self-help methods that will let you convert distress (harm) into eustress (growth). These are all tools you can apply in a matter of minutes or up to an hour. Most of the methods can be implemented anytime, anywhere including your place of work. In fact, the last segment of the chapter is devoted to stress management strategies you can apply on the job.

The methods in this chapter work to dismantle the stress response at one or more of three stages: reprogramming the distorted thinking that fuels negative emotion, alleviating negative emotion once it has risen, and gaining fast relief from the symptoms of stress. Try experimenting with all the methods. Their power grows with practice. Some methods may work extraordinarily well for you, while others provide only mild relief. Experiment with them and you'll find the right prescription for "treating" your stressful challenges.

Scientific Affirmations

An affirmation is a declaration of truth. Scientific affirmations are declarations of truth designed and applied in a way that infuses your mind with positive thoughts, beliefs, attitudes and expectations. If applied correctly they work as an antidote for distorted thinking, which means you won't be swamped by negative emotion. They also serve to awaken and amplify the heroic attitudes of courage, faith, hope and love. Used rightly they have the power to convert distress into eustress.

Scientific affirmations have the power to saturate the mind at multiple levels, which makes them vastly more powerful than "positive thinking." With positive thinking you are only affecting the conscious mind – the weakest part of the mind. With scientific affirmations you activate the power of the mind at three levels: the conscious, subconscious and individual super-conscious minds.

To begin using this powerful tool, start by designing one or more affirmations. Research in mind-body medicine over the last 50 years shows that effective affirmations possess certain key characteristics. They are short, epic, first person, present tense and contain only positive words. The logic behind this formula is actually simple. A good affirmation is short, which makes it easy to remember and repeat. It is "epic" in the sense that it expresses a heroic or lofty truth. You don't want to think small with your affirmations, or a small response is what you'll get. Remember, "As you think, so shall you be."

Scientific affirmations must also be in the first person, which means they are "I" statements like "I am courageous." They must also be in the present tense, as if they are happening now. For example, the affirmation "I am courageous" is much more powerful to the mind than the declaration "I will be courageous" or even the emphatic "I shall be courageous." The latter two declarations introduce some measure of doubt to the mind because in fact they haven't occurred yet. Even more important for our purposes, a present tense affirmation is identical in expression to the "instantaneous knowing" of the individual super-conscious mind, or soul. It therefore taps the power of the soul.

Lastly, an effective affirmation should not contain any negative words. For example, consider the declaration "I am not afraid." If you repeat this declaration, your subconscious mind will hear the word "afraid" over and over again, and become saturated with the idea of fear. This outcome is what you wish to avoid at all costs! So you need to be sure that your affirmations contain only positive words like, "I am brave!"

Affirmations work best if they directly counter the negative thoughts, beliefs, attitudes and expectations that are fueling your distress. For example, if you are fearful because you expect to be hurt, you might choose an affirmation like "God and I are one." This affirmation instills your mind with the belief and expectation that no circumstance on earth can hurt you because the cosmic mind is your very self and protector. Similarly, if you are afraid of losing your job and you feel angry at the injustice of it, you might use an affirmation like "I am infinite peace and master of my destiny." If your life is fraught with unmet needs for the basics in life and you feel powerless to do anything about it, you might use "God's infinite prosperity is mine." If you are prone to grief and sadness, you might try "I am eternal, ever new joy." If you are physically ill, you might try "I feel great."

These are just examples, but they are good examples. They meet the key criteria for effective affirmations, remind you of your limitless nature and affirm your connection with the cosmic mind. In designing your own affirmations you'll want to use language that fits your own philosophical and religious values. You can also choose to use an affirmation developed by a guru, master, teacher, priest or rabbi of your faith, many of which can be found in print. A short line from scripture may be perfect ("The Father and I are One"). Whatever you choose just be sure it meets the scientific criteria for effective affirmations.

Once you've chosen your affirmation you are ready to put it to work on your behalf.

Scientific affirmations should be used at the end of meditation, when they are extremely powerful and then anytime you begin to feel negative emotion rising. You'll want to use just one affirmation each time you meditate. If you try to use multiple affirmations during meditation, chances are you will dilute their impact. You can use multiple affirmations, but be sure to employ just one affirmation each time you meditate.

To use affirmations successfully you need to attain a deep meditative state. If you are an advanced meditator use your own meditation technique. However if you are new to meditation or have trouble meditating deeply, use the hypnotic meditation method I provided in Chapter Seven. It will let you attain the depth you need for success with very little effort on your part, very quickly.

Using your own method or mine, meditate until your mind is very calm and you feel the first fruit of soul contact: a deepening peace. It's a good idea to use affirmations near the end of your meditation, when your mind – at all levels – is like an open book. Now, while keeping your eyes focused on your Third Eye (the point between the eyebrows), begin silent, slow recitation of your affirmation. Be sure to concentrate on the words and their meaning. If you repeat them "mindlessly" they won't do you much good. Some people recite their affirmation only while they breathe out. Some people split their affirmation between the in-drawn and outgoing breaths, as would be the case if you recited "God and I" on the in-breath and "are one" on the out breath. Either of these approaches will work. Just be sure to concentrate on the words and their meaning. You will need to repeat your affirmation slowly 12 times for maximal effect. When you are finished, offer a prayer of thanks and open your eyes. You should feel noticeably better.

With recitation and concentration you force your affirmation into your subconscious mind where it begins to compete with the distortions in your thinking that are fueling your distress. With continued practice your affirmation will push through your subconscious into your individual super-conscious mind. Once there it will tap the awesome power of your soul to help you adopt the new, distortion-free beliefs and expectations.

If you employ this technique correctly, you should feel a discernable measure of relief from your distress right away. However, if the distortions in thought that are driving your distress are firmly entrenched in your subconscious, you may have to use your affirmation in meditation several times a week over a period of time before you no longer feel the hurtful emotions that give rise to your distress.

As you practice scientific affirmations in meditation you will train your mind to resonate with the affirmation and the technique you are using to employ it. Once the mind is trained in this way you will be able to use the affirmation outside of meditation to great effect. To obtain best results you want to use it as soon as you start feeling bad, so you need to stay aware of your feelings to employ the technique effectively. As soon as you notice negative thought or emotion, slow down for a moment, put your attention on your Third Eye and recite your affirmation 3 to 5 times. Coordinate your recitation with your breath in exactly the same way you do when you're meditating. You don't have to close your eyes. However, if you are in a private place, go ahead and close them. It will help you concentrate. You should notice immediate relief from distress when you use this technique.

Venting Negative Emotion

Any activity that helps you release negative emotion will truncate the stress response and help convert distress into eustress. Some years ago, a man in his early 50s came to see me for anger management. In addition to his emotional issues he suffered from osteoarthritis in his neck and lumbar spine. He was hunched over and in a lot of pain which made him extremely irritable. His job was on the line because of his anger and his firm's human resource specialist had directed him to me for help.

This man was not so unlike many people who have legitimate gripes in life. His dad was an absentee father who drank too much. His mother put a lot of pressure on him to be the man of the household and be a dad to his little brother, so he was never allowed to be a kid. As a young man he'd married a woman who was a good bit like his mother and who put even more pressure on him to perform. Life had abused this man and he chose to get angry in response to it. In fact he'd become so obnoxious and offensive that no one wanted to listen to him. He had no one to talk to and had repressed his feelings for more than three decades. By the time he walked into my office he was like a dormant volcano waiting to explode, to the point that he was a danger to himself and others.

Over two months of weekly therapy with me this man poured out his life story. By the end of the two months he was no longer angry. All he *really* needed was to vent his feelings. In the few sessions that followed we used talk-therapy to help him come fully to grips with his *Story Behind the Story* and move into peace. As he did so, his back and neck problems went away entirely. They only existed in the first place because he felt as though he was carrying the weight of the world on his shoulders.

I share this particular story because it illustrates how important it is to release pent-up negative feelings. It is not enough to carry powerful feelings and thoughts inside while you try to sort them out in the privacy of your own mind. That will keep you wrapped up in distorted logic and emotion, like a mouse running around in a maze. You must get your feelings and thoughts out. My client could not attain freedom from emotional and physical pain until he had a chance to release the emotional burden he was carrying.

Whether the negative emotion you carry is old (it has haunted you since you were a kid) or whether it arose this afternoon (you had a fight with your husband or your boss berated you at work), you need to release it, and the more physical the release the better.

The act of releasing negative emotion is called *catharsis*, a concept I introduced in Chapter Eight. There I touted the use of physical exercise as an outstanding method for achieving catharsis, but there are two other effective methods you can use to get free of negative emotion: venting your feelings aloud and writing out your feelings.

To vent your feelings aloud tell an adult family member or a friend you really need to vent your feelings and ask if they will listen. Assure them they are not to take anything you say personally – you just need to vent. If they agree to be your sounding board then take several minutes to let your feelings fly. The important thing is for you to vent your feelings exactly as they are, whatever they may be: frustration, fear, rage, grief, shame, guilt, whatever. Be sure to tell it exactly like it is, even if it's irrational, hurtful or repugnant. You won't get the release you need otherwise. It takes a very patient and understanding friend to act as a sounding board for this kind of release, but what is love for? All they have to do is listen compassionately. Sometimes they have good advice. Sometimes they're a shoulder to cry on. Sometimes that's just what you need.

If you can't find a friend or a family member who will listen, then vent your feelings out loud to no one in particular. All you need is a set of working vocal cords and the ability to overcome a quirky social taboo. After all, only crazy people talk to themselves, right? Or maybe you believe it's all right to talk to yourself, as long as you don't talk back.

Actually it's OK to talk to yourself and equally OK to talk back. They're both healthy and natural. Just find some private time and simply speak the thoughts and feelings that are traveling through your mind. Remember, what you think and feel will only find full release if you vent your thoughts and feelings *exactly* as they exist in your mind. If your feelings are powerful feel free to put some "oomph" behind your oral expression. If you do it right, expect this technique to lead to tears, shouting, slamming your fist on the table or other forms of physical release. Do whatever you need to do. That's the point of the technique. Take every opportunity to vent your feelings aloud until you find the release you need – just don't hurt anyone in the process.

You can also write-out your thoughts and feelings. To get the benefit of this technique you have to write *exactly* what you think and feel. This is a "your-eyes-only" exercise so you can afford to be honest and entirely truthful. If you try to make it nice, it won't work.

To write for emotional release, simply set aside some time. Get out paper and pen or turn on your computer. Start writing a "stream-of-consciousness" about the thing or things that are troubling you. Describe what has hurt you (events, relationships, illness) and the toll it's taken. Write down how you feel, any thoughts related to your feelings or anything related to why you feel the way you do. You should also ask yourself what you need to feel better and write about that too.

To get the benefit of this technique I usually recommend a half hour of writing every day or every other day for about two weeks. You'll need that much time to address levels of thought and feeling that lie underneath the surface layers.

If an important relationship has been a major source of pain in your life, you can choose to write a letter – one you will never send – to the person who has hurt you. Feel free to explore all your anger, frustration, fear, longing or loss, or to demand restitution or express forgiveness, whatever applies. Just tell it like it is and you'll get the release you're looking for. If the person you need to communicate with is no longer alive or if your issues crosscut many years of strife, consider writing your letter to God or to the Universe.

If it's been a long time since you dealt authentically with your feelings, you might need some "props" to help you engage your emotions fully. Before you sit down to write for cathartic release, you could spend some time going through old photographs or mementos. Or dig out some of your old music to listen to songs that had significance for you at a difficult time in your past. Such props are powerful triggers of memory and emotion.

Writing for emotional release is not the same as journaling. Journaling is a therapeutic art and there are several styles. However, basic journaling is easy. To do it get a blank journal or notebook and start writing about how you feel right now. Describe your history and important relationships and the impact your past has had on who you are today. Be sure to chronicle the positive and the negative. Having explored your life story a bit, come back to the present. Then at regular intervals (for some people, daily) chronicle the major events in your day and how you feel and think about them, along with how you behaved and why. In doing so you'll gain frequent release of otherwise difficult thoughts and feelings, and you'll identify patterns – repetitive ways of relating to others and of feeling, thinking and behaving – in response to specific stressors in your environment. You'll be able to see with stark clarity just how much your past is influencing who you are today. This self-insight will give you another angle on your *Story Behind the Story*.

Creative Expression

The word "therapy" comes from the Greek word *therapeia* which means to nurse or cure through creative expression – the arts, writing, music, dance, drama, gardening, hobbies and creative play, just to name a few. You can use creative expression to attain cathartic release of old pain, symbolic resolution of unresolved conflict and distress from the past, deeper self-knowledge, joy and a clearer understanding of your *Story Behind the Story*. There are several creative means you can use to obtain these benefits. Here are some examples:

Artistic Expression

The benefits of artistic expression are numerous: inner conflict resolution, release of negative emotion, enhanced self-awareness, a positive change in attitude, an increase in emotional wellbeing, and higher levels of inspiration, optimism and personal growth.

With artistic expression the focus is on the change that comes to you through the process of creating a piece of art, *not* on the aesthetics of the final product. You do not have to be a Husain to get the benefit.

I'm no artist, but I used painting to release my own emotions during my years at college. I would stretch out a huge canvas on the floor and toss large amounts of paint onto it. I didn't use paintbrushes but I would swirl the paint with a spatula or other objects. My approach (as I was to learn later) maximized what art therapists call "flow," a natural hypnotic state that focuses you entirely on a single task – a naturally restful and healing state. My painting took an interesting turn during those years. It began with loud primary colors and harsh abrupt patterns – an expression of my angst in college. But I eventually found I preferred working with pastels using fluid patterns – an expression of my maturation into peace and joy and a more sensual appreciation of what life has to offer.

As I did in this example, you might consider the arts (drawing, painting, photography, collage, mosaic work, sculpture, flower arranging, weaving, ceramics, carving and the like) as a means to access deep levels of self-expression. Recall the language of the subconscious mind consists of symbols, metaphors and stories, so art provides a natural gateway for subconscious expression. Furthermore, time spent focusing on art will take your mind off what's stressing you. Just the act of having an artistic avocation can make you feel more harmonious and provide you with more enjoyable downtime.

Studies show that artistic endeavors shift the body's physiology away from stress to one of deep relaxation by fostering different brain wave patterns, improving autonomic nervous system functioning and increasing the production of certain neurotransmitters in the brain. These changes boost immune system function and blood flow to vital organs. Studies with women also show that artistic expression improves hormone balance, which can reduce the unpleasant emotional swings associated with pre-menstrual syndrome and menopause.

Creative Writing

Creative writing is another very effective means for achieving emotional release, mental clarity, peace of mind and a better perspective on your *Story Behind the Story*. It is a technique that works especially well for people who've experienced highly stressful events in life.

Creative writing has many forms. You could choose to write out your story as if you were a biographer or a screenplay writer looking at your life from the outside (like we did in Chapter Six). One approach focuses on creating a dream-list – what you would do if you could do anything you wanted to. Some people enjoy fictional writing, which is a powerful means for self-expression because of its mythic heroic quality. The subconscious mind loves to communicate with stories – the more symbolic and metaphorical the better. With fiction you can feel free to explore archetypal trends in your life, change your story, endow yourself (the hero or heroine in your story) with superhuman qualities, change your gender, height or looks or exaggerate the fiendish nature of the people or events that have plagued you. Far from being fantastic nonsense this type of fictional exercise will help you make sense of your struggle and/or purpose in life, boost your self-esteem and inspire you to live out your dreams.

Poetry in all its forms provides a unique means of release and expression because of the special role that rhythm plays in writing – poetry tends to move the writer from one level of inspiration to another while expressing feelings at the same time. As with all of the other expressive techniques we're discussing here, you don't need to be a Tagore to benefit from writing poetry. What you experience through the process is much more important than the quality of your finished product. Besides, you might find you are a poet. If you don't challenge yourself to try new things, you'll never know how gifted you are.

Regardless of how you approach it, creative writing is a process that brings release, clarity, and perspective to feelings, events, and directions in life that are otherwise chaotic, "unknowable," and stressful. It can take the form of writing or you can combine it with sketches, paintings, photographs, mementos or art clipped from magazines. It is a particularly dynamic form of self-expression and you can easily tailor it to your interests and personality type.

Music

Perhaps you have heard of the "Mozart Effect," the power of certain music to reduce physical and mental stress. Music – whether you listen to it or create it – has several benefits. Research shows that it stimulates the body's natural "feel good" chemicals (opiates and endorphins) and subtly improves blood pressure, pulse rate, breathing, immune system functioning and posture. Certain forms of religious music and chants are well-known for their ability to calm the mind and body, as well as elevate and expand our awareness.

You may like the soaring strains of classical music, or you might be the type to blast popular rock and roll. With music, it's different strokes for different folks. Just watch out for harsh discordant sounds – this type of music is good for release of powerful emotion but a steady diet of it will drive too much negative energy into your subconscious mind.

Dance

I have trouble listening to music without dancing. I'm not the world's best dancer. I dance because it makes me feel good. Sometimes at night my wife and I will play our favorite tunes and dance around together in the kitchen. I never miss a chance to dance at a party. Sometimes I even dance while I'm walking along. It's hard to be unhappy while you're dancing.

Dance is therapeutic because of the vital connection between movement and the emotional, intellectual and physical energies that make up body and mind. Rhythmic movement works to integrate and harmonize the emotional, physical and cognitive facets of "self." Movement also provides a kinesthetic pathway for subconscious memories, conflicts and issues to express and release (in much the same way exercise does). Those who are recovering from physical, sexual or emotional abuse find this expressive technique especially helpful for gaining a sense of ease with their own bodies.

Not everyone is able to dance in public. If this is you, when nobody's watching, play some music and give yourself permission to move in whatever way you feel like moving. You can choose to dwell on a particular situation, thought or emotion as you're dancing or you can simply move with the music. The amount of emotional release you enjoy might surprise you. Symbols, metaphors, or old memories might crop up as you move. You might feel like shedding a tear, begin to feel downright joyful or both. Those of you who need a structured setting in order to "move" might consider a dance class, dance therapy or even taking a class in yoga, Tai Chi, or aikido.

Dramatic Expression

Aristotle first mentioned the word *catharsis* to describe emotional release in audiences watching tragic Greek plays. Dramatic expression, whether you watch it or you do it, facilitates emotional release, personal growth and physical health.

You can use expression through drama to achieve *catharsis*, solve a problem, delve deeply into truths about yourself, understand personally-resonant images or transcend unhealthy patterns of interaction. There are formal "drama therapies" used in hospitals, schools, mental health centers and businesses. Here, psychodrama, role-play, theater games, group-dynamic games, mime, puppetry, improvisational techniques and even stand-up comedy are used, not only to help individuals resolve conflicts, but to help groups of people learn how to function together like a well-oiled machine. You might consider getting involved in a drama class or club to get these benefits.

You can also get the benefits of drama by weaving a little dramatic expression into your day-to-day living. Try experimenting with role-play, comedy and improvisation. There is an old adage that "more truth was said in jest than ever was said in sorrow." In the late evenings my family often gathers in the kitchen. If one of us has had a hard day, that person may "act out" his or her dilemma with tremendous theatrical or comic exaggeration, while the rest of us join in the show. An ordinary exercise in "kitchen drama" like this can achieve a great deal of cathartic release, healing and understanding.

You don't have to do drama to get the benefits of dramatic expression. You can obtain its benefits just by attending a good play, ballet, opera, musical production or movie. Audience members get deeply involved in the plot of a good performance. By connecting in a mythic archetypal way with the struggles and triumphs of the main characters, members of the audience are able to live out their own emotional issues and, on occasion, revive their dreams.

Create or Build Something

You can gain the benefits of cathartic release through any endeavor that involves the use of your hands, whether it's building an addition on your home, gardening or even cooking a gourmet meal. Working with your hands to create something is cathartic, restful to mind and body and *grounding*, meaning it connects you into the here and now and dramatically alleviates stress. Feelings of appreciation, tranquility and joy tend to accompany a creative act, especially if you are concentrating fully on your enterprise. Concentration on one activity to the exclusion of all else is a natural hypnotic state that is extremely restful. Gardening is particularly good for this because it combines elements of exercise, concentration and creativity in a healthful outdoor setting. Studies indicate that gardening reduces blood pressure, alleviates negative emotions and stressful thoughts, boosts mood and brain functioning and improves motivation and morale.

Peer-Based Group Support

"No man is an island." This quote from the famous philosopher John Donne reminds us that individuals cannot thrive if they are isolated from other people. This is an important religious and philosophical tenet, and research in mind-body medicine proves it to be true. It turns out that group support is critically essential to human health and wellbeing. Study after study reveals that people who are part of a regular continuous group enjoy much lower levels of stress and are healthier and happier than people who are socially isolated. For example, one recent study showed that women with breast cancer who are part of a support group have a much longer lifespan than women with cancer who are not part of a support group. That's astounding.

Support groups consist of individuals who have shared interests or needs. They can be formally structured, in which case they may have one or more facilitators, or they can be informally structured – just a group of friends who get together regularly to dialogue. They can be organized around a profession (like public service), age or gender (a teen group, or women's group), a diagnosis (like heart disease), or an interest (like environmental health). Many health clinics, universities, religious groups, social organizations and businesses maintain support groups for their patients, students, members and employees.

A hallmark of group support is the ability to express and release thoughts and feelings about one's own experience in a non-judgmental environment. Support groups allow people to explore difficult issues in a supportive social context, observe and reflect on others' means of coping and give and get immediate feedback about concerns and problems affecting one's life. Group members benefit not only by working through their own issues but also by helping others. One of the best things about being a member of such a group is that you can observe other people coping with distress and striving for harmony and say to yourself "He's doing it. She's doing it. I can do it too." For all these reasons, if your distress is moderate to high, you should consider becoming part of a support group or perhaps establishing one of your own.

Quick-Hit Stressbusters

This section is devoted to fast, easy techniques you can use anywhere, anytime to mitigate your distress when it is rising. Use them whenever you feel any of the symptoms on the symptom checklist in Chapter Four. While they are not a permanent cure for distress they work almost instantly to reduce its symptoms, so they are indispensable when distress arises to assail you.

Diaphragmatic Breathing

When you're distressed, you become anxious and your breathing gets shallow and fast. This type of breathing causes you to take in too little oxygen and retain too much carbon dioxide, the gas you breathe out when you exhale – it's not supposed to remain in your body except in small trace amounts. The resulting imbalance between oxygen and carbon dioxide will perpetuate anxiety and distress. You can reverse this situation with a few minutes of diaphragmatic breathing.

Diaphragmatic breathing is sometimes called "stomach breathing." This type of breathing relies on the diaphragm, a strong dome-shaped muscle located under your ribs, just above your stomach. To breathe diaphragmatically, breathe in slowly and deeply through your nose while allowing your diaphragm to push down and your stomach to expand outward. Your chest should remain still. Then breathe out slowly through pursed lips and as you do, tighten your stomach muscles, letting them fall inward. Breathe in this way until you feel calmer, usually 2 to 4 minutes. You should notice that diaphragmatic breathing has a secondary and beneficial effect: it causes the muscles on the floor of your pelvis (the psoas, which traverse the area between your hips and bottom) to relax deeply. This will also help to lessen your distress.

Try to catch yourself whenever your breathing starts to get rapid and shallow, recognize it as a sign that distress is rising, and immediately shift to diaphragmatic breathing. In fact, it is a good idea to breathe diaphragmatically before and during any event which you assume will be stressful – an important meeting with your boss or your in-laws for example.

Meditative Breathing

This technique is even more powerful than diaphragmatic breathing, but to apply it you have to be a meditator. If you are a regular meditator, use of this technique anywhere at any time will induce the healthful effects of meditation. It's simple. All you need to do is breathe exactly the way you do while you're meditating. If you use the meditation method in this book, this would mean you put your attention on your Third Eye (the point between the eyebrows), draw in a deep breath and as you breathe out, silently chant the sound *Om*. You can do this with your eyes open or closed. Closed eyes are preferable for novice meditators because it's easier to concentrate with your eyes closed. Advanced meditators can do it successfully with their eyes open. Either way, if you do it for 2 or 3 minutes you'll enjoy the peace and relaxation of a "mini" meditation. The breathing technique in Chapter Nine: Moving Energy with Your Mind is an even more sophisticated form of meditative breathing. If you use it you'll get great results.

Jacobsonian Relaxation

This method is for people who carry a great deal of physical anxiety or tension. It involves the progressive tensing and relaxing of the major muscle groups in the body. You can do it standing or sitting and it takes less than 2 minutes. To do it, begin with 1 minute of diaphragmatic breathing. Next, tense the muscles in your feet. Then relax them. Then tense the muscles in your calves and relax them. Continue to consecutively tense and relax all the major muscle groups in your body in the following order: thighs, buttocks, lower stomach, diaphragm and back, chest and shoulder blades, shoulders, upper arms, forearms, hands and fingers, neck and face. That's the method, start to finish. If you use it be sure not to tense your muscles too quickly. If you "jerk" your muscles into a state of tension you could impair your circulation, even damage your heart or injure a muscle, ligament or tendon. Use a smooth, fluid motion, taking two or three full seconds to tense and relax each muscle group. It's a good idea to follow this exercise with one full minute of diaphragmatic breathing.

The "Ten-to-One Countdown"

This method involves the use of guided thought to relax mind and body. It takes about 4 minutes to complete. To do it, sit back and relax comfortably in a chair or recliner and close your eyes. Next, comfortably and slowly draw in a deep diaphragmatic breath and then release it. As you release your breath silently say the word "ten." Draw in the next deep diaphragmatic breath and as you release it, silently say the word "nine." Continue this process, synchronizing your breath with each count, until you get to one. The key to success with using this method is to focus your attention on your breath as it flows in and out and on the numbers in the countdown. If you lose your place in the countdown, which is usually a sign you are starting to relax, simply start again with 5 and keep counting down.

Progressive Relaxation

This method relies on the power of the imagination to relax mind and body. It takes about 4 minutes. To use it, find a few minutes of privacy, sit comfortably in a chair or recliner, and close your eyes. Draw in one deep diaphragmatic breath and let it flow out. Then just let your body breathe on its own. Next put your attention on your toes and imagine a warm peaceful relaxing feeling beginning to flow into your feet through the tips of your toes. Then imagine it is flowing through your feet, then up through your calves, knees, thighs, buttocks, waist, diaphragm, back, chest and shoulders. From your shoulders, imagine it is flowing down through your arms to the tips of your fingers. Then return your attention to your shoulders and imagine it is flowing up through your neck, through the back of your head, then the top of your head and lastly, down through your face. Then open your eyes. You should feel much more relaxed.

Feel free to imagine the "flow" of warm relaxation in any way that works for you. Some people prefer to imagine a healing light flowing into their body, filling every cell of the body with light as it flows. More cognitive types tend to "think" of perfect relaxation moving into every muscle, nerve and fiber of the body as it flows. Either of these approaches or a similar approach will work.

Guided Imagery

This method uses the power of imagery to take your attention away from what is distressing you and place it on something pleasant, relaxing and joyful. It takes about 6 minutes. To use it, sit back comfortably and close your eyes. Begin with 30 seconds of diaphragmatic breathing. Then let your breath move in and out on its own while you begin to imagine being in a time and place where you have experienced the most relaxation and joy. This might be a place you went on vacation, a very happy memory from your past or even a fantasy location – something you saw in a movie or read about in a book. Whatever and wherever it is, imagine you are there. Try your best to imagine the sights, sounds, smells, tastes and feelings associated with being in your "happy place." Allow yourself to luxuriate in these thoughts and feelings for at least 5 minutes. Then open your eyes. You should feel much more relaxed and happy.

The Dive Reflex

This technique is extremely simple and fast. It is based on research which shows that very cold water applied to the face mimics "the dive reflex" – a natural biological response to head-first submersion in cold water. If you dive into a cool pool of water, the cold on your face will improve blood and oxygen flow to your brain, which will lower your stress. To mimic the dive reflex, just put some ice in a basin or bowl of water. Then splash your face with it, especially your eyes and forehead. You can also soak a cloth in very cold water and apply the wet cloth to your forehead and eyes. Keep the cold on your face for at least 2 minutes. You should feel better right away.

How to Combat Work-Related Stress

People who are employed spend the vast majority of their waking hours at work so it's important to do what you can to ensure your work life sustains your peace of mind. Here I've listed a variety of simple strategies for minimizing work-related stress.

Make Your Work Area Your Own

To the extent you can, arrange your workspace so it is comfortable and comforting. If your chair has a hard seat and back for example, get a pad to sit on and one to cushion your lower back. It is stressful to the body to sit on a hard chair for hours at a time. If your work area is noisy, do what you can to dampen the ambient sound even if it includes asking your colleagues to stop talking so loud. If you can't cut the noise get a pair of headphones to wear when you really need to concentrate. It is stressful to the mind to attempt to concentrate on a task with too much background noise. Also consider personalizing your workspace with tokens, art or books that resonate with your personal beliefs and aspirations. Frame a picture of your family or friends and put it where you can see it. It also helps to have a flowering plant nearby – a constant reminder of life and beauty that will help keep the air clean and oxygenated.

Don't Be Tied to Your Work Station

To minimize work-related stress you don't want to stay tied to your desk all day. Always take a break for lunch and try not to eat at your desk. Punctuate each morning and afternoon with a small break. It's a good idea to get up and leave your workstation during your breaks and if you can, to walk briskly outside in the sunshine for a few minutes. During breaks turn your attention to something that interests you that is not work-related. If you are stuck at your desk for extended periods, employ one or more of the "Quick-Hit Stressbusters" in this chapter every hour or two to prevent stress from building.

Connect with Colleagues

It's good to connect with your colleagues on a personal level. You don't want to overdo it to the point you aren't getting your work done and you don't want to share inappropriately, but you should feel part of a team of people who know and trust one another. It is stressful to feel alienated and alone. Besides, in sharing with your colleagues you might learn some useful information that will help your career. Always share in a virtuous way, always be respectful and *never* gossip – it is highly destructive. If you are part of an organization that gossips don't give in to it. It will contribute to institutional stress and hurt your career.

Maintain a Positive Attitude

If you don't like your work or you find it boring, change your orientation to it by affirming that it has value – it is helping your firm, helping the Indian economy and helping you to build a future. Let's face it, you are fortunate to have a job! Whatever you do resolve to do it with a good attitude and take pride in doing it. If you are bored, ask for tasks that are more challenging. Work on improving your skills so you can handle different, more interesting job duties as soon as the opportunity arises.

Try Not to Multi-task

If your work is hectic and overwhelming, do everything in your power to get better organized, then prioritize your tasks and tackle them in order of importance. Try to finish one job completely before moving on to another. While this is not always possible it will minimize your stress and maximize your efficiency. It is ironic that multi-tasking is so highly valued in today's workplace. I do not know of one single study which shows it is effective or efficient. To the contrary there are a host of studies which show that efficiency and output are maximized when a person is able to concentrate on one task at a time without interruption until the task is completed.

One recent study concluded that multi-tasking is not only highly stressful, it is counter-productive. This study, which focused on U.S. workers in white-collar jobs, showed that the average office worker gets interrupted and re-directed to focus on another issue, call or task every 4.5 minutes. It takes 1.5 minutes to regain concentration on a project once you have set it aside to address another task. What this means is that the average worker in a multi-task office environment is losing about one-quarter of their productive time and energy every day. Keep this in mind and do what you can to minimize interruptions at the office. Make time for your boss and take care of emergencies when they arise but otherwise you should "block-out" chunks of time to focus on your most important projects – time when you don't allow interruption. Don't hop back and forth quickly between different responsibilities if you can help it.

Do the Toughest Thing First

If you have a task you do not want to do, tackle it early in the day when you're fresh. This way you can deal with it when your energy reserves are high and get it over with quickly. You'll feel less stress if you don't put it off. Ask your colleagues for guidance or assistance if you need to, but get those unpleasant things completed so you can get them off your desk and off your mind.

Rely on Your Supervisor

Frequent accurate communication with your supervisor is key to effective stress management in the workplace. Don't fail to rely on him or her for help if you need it. Your supervisor gets paid more than you do to handle pressure, so if you have more work than you can reasonably accomplish tell your supervisor and ask him or her to set your priorities. If a problem is brewing don't wait too long to bring it to the attention of your supervisor, along with your approach to resolving it if you have one. Small problems only get bigger if they are ignored. A problem you share with your supervisor or colleagues is one less problem that will keep you up at night.

Without being obnoxious or self-aggrandizing make sure your supervisor knows how much you are accomplishing. Don't be so humble that you fail to claim credit for your achievements. At the same time, be quick to acknowledge your subordinates, colleagues and supervisors for a job well done and never claim credit for someone else's work.

163

Negotiate for Your Needs

Negotiate for the resources you need, whether these be more time, more staff, better technology, a pay raise or some time off. Your supervisor or firm may not be able to grant your request but it's good to articulate your legitimate needs to your supervisor. There is a big difference between being a team player – the type of person who works hard without many complaints – and a martyr – the type of person who fails to exercise righteous insight, expectation and action on their own behalf.

It's Lonely at the Top

If you are a top executive the stress of your employees and the stress of your board (or governing body) ends up becoming yours. You get "pinched" by pressure from the bottom up and the top down. Top executives often feel as if they are an island unto themselves for this reason. They are compelled to "keep a stiff upper lip" and "show no fear" because they are conscious of the responsibilities of leadership and unwilling or unable to share their burdens with others. They also tend to be stubborn as a lot and not very prone to taking it easy. Most people in this position work hard and play hard and have difficulty relaxing. For all these reasons, they suffer disproportionately from heart attack, stroke, diabetes and other stress-related illnesses, including cancer.

If you are a top executive you need to be doubly concerned with doing what it takes to ensure your health and harmony. Your *Story Behind the Story* is calling you to get things in better perspective. Let's face it: your work will be here today, tomorrow and forever – even when you are dead and gone. A lot may be demanded of you from all sides but only you have the ability to take control of your life and put your own wellbeing first. Otherwise your health will deteriorate, at which point you will conclude that the world got a much better deal out of you than you got out of it.

Apart from the self-help methods I describe in this book, you should consider consulting with a qualified counselor, a psychologist for example, or a bona fide spiritual advisor from an established religious order. You might also consider becoming a member of a group of like-minded professionals who have similar challenges. A peer support group of this nature could be formally structured, or it could just be a group of trustworthy acquaintances who get together to "talk shop" every now and then.

The Saint's Conundrum

If you are responsible for the welfare of others – a nurse, doctor, psychologist, social services provider, priestly healer, emergency services worker, educator of the poor, or any caregiver – you must be especially wary of stress. People with jobs like these tend to succumb to *compassion fatigue*, a form of secondary post-traumatic stress wherein the stress of the person being cared for, or even the stress of an entire segment of society, gets transferred onto the caregiver.

Compassion fatigue used to be called "burnout," and for good reason. It will leave you brokenhearted, unhappy, hopeless, chronically-fatigued, depressed, anxious and physically ill. Ironically, the most compassionate caregivers will lose their compassion, not because they give too much to others but because they will not take enough for themselves. Selfless service to others therefore requires a unique form of self-interest.

"That which gives light must endure burning." This is a quote from Viktor Frankl, the famed psychiatrist who gave of himself tirelessly, even while he was interred in a concentration camp during World War II and despite the fact his family had been murdered. Are you a caregiver? If so, meditation, good self-care and a harmonious lifestyle are absolutely critical for you or you will not be able to "endure burning." You cannot give light to others without taking excessive amounts of light for yourself. Your own harmony must come first and foremost or you will "burn up" early in your career and be of no use to yourself or anyone else.

There is another deeper level of truth behind Frankl's metaphor. If you are dedicated to selfless service you should be aware of it. Dr. Frankl was able to serve others under the most tragic circumstances imaginable because he was a man of God. Only someone who has attained enlightenment has the ability to give tirelessly to others without a substantial loss to themselves. Being one with the cosmic mind, they are able to tap its infinite power to accomplish any task under any circumstance. All this is to say, if you are a truly dedicated servant of humankind, enlightenment must be your goal. It is the only sure way to avoid *The Saint's Conundrum*.

13

Preparing to Meet Your Destiny

The science, philosophy and methods in this book equip you with everything you need to live out your highest personal destiny – a future far beyond what the ordinary person can imagine. You came on earth to defy the illusion that you are a mere mortal, to live your life as a joyful adventure in pursuit of your dreams, and if you so desire, to change the world. Distress in any form is simply a sign that you haven't quite figured out how to do it yet. The methods in this book will change that.

The methods are powerful. You won't know just how powerful they are until you use them. They are the closest thing you will find to a "magic pill" that will make you impervious to fear and deliver the power you need to live out your dreams. My purpose in writing this book is to put these methods in your hands. As a perfect blend of hard science and eastern philosophy, they take their inspiration from the relationship I have with my guru Sri Paramahansa Yogananda. It was he who taught Gandhiji Kriya Yoga. Yoganandaji's love for India and her people remains eternal and infinite.

Those of you who came to this book to get help with managing your distress have discovered it is not merely a stress management manual. It's a "how to change your life and your world" manual. The two – distress, and failure to live out your own highest destiny – are intertwined. They are two sides of the same coin. This is an essential truth that is critically important for you to grasp, not only for your own sake but because you have a special role to play in the redemption of our world. You count. India needs you, and the world needs India. She has a very special destiny to fulfill as a world leader, one that was mapped out millennia ago when the Rishis and Rishikas first unraveled the secrets of the cosmos – a subject I will return to later in this chapter.

Your Prescription for Living an Epic, Heroic Life

The tools in this book will let you do three things that are essential to your ability to live a heroic life, free of distress:

1. *Maintain the Right Attitude* – You must dare to dream. You are a god who was born in human form for the purpose of living an epic, heroic life – a life characterized by nothing less than total fulfillment, harmony, love and joy.

2. *Gain Your Freedom* – You must understand the themes, long buried memories and unacknowledged lessons you learned from others that have distorted your thoughts, beliefs and expectations about who you are, what you can do and how fun life can be.

3. *Claim Your Power* – You must access the super-conscious dimensions of your mind where you will find your heroic nature, insight regarding your *Story Behind the Story* and the power you need to live out your dreams.

Now let's look at how to use the methods in this book to accomplish these three goals.

Maintain the Right Attitude

Essentially two kinds of people come to see me. The first kind want to maintain their lives pretty much the way they are with a few improvements. Perhaps they want better physical or mental health, a better marriage, higher income, more power or prestige. For these folks the purpose of life is to go with the flow, enjoy life's pleasures and not question the way things are. The second group is composed of the heroic adventurers. They love to blow the lid off the status quo. They want to know what comes next, whatever it may be, and they want to go for it. They're interested in reinventing their destiny more than once if need be and they don't care much about cultural stereotypes of "the good life."

Why can't you do both? You don't have to be caught in the "Alexander Dichotomy," opting for a short glorious life and an early demise like Alexander the Great. Nor do you have to settle for a conventional long life of measured increase in worldly achievement. Using the methods in this book you can easily unleash enough mental power to do both: live a long life without limits of any kind.

What is your attitude toward life? Whatever your highest destiny may be you can't fulfill it if you don't have the hero archetype: a drive to explore life with gusto, courage, determination, faith, hope, love and joy. To be certain, you possess a heroic nature – it is an innate characteristic of your soul. The soul is utterly fearless, always joyful, aware of its immortality and its power and open to adventure. So believe me when I say you have the power and qualities of a hero. Your conditioned habits of thought, past trials and limiting present circumstances may be obscuring it for you, but it is there.

If you already possess the hero archetype, then you already have the winning attitude required to fulfill your highest destiny. If you would like to have this attitude but you just can't summon it within yourself then you should meditate every day. Daily meditation for 30 minutes will deliver enough soul awareness to break you out of your lethargy and the illusion that you are a mere mortal. Use the hypnotic meditation method in Chapter Seven every day and you will be able to do this with ease. It won't be long before you feel so powerful and strong that your self-doubt will melt away, replaced by a fearless joy and all the courage and determination you need. Obstacles which threatened you before will start to seem trivial. You will actually experience the power of your own soul, know it in your bones. You will be awed by yourself and your possibilities then and find it natural to adopt a heroic attitude.

If you do not possess a heroic attitude and have no interest in adopting one, you need to ask yourself why. Too much unresolved distress from the past is the most frequent cause of such ambivalence. If you are presently poor, ill or exhausted from overwork, perhaps you think the idea of a heroic life is a hoax. If this is you then you must do the most courageous thing imaginable: decide to adopt a heroic attitude as an exercise of your own free will, despite your doubts and beliefs to the contrary, your meager resources or failing health. Do it as an act of blind faith. Then employ the methods in this book in the order I describe below. They will free you from doubt by liberating you from the things that are holding you back and by demonstrating, beyond a shadow of a doubt, that you have what it takes to re-create your destiny. Your success using the methods will prove to you that your leap of faith was well worth it.

Gain Your Freedom

Distorted thinking is the nemesis of every would-be hero. It results from unresolved historical conflict and culturally-imposed "small" ideas of self that have been drilled into us from the time of our youth – in other words, historical distress. These distorted, conditioned habits of thought are driving your karma, keeping you susceptible to distress and prohibiting you from realizing your potential. They are effectively deluding you into believing you are a mere mortal and holding you back, so they have to go. To gain your freedom from delusional thoughts, beliefs, perceptions, attitudes and expectations, rely on the following prescription. I have listed each method in order of importance, with the most powerful methods first:

1. ***Establish a harmonious lifestyle with daily meditation as its hub.*** A harmonious lifestyle (Chapter Eight) will ensure work-life balance and provide your body and mind with the fuel they need to maintain overall health and wellbeing. Daily meditation (Chapter Seven) will open the door to wondrous levels of insight, power and the heroic qualities you need to realize your highest destiny.

2. ***Employ hypnotic regression.*** Use the hypnotic regression method according to the instructions in Chapter Eleven: once per week for four consecutive weeks for initial release of old emotional pain and freedom from distorted thinking. Then use the method weekly to perfect your freedom and build self-insight. Remember not to use it without assistance from a mental health professional if you have suffered a lot of trauma or if you are unable to control your emotions.

3. ***Practice cognitive reprogramming.*** Everyone can benefit from using the cognitive reprogramming method, especially those of you who "think a lot." Use this method according to the instructions in Chapter Ten until such time as you no longer feel burdened by negative emotion and feel a rising optimism, determination and courage. Then use it anytime you become aware of emotional distress or want more mental power and focus.

4. ***Use scientific affirmations 2 or 3 times per week.*** Use the guidance in Chapter Twelve to employ scientific affirmations on the heels of your daily meditation two or three times per week. When used correctly affirmations have the ability to penetrate deeply into the mind to reprogram the conditioned, distorted habits of thought that are causing your distress and keeping you from realizing your potential. Affirmations also help activate the heroic attitudes you need for success.

5. ***Employ cathartic release methods and expressive techniques.*** Experiment with these methods, per the instructions in Chapter Twelve, until you find the ones that work best for you. One or more of these methods can easily be built into your daily lifestyle. Many of them are downright fun. All will bring measurable relief from negative emotion as well as resolution of historical distress and more clarity with regard to your *Story Behind the Story*.

6. ***Become part of a group.*** Using the guidance in Chapter Twelve, find or create a group of like-minded peers with whom you can share your challenges and perspectives. The resulting inspiration, insight and support you receive will be well worth the effort. You

might even consider creating a group that's chartered around use of the methods in this book.

Claim Your Power

You must access the power that is secreted away in your super-conscious mind: your own soul-force, as well as the infinite power of the universal super-conscious mind (God). With this power you will be able to achieve any noble goal and conquer any obstacle that stands in your way, including your distress. Without it, you will remain ensnared and confined by your mortal existence. Even a little taste of your own soul-force will give you new hope, optimism, and courage and convince you that you can accomplish your dreams.

You must understand what power is in its purest form. Most people get hung up about power in the worldly sense so they end up craving things like monetary wealth, political clout and social prestige. But worldly forms of power are personal, tied to a single individual and circumstance and have no lasting value – you can't take them with you when you go. Real power is not personal and not tied to specific persons or their accomplishments. It's like a cosmic battery, available in unending supply from the universal mind. Anyone can have as much of it as they like, regardless of their circumstances, status, gender, age or worldly achievements. Real power will let you achieve your own noble dreams, heal the world if you chose and ultimately lead you into enlightened awareness. This is the ultimate power play, the only one that delivers infinite power you can share with others – power you can take with you when you go. To access this power, rely on the following prescription:

1. **Daily scientific meditation.** Only meditation will deliver access to the limitless power of the super-conscious mind. For this reason, if you were to choose just one method from among the many methods in this book, it should be daily meditation using a proven method like the one in Chapter Seven. Start meditating every day. Make it your goal to get to the point where you're spending one hour each day in meditation. It will lead you into heroic levels of self-knowledge, courage, faith, hope and love. It will give you the insight and the power you need to live out your *Story Behind the Story*, to change your destiny or to change the world. It will make you immortal.

2. **Energy healing 2 or 3 times per week in meditation, and in between.** Using the method in Chapter Nine, tack energy healing onto your daily meditation 2 or 3 times per week. Focus first on yourself, then tackle each of your noble goals – the things you want to change. Use the method to achieve one goal at a time,

and stay with the method until you see the results you're looking for. Use the method outside of meditation too, as you move about during the day. The amount of power you're able to focus on your agenda for change will increase exponentially as you practice the method.

3. **Hypnotic regression.** Hypnotic regression lets you free yourself from the past and it also opens the door to super-consciousness. After you've used it to find freedom from unresolved historical distress, keep using it once a week to make continual gains in soul-level insight and power. It will help you gain access to your *Story Behind the Story* and the power you need to fulfill it or change it.

The remaining methods in this book, specifically the Quick-Hit Stressbusters in Chapter Twelve, are good palliatives, which means they'll help you overcome distress as it is rising and convert it into eustress. Use them whenever the need arises. Unlike the methods listed above, they do not have the power, in-and-of-themselves, to dismantle the original cause of your distress. However, they will make a big difference in the moment. Sometimes, that's all you need.

Your Eight-Step Strategy for Fulfilling your Destiny

Here is a checklist that summarizes all the guidance so far in this chapter – the components of a strategy that will enable you to live life heroically, free of distress. The methods are listed in order from most important to least important.

- A harmonious lifestyle with daily meditation as its hub
- Hypnotic regression once a week
- Energy healing 2 or 3 times weekly as part of your daily meditation
- Scientific affirmations 2 or 3 times weekly as part of your daily meditation
- Cathartic release methods (your choice), as needed
- Creative expressive methods built into your lifestyle, as needed
- Peer group support
- Quick-hit Stressbusters, as needed

This seems like a lot to cram into one person's busy schedule. However I assure you that if you start down this path, your soul will be so delighted that the universe will bend the laws of time and space to make way for the implementation of your strategy. Not only this, but you'll find that the benefits far outweigh the hassle of building this routine into your lifestyle. You really can't put a price on your own immortality. When you attain it, you'll realize it was worth a thousand times the effort you put into getting it.

Don't even try to bite off the entire strategy at once. Start by establishing a harmonious lifestyle with daily meditation as its nucleus and work down the list from there. Daily meditation is the utmost key to success. Meditate every day using a proven method and your *Story Behind the Story* will unfold, along with an endless stream of possibilities and the power to bring them into realization. Meditate and you will directly experience your own infinite eternal nature. Health, wealth, possessions – even a great love in your life – all take a backseat to the ultimate *Story Behind the Story*, which is to discover just how powerful you really are.

After you've established a harmonious lifestyle that includes daily meditation it's easy to start building the other items on the checklist into your routine. Finding an hour in your week to use the hypnotic regression method might be a little challenging at first but after you use it you'll be so thrilled with the results that you'll hunger for the week to go by so you can use it again. Hypnotic regression is extremely powerful. You'll want to use it once a week for at least one month to get a big "jump" on gaining your freedom before you start experimenting with the other methods.

Next in importance come energy healing and scientific affirmations. These are specialized techniques that you fold into your daily meditation. Use of these two methods won't take any additional time away from your busy schedule and they'll deliver observable change. Once you instill these methods into your daily routine, move on to experimenting with the cathartic release methods and creative, expressive techniques as you see fit. Use the quick-hit stressbusters to alleviate distress anytime, anywhere. When you can see your way clear to do it, consider becoming a member of a group of like-minded peers.

Whatever you do, don't turn the implementation of this strategy into a job. Have fun with it. Experiment with the available options. Let it unfold naturally. Your own soul – the sleeping giant within you – will awaken to provide you with the guidance you need. Trust your own internal compass and do what you can to make progress with implementing your self-styled strategy. Then enjoy the ride.

What To Expect

People often ask me, "Why do some people get a sensational, miraculous benefit from the methods, while others have to work with the methods for a while?"

Two factors will determine how quickly you get results from the use of these methods:

- The degree to which you are engaging your *Story Behind the Story*, and
- The degree to which you maintain a receptive attitude.

The first factor has to do with how well you're working with your highest purpose for being here. If you are moving in tandem with it you will make rapid progress. If you resist your lessons, you'll find your progress is slow and incremental. The reason why is that your subconscious mind will slow you down in order to get you to connect with your *Story Behind the Story*. If your progress is very slow, in all likelihood it's because you're not seeing or acknowledging something important about your lack of internal harmony. For example, if your sole motivation for using the methods is to make lots of money, when in fact you should be concerned about your uncontrollable anger and the distortions in thought and feeling that are driving it, your progress is likely to be slow. You do not have to be problem-free in order to use the methods to great effect – not by a long shot. However, you *do* need to pay attention to your need for attaining internal harmony. Your progress will depend on it.

The second factor that will impact your rate of progress is your level of receptivity toward the methods and the science behind them. These methods are powerful and the science that backs them is solid. They are like a seed that carries the potential to become the most majestic tree in the forest. But there is the power of the seed and then there's the receptivity of the soil. If you are receptive to the power of these methods and to your own power – if you think in very expansive terms about what you can do – your progress will be meteoric. Remember *as you think, so shall you be*.

The methods in this book are accompanied by a new, more accurate and scientifically validated world view. They will let you do things that have never before been credibly considered possible. You can influence your own mind-body connection to dramatically improve your health and wellbeing, even cure yourself of things like heart disease and cancer. You can use the power of your mind to affect the energy fields associated with other people, places and things in order to make your noble dreams come true. You can heal the world around you. You can rapidly come into enlightened states of awareness. Using these methods what used to take 30 to 40 years of intense discipline can now be accomplished in one to two years, or even a matter of months if your mind is receptive and you're willing to engage your *Story Behind the Story*. Armed with these methods your possibilities are truly endless.

A New World Order

We are now entering a golden age of unprecedented human evolution. It will be an age in which there is no longer an us-versus-them mentality, one in which everyone realizes we are all part of the same vast soup of intelligent energy – all of us equal and united as one. In this age people will use the power of their minds to create justice, harmony and prosperity for all and we will heal the earth from the ravages of pollution, global warming and warfare. In order to get the job done the world needs enlightened people at all levels within society and it needs them now. India needs them in the particular because she has a special role to play in the redemption of our world, and so do you.

The methods in this book will help you usher in this new era. Use them to heal yourself, live out your noble dreams and become an eternal, immortal being. Then join us in creating the next age of humanity by helping to forge harmony, justice, compassion and prosperity for all. The same methods in this book, when used collectively, have the power to redeem our world and transform it into heaven on earth. I am inviting you to use them in precisely this way and become a member of the new world order. It is not hard to do. You can start by using the following exercise, then share it with family and friends. It has the ability to redeem Mother India from the things that plague her and to heal the world we share.

A National De-Stressor

There are problems in India that are responsible for fueling a national epidemic of distress – problems which share a common cause that transcends geography and time. The first problem consists of terrorism and acts of inter-cultural and inter-racial violence. The second problem is poverty and its ugly antecedents: illiteracy, disease and caste-based oppression. The third is gender discrimination. India also needs more wealth to surmount her challenges. If these concerns matter to you then you need to know how they arose and how to heal them.

To understand the cause of these problems recall that every person, place and thing in existence is made of energy and there is a single intelligent, *alive* energy field that spans the entire universe. Within the universal field everything is connected to and reacting with everything else simultaneously. This is a fact proven by modern physics and paralleled in the teachings of the Rishis, the Buddha, the Prophets of Israel, the Sikh Gurus, Mahavira, the Sufi Teachers of Islam and Jesus Christ. Science and religion concur on this point.

The world-wide energy field provides the necessary ingredients for our enlightenment as individuals and as a species. Within it there are energetic forces that strive to lead us away from God by forging disharmony, destruction, the alienation of individuals and entire cultures *(avidya)*. There are also energetic forces that work to lead us into unity by promoting the nobility of every soul and the essential oneness of humankind *(vidya)*. The worldwide energy field constitutes a "learning laboratory" within which we are supposed to discover our highest nature as the sons and daughters of God. We have the ability to wield the sword of *vidya* on the battlefield of life until there is unity, peace, love, justice and prosperity for all as necessary means for enlightenment.

Avidya concentrates anywhere in the world where there has been great suffering, usually brought on as the result of greed and injustice perpetrated by an oppressor or oppressive force – a foreign invader, a selfish potentate, a business conglomerate or nation that is preying on another population for financial gain. The energy of oppression creates a powerful, negatively-charged *avidya* force. *Avidya* naturally concentrates among the oppressed and once ignited, transmits instantaneously throughout the world-wide energy field. Thereafter it will focus as specific acts of oppression in places that are the most vulnerable, and it will directly attack any concentration of *vidya* virtue in an effort to destabilize it. This is just the nature of *avidya*, which always seeks to harm, destabilize and destroy the weak and annihilate virtue.

The ancient Rishis of India created a powerful concentration of *vidya* virtue. Because of their efforts India was and still is destined to illuminate the world. Unfortunately, the virtue that was ancient India became a natural target for its energetic opposite: *avidya* evil. It is no accident that India has suffered the scourge of oppression from innumerable foreign invaders over centuries, ending with the British Raj. The concentration of *avidya* they helped create, and its effects, will be obvious to any elderly reader or any student of Indian history. The heartbreak of Partition for example, was the direct result of centuries of oppression on the Subcontinent and the *avidya* energies behind it: destructive energies that pitted neighbor against neighbor, held the caste system in place long after its due and perpetuated the second-class status of women and girls.

That brings us to the present day. The enlightened individual understands that terrorism, violence, poverty, caste-based oppression and sexism in India are all functions of *avidya* and its nefarious goal to dissolve India's unity, make a sham out of her pure philosophy and prevent her from fulfilling her destiny as a world leader. The cause of India's distress is not the foreign rulers or governments that have occupied her, nor the business conglomerates who've taken advantage of her wealth, nor the terrorist, nor the gangs who rise up to assault their neighbors, nor the poor man who can't feed his family – all of whom have succumbed to the forces of *avidya* themselves via fear, ignorance and suffering. The only real enemy is *avidya* (evil) itself.

India's challenges are therefore not exclusively national problems and cannot be solved entirely at the national level. Every disorder on our planet – from poverty to disease, war to famine – has come into being because of greedy, isolationist thinking on the part of the world's citizenry over thousands of years. This type of thinking invites, then spreads, destructive *avidya* energies throughout the world-wide field. Once in the field these negative energies impact the hearts and minds of people everywhere, fueling a global epidemic of fear, rage and aggression. They also penetrate the energy fields associated with the earth and its biosphere to increase the frequency and intensity of floods, storms, famines, earthquakes and other natural disasters.

Thankfully this generation has the power to undo what past generations have done. Owing to God's influence whenever there is a rise in *avidya* darkness there is a rise in positive *vidya* energies to thwart it, usually triggered by the prayers and meditations of devout people. At present a rise in *vidya* energy is well underway and clearly evident in the thousands of global, national and regional initiatives designed to promote peace, justice, compassion and healing. The ultimate goal is simple: if every one of us thought of every other living person as a member of our own family – with the same concern and care we reserve for our loved ones – the whole world would become free of violence, poverty and oppression virtually overnight.

For all these reasons, the only effective strategy for healing India of her distress is to saturate the whole country and the world-wide energy field with *vidya* – the peace, compassion, love, justice and power that will lift every man, woman and child into unity with one-another and with God.

The tactics applicable under this strategy are twofold. The first tactic exists at the level of changes in thought and behavior. People need to stop thinking of themselves, their families, their culture or even their needs and desires, in isolationist terms. This creates an imbalance in the field that will come to roost somewhere in the form of more violence, poverty and oppression. At a behavioral level people from opposing groups need to find humane ways to come to know each other. It could be something as simple as a shared meal or as structured as a formal dialogue across cultures or social class boundaries. No act is too small.

Owing to the existence of the field, a small act of kindness in a remote village in India will transmit instantaneously to every corner of the nation and then spread outward to embrace the world.

The second, far more potent tactic, involves the use of super-conscious thought to shift the energies in India and the world-wide field into *vidya* (a unifying energy of Divine love, justice and compassion for all) and away from *avidya* (an alienating, violent sense of selfishness and opposition). To do this you can use a variation of the same method I describe in Chapter Nine: Moving Energy with Your Mind.

To use the method to heal India's distress you must be able to meditate very deeply. If you are an advanced meditator use your own method. If you are new to meditation or have been unable to attain a deep meditative state, use the Hypnotic Meditation method I provide in Chapter Seven. It will let you sink deeply into a meditative state with very little effort on your part.

Using my method or one of your own, begin by meditating until your mind is very calm and you feel the deepening peace that signifies soul contact. This is the time to ask God or your guru or teacher to aid you in your efforts. Now use this simple guided thought process to liberate India from the political, economic and social problems that besiege her. Start by allowing yourself to sense the thousands of people who are already using meditative action to shift the energies in the world-wide field. If your mind is extremely calm you will be able to feel their activity or if not, just imagine the throngs of people who are working on the problem and see yourself merging with this collective effort. Realize that God is with you and so is the world-wide field, which always seeks for the wholeness of humankind. Recognize you are an agent of Divine will. Now you are ready to intervene.

Begin with the most obvious expression of the problem you are aware of – the terrorist action in Mumbai, the slums in your community or perhaps your family has been involved in one of the domestic riots that have scourged India. Whatever it is, focus on it and think "I am routing out the enemy with love and compassion." Remember, the enemy you are focusing on is *avidya*, or evil, not the particular souls involved. They deserve liberation. One way to do this is to visualize your target first then imagine you are sending pure white healing light into it until it is radiant with *vidya* virtue. Alternatively you can just "think" of the forces of darkness within society dissolving away and giving rise to the forces of love, compassion, prosperity and justice for all. Do this for several minutes. Do not bring any anger or fear or resentment into the exercise. You must approach this endeavor with a calm mind and compassion. To do otherwise will only fuel the forces of destruction and create a greater imbalance in the field.

Now let this part of the exercise go and return to your meditative practice. If you use the method I suggested in Chapter Seven this will be silent chanting of *Om* on the out-breath. When your mind is calm again move to the second stage of intervention. This time you will focus healing energy on all of India. Concentrate on this for at least five minutes. Use your mind to saturate every corner of your country – every mountain and stream, every human being and every living thing – with the energy of love, peace, compassion, and justice.

Next let this part of the exercise go and return once again to your meditative practice. When your mind is very calm move to the third stage of intervention. In this stage you will spread healing energy outward from India in all directions to span the entire globe. Think "Let God's will be done" and imagine that the white healing light of Divine love, peace, compassion and justice is moving into all that is. Concentrate on this effort for up to 10 minutes, more if you can, until you are certain that every person, place and thing on earth is saturated with *vidya* virtue.

At this juncture you will want to thank God and the enlightened beings world-wide for their fellowship in your efforts. Then open your eyes. You will notice you feel extremely peaceful, perhaps even blissful at the end of this experience. Any act of unselfish compassion conveys a reciprocal gift to the healer because of the existence of the field and your relationship with it. You are a co-creator of the field and your power to influence it is exponentially greater than you think. At the end of the exercise, as you feel the positive energy flowing into you, realize you just conveyed a substantial degree of healing to every Indian citizen, every being on the planet and the earth itself. Don't think for a moment that your help is insignificant. Mother Teresa said that when we give purely God makes the effect infinite. She was right. If you want to propel India into her highest destiny you should conduct this meditative exercise twice a week and enlist your friends and relatives in the effort. The cosmic mind of God, the enlightened Masters of India and the earth itself will rise up to ensure your success.

In Conclusion

Have faith in yourself, in God and in your own infinite potential. Employ the methods in this book to heal yourself, annihilate distress, access your power and discover the thrill of adventure. Live a heroic life true to your own noble hopes, dreams and ambitions. Become immortal. Help usher in the next wondrous age of unity and prosperity on earth. Have it all: a worldly life of adventure, enlightened awareness and a key role to play in the liberation of humankind. Do it all. Be it all. This is your destiny if you choose it.

Welcome to a life without limits.

Appendix
Stress-related Causes of Illness

Appendix
Stress-related Causes of Illness

This Appendix lists the most frequent underlying psychological or spiritual causes for 48 common ailments, including mental and emotional disorders. *Your cause may vary.* To get to the heart of your unique situation you will need to look at your *Story Behind the Story*: the challenges you've faced and how you reacted to them, the nature and intensity of the distress you carry, and the degree to which you are living out your highest dreams and aspirations. If you don't see your ailment email DrLevy@TheLevyCenters.com. I will help you pinpoint the cause of your issue.

I provide this guidance because it has the potential to vastly increase your power over your own wellbeing. It is not designed to replace competent medical care. If you are unwell please use the tools in this book as an adjunct to a responsible healthcare programme prescribed by a properly credentialed health professional (a physician, physician's assistant or doctor of mental health).

Allergies

People who suffer from allergies are typically launching a mild attack upon themselves. They are irritated (with themselves, with others or with circumstances), hypersensitive and they tend to have low self-esteem. As a result they turn their irritation inward in the form of a histamine reaction to miniscule irritants in their environment.

Self-help Tip: If this is you, you need to deal with the people, events and underlying emotions that are causing your irritation, free yourself from their influence and stop punishing yourself.

Anger

Healthy anger is a natural response to a perceived threat: if something is attacking or hurting you and your self-esteem is solid, you get angry in order to fight it off. Healthy anger takes indwelling negative emotion (like fear) and turns it outward into the world in the form of action that's designed to stop a painful experience. It comes in handy: it can solve a problem if it's used wisely, even save your life.

Unhealthy anger is a different thing altogether. It is chronic, intense, damaging and often out of control. If this is you then you need to look deeper. Anger is a secondary emotion, so you will find another emotion behind it that is keeping it alive. The number one emotion that's responsible for fueling chronic anger is fear. If this is you, you've probably had to endure a lot of emotional pain over a long time, so much so that you finally got furious. The next most frequent cause of anger is shame. If this is you, events or other people have made you feel like you're just not good enough and you're intensely angry at the unfairness of it all. Chances are you've been trying to do good and be good but things still haven't worked out. Chronic physical pain is also a cause for unhealthy anger: the sustained anguish it generates would drive anyone to rage now and then.

Self-help Tip: If unhealthy anger is your issue then you have to find the underlying cause and free yourself from it once and for all. Also read the content for **FEAR** and **SHAME**.

Anxiety

There are three main types of anxiety:

1. People who suffer from generalized anxiety problems typically have a history of being hurt and a chronic fear of getting hurt yet again, accompanied by a feeling of helplessness and an inability to exert control over their environment or relationships.

2. If you suffer from a specific anxiety disorder such as fear of heights look for its symbolic significance: people with a fear of heights have a fear of falling and being hurt; people with a fear of public places tend to have a fear of being exposed; people with a fear of tight spaces (like elevators) have a fear of being trapped and so on. Past traumatic events (like falling from a high place) can make this type of anxiety worse but they are not the original cause of the anxiety.

3. Post-traumatic stress disorder – for those who have been repeatedly exposed to extreme trauma (as in the case of natural

disaster, war or a long history of abuse) their fear of being mortally harmed is so firmly embedded in the subconscious mind that it invades the conscious mind: they have the conscious expectation that everyday occurrences will be life-threatening.

Self-help Tip: If you suffer from anxiety your goal is to free yourself from the underlying causes (fear or shame) which typically have a strong root in the subconscious mind, our storehouse of memory. Also read the content for **FEAR** and **SHAME**.

Arthritis

Arthritis typically evolves in people who lack emotional and cognitive flexibility in response to stressful situations – the unresolved psychological stress then gets focused inward in a form of self-attack that manifests as inflammation and physical inflexibility. Arthritis frequently arises for people who were extremely stressed early in life owing to hardship, physical trauma, abuse or neglect. Children and adolescents do not generally possess enough emotional or cognitive sophistication to deal effectively with acute stress so they internalize it. If it is never dealt with it will eventually somatize (become cellular) in the form of arthritis or other stress-related illnesses.

Self-help Tip: If you suffer from arthritis your goal should be to free yourself from negative emotion that may have arisen due to stress early in life and find healthier ways to manage stress as it arises in your day-to-day experience.

Auto-Immune Disorders

Auto-immune disorders typically arise in people who have very low self-esteem, to the point they feel so unworthy they deserve to be punished. This translates into a self-attack on the immune system, chronic fatigue, muscular pain and adrenal suppression. The psychological pattern for these disorders usually gets established early. If this is you look to your early childhood history for repeated messages from parents and significant others that you didn't measure-up and that no matter what you did, life would still be difficult.

Self-help Tip: If this is you, your goal should be to free yourself from the emotional pain and distorted thinking that keeps you locked in a cycle of self-deprecation. Also read the content for **SHAME**.

Back and Neck Pain

Pain in the spine (and associated illness or injury) typically arises for people whose responsibilities outstrip their physical, mental or financial resources.

This problem is typical for strong-willed people who tend not to dump their problems on others but instead try to shoulder their burdens alone. People with lower back pain tend to respond to this challenge by "getting their back up" to confront the onslaught – they live in a warrior posture with their lower back girded to "heft" the demands of life. Alternatively people with neck pain tend to be people who are always "sticking their neck out" or who feel that "life has become one big pain in the neck." If you've suffered an injury to the spine, chances are you fit one of these categories and the accumulated stress in your spine made it prone to injury.

Self-help Tip: If this is you, your goal should be to free yourself from the accumulated stress in your spine, find healthier ways to manage stress, share your burdens and simplify and realign your life so it is more consistent with your highest dreams and aspirations.

Bipolar Disorder

Bipolar disorders have a hereditary basis but the psychological component tends to consist of intense, repressed early childhood anger, as would be the case for kids who grew up in families that were highly volatile, abusive, neglectful or controlling. Most people have a natural rise and fall in mood but with bipolar disorder there is so much repressed anger that people go to the extremes of high and low, much like their emotions are riding a roller coaster.

Self-help Tip: If this is you, your goal should be to discover and release the old anger that is fueling the rise and fall of your emotions. Usually, it is rooted in the subconscious mind (our storehouse of old memory).

Cancer – All Types

The psychological cause for all cancers consists of strongly repressed negative emotion that is being used (consciously or unconsciously) to attack the self. The particular type of negative emotion and the thoughts associated with it will determine the location and type of cancer.

Self-help Tip for All People with Cancer

Your goal should be to discover the deep-seated negative emotions that are fueling your illness, free yourself from them once and for all and stop the self-attack. You also must find more meaning, purpose, love and joy in life. Also read the content below, as relevant, for your type of cancer.

Cancer – Bladder

With bladder cancer the overall thrust of negative emotion can be summed up in the phrase "I'm pissed-off."

Self-help Tip: Read the content for **ANGER**.

Cancer – Bone

With bone cancer the overall thrust of negative emotion is usually related to anger and intense fear, which runs very deep and therefore attacks the structure of your being, as in the phrase "I am shaken to the bone."

Self-help Tip: Read the content for **ANGER** and **FEAR**.

Cancer – Breast

With breast cancer the overall thrust of negative emotion is usually related to fear, anger, guilt or shame around issues having to do with one's own sexuality, in particular with receiving and giving nurturance. Often it is associated with a history of sexual abuse.

Self-help Tip: Read the content for **ANGER, FEAR** and **SHAME**.

Cancer – Cervical

Women with cervical cancer tend to carry a great deal of strong repressed negative emotion (fear, anger, guilt or shame) around their sexuality. This is usually true for women who have been abused sexually or who have been denigrated, minimized or objectified based on their sexuality (in or out of marriage). Sometimes the negative emotion is focused exclusively around the idea of giving birth.

Self-help Tip: Read the content for **ANGER, FEAR** and **SHAME**.

Cancer – Colorectal

With colon and rectal cancer the overall thrust of negative emotion is usually related to one or both of two things: a deep despair that life is really shitty (nothing ever goes your way) or the feeling that you just can't eliminate things from your life that are harming you (people, relationships or responsibilities constantly cause you pain). There is usually a fair amount of repressed anger associated with the unfairness of it all.

Self-help Tip: Read the content for **ANGER, FEAR** and **SHAME**.

Cancer – Kidney

With kidney cancer, the overall thrust of negative emotion can be similar to the feelings associated with bladder cancer - a feeling of being "pissed-off" that is usually mixed with fear, or more specifically a "fear of being pissed-off." This would arise for a person who has been exposed to the toxic nature of anger, is fearful of it and afraid to unleash it in themselves.

Self-help Tip: Read the content for **ANGER** and **FEAR**.

Cancer – Leukemia

Of all the cancers leukemia sufferers tend to be people who carry the most strongly suppressed fear, anger, guilt or shame. Negative emotion is so suppressed there is seldom any evidence whatsoever of it, so most leukemia sufferers seem reasonable and well-balanced. The negative emotion is there however and powerful enough to run right at the stream of life: the bloodstream. Spiritual sadness, detachment and alienation may also be a factor for the leukemia sufferer, who usually finds little meaning and purpose in life.

Self-help Tip: Read the content for **ANGER**, **FEAR** and **SHAME**.

Cancer – Liver

People with liver cancer tend to be people who have a bilious attitude toward life, or a pissed-off attitude that's being repressed and directed inward. Liver cancer is one of the most serious and difficult to treat cancers. It runs right at every cell in the body by causing toxins to build up systemically. If you have this form of cancer you should ask yourself in all candor, "Do I really want to live?" Your healing will begin with honesty about the weight of the burden you have been carrying.

Self-help Tip: Read the content for **ANGER**.

Cancer – Lung

With lung cancer, the overall thrust of negative emotion has to do with an ambivalence or dislike around the idea of staying alive, a "dis-ease" with drawing the breath of life or with being "in the flow" and rhythm of life. Poor self-esteem, too many messages received early in life that you just couldn't measure up and a sense that "life is just too big a burden" are often involved.

Self-help Tip: Read the content for **ANGER**, **FEAR** and **SHAME**.

Cancer – Pancreatic

People with pancreatic cancer are similar to people with diabetes – they have trouble digesting the sweetness of life (the pancreas produces chemicals that allow us to metabolize sugar). But unlike people with diabetes, the pancreatic cancer sufferer tends to carry much more self-directed anger and fear which are being more strongly repressed.

Self-help Tip: Read the content for **ANGER** and **FEAR**.

Cancer – Prostate

People with prostate cancer tend to hold back their emotions, anger in the particular, which they concentrate in the area between the genitals and the anus – in other words, they become a "tight-ass." Men who suffer from prostate cancer can usually look back on life experiences that left them feeling emasculated, have trouble with deep levels of intimacy and trust, and do not have a good ongoing healthy sexual relationship in their lives.

Self-help Tip: Read the content for **ANGER** and **FEAR**.

Cancer – Skin

People with skin cancer are generally people who are highly sensitive, so much so they don't like to feel what it's like to be in their own skin. Like other cancer sufferers they are repressing negative emotion but to a less intense degree – their emotions tend to lie "right on the surface."

Self-help Tip: Strive to develop stronger emotional boundaries. Also read the content for **ANGER, FEAR** and **SHAME**.

Cancer – Stomach

People with stomach cancer tend to have had a belly-full of problems in life and are carrying so much anger, fear and shame that they just can't stomach it any more.

Self-help Tip: Read the content for **ANGER, FEAR** and **SHAME**.

Cancer – Thyroid

The most frequent underlying issue for people with thyroid cancer is that they carry powerful negative emotion (i.e. anger, fear, sadness, shame, guilt) that cries for release, but the person is withholding self-expression (they cannot or will not speak of the things that trouble them). The result is that negative energy associated with these emotions ends up collecting in their throat and neck.

Self-help Tip: Read the content for **ANGER, FEAR** and **SHAME**.

Cancer – Uterine

Women with uterine cancer tend to carry a great deal of strong repressed negative emotion (fear, anger, guilt or shame) around their sexuality. This is usually true for women who have been abused sexually or those who have been denigrated, minimized or used for their sexuality (in or out of marriage). Sometimes the negative emotion is focused exclusively around the idea of giving birth.

Self-help Tip: Read the content for **ANGER, FEAR** and **SHAME**.

Colds and Flu – Chronic

Chronic colds and flu typically arise in people who desperately need some rest and relaxation, but don't feel they have permission to rest unless they get sick. A lot of people will take a mental health day when they need it but sufferers of chronic colds and flu do just the opposite – they tend to be workaholics who won't take time off, no matter what, until they get sick. A minority of chronic cold and flu sufferers get repeatedly ill because, at a psychological level, they just can't face the stress of day-to-day existence, especially work-related stress. They get sick so they can take a break.

Self-help Tip: If this is you, your goal should be to examine your thoughts and feelings as they relate to how you deal with life's challenges, reprogram them and find a healthier way to manage stress. Also see the content for **STRESS**.

Congenital Illness and Disabilities

Congenital disorders, including disabilities, are chosen by the soul of the individual for a higher purpose. There is a tendency among the masses to assume that when people are born with congenital health problems they are being punished. This is untrue. The reasons why a soul might choose to be born with a congenital illness or disability are varied but they are all noble. The soul might desire an intense lesson in the development of humility or super-charged willpower for example. Some souls make this choice because they wish to compress many lifetimes of growth and evolution into one (struggle and expansion are closely related). An advanced soul might choose this type of incarnation in order to teach their families, teachers, classmates, doctors and neighbors about the true meaning of compassion and unconditional love. In some cases very evolved souls choose to be born in the humble disguise of a broken body so they can secretly effect a major overhaul of our educational, medical, social or political institutions. Extremely rarely, a congenital illness or disability can be the product of past-life trauma that has not been completely resolved.

Self-help Tip: If this is you and you are able to do it, you should learn to meditate regularly. It will bring you into peace and joy, provide you with the insight you need to exert more control over your destiny and deliver the power to heal yourself. If the reader has a loved one who is too disabled (or too young) to employ meditative healing techniques on their own behalf, **you** should use meditation and subtle energy healing to help them.

Degenerative Disc Disease

Degenerative disc disease typically arises for people whose responsibilities outstrip their resources (physical, mental or financial). If this is you, you are probably a strong-willed person who tends to shoulder your burdens alone. Such people tend to have a military posture toward life. They always "have their back up" to confront the battle or feel as though they're "sticking their neck out" all the time. They end up storing unbelievable amounts of stress in the spine. If you've suffered an injury to the spine, chances are the accumulated stress in your spine made it prone to injury. Once the spine is injured, the probability of degenerative disc disease increases.

Self-help Tip: If this is you, your goal should be to examine your thoughts and feelings as they relate to how you deal with life's challenges, slow down and smell the roses, rely more on others and find healthier ways to manage stress.

Depression

There are two main types of depression. One is a deep sadness – usually brought on by too much unresolved emotional pain and suffering – which creates anger toward others or the world around us. However, instead of expressing this anger we turn it inward. This type of depression is typically associated with feelings of unworthiness and low self-esteem. If things are going bad we get mad at ourselves because we don't deserve any better.

The second type of depression is called vegetative depression. This is a case where we are slowing down, either because we've made the decision to give up on life (consciously or unconsciously) or we're just getting worn down by the demands that life is placing on us, or both. You don't have to be sad for vegetative depression, you may just feel tired and ambivalent about living. If this is you, you should see a physician and have a good physical because chances are your depressed state has affected particular organ systems that are now helping to slow you down. Your physician will want to check your thyroid, adrenals, kidneys, liver and heart. A vegetative depression will affect one or more of these systems. The content of your emotional pain will determine where your body will be affected. For example, if you carry a lot of unresolved anger your liver and kidneys are at risk; too much emotional pain from harmful relationships will affect your heart; too much withholding of self-expression will go to the thyroid, and so on.

Self-help Tip: If this is you, your goal is to discover and release the underlying emotions that are fueling your depression and free yourself from them once and for all. Also read the content for **ANGER, FEAR** and **SHAME.**

Diabetes – Adult

People with diabetes are usually those who have trouble digesting the sweetness of life. Often they are obsessively organized and/or angry and not able to relax and flow or feel joy just being alive. They can easily enjoy the big victories in life but they can't slow down long enough to smell the roses, or savor a good meal, or take joy from holding a small child's hand.

Self-help Tip: If this is you, your goal should be to free yourself from the underlying negative emotions that are fueling your driven approach to life. Also read the content under **ANGER.**

Dysmenorrhea

Dysmenorrhea sufferers are typically women who hold repressed negative emotion around their own sexuality. Fear is usually the predominant emotion (literally fear of one's own sexuality), followed by shame, both of which lead to self-disgust or self-loathing. It is prevalent in women who've been sexually abused (physically or emotionally) or who have been denigrated, minimized or objectified based on their feminine attributes. Current stress levels are also a factor.

Self-help Tip: If this is you, you need to free yourself from the negative emotion that is fueling your illness once and for all and find healthier ways of managing stress. Also see the content for **FEAR** and **SHAME.**

Eye Disease – Vision Problems

Eye disease usually affects people who've known a great deal of suffering. It is typically a function of repressed fear related to excessive suffering in the past and fearful expectations about a future that you don't want to see.

Self-help Tip: If this is you, you need to come to grips with your old fear, free yourself from it and gain confidence that your future could be anything you make of it. Also, read the content for **FEAR.**

Fear

Just like you have pain in your body to alert you to illness or injury, you have fear in your mind to alert you to a threat to your safety. It's an early warning system that's useful if you can put your finger on the source of the fear and do something constructive about it. For chronic fear sufferers however, fear is frequent, serious and out of control. If this is you, you probably have been exposed to too much trauma, loss or abuse and never got the help you needed to deal with it. When any challenge arises, in the back of your mind you're thinking "Oh no, here it goes again" along with the expectation that you'll end up hurt and there's nothing you can do about it. Your alarm system has become way too hypersensitive because of what you've been through and it's always on red alert.

Self-help Tip: If this is you, you need to stand down your alarm system. You can take the heat out of it by freeing yourself from the old fear and the distorted thinking that goes along with it.

Gastro-Intestinal Problems

GI problems always signify the presence of repressed emotion. Where and how it lodges in the digestive system will be determined by the type of emotion that is being repressed and the thoughts associated with it. Upper GI problems like ulcers and acid reflux disease usually involve a lot of chronic stress and fear. This wears a person down over time until they are literally burned-up with irritation in the form of excess stomach acid. Lower GI problems like Spastic Colon, Irritable Bowel Syndrome and Crohn's Disease are similar to upper GI problems, but they tend to involve a more "visceral" anger – the worse the anger, the more severe and chronic the problem.

Self-help Tip: If this is you, your goal should be to discover the underlying emotions that are fueling your problem, free yourself from them once and for all and find some happiness and peace in life. Also read the content for **ANGER, FEAR** and **SHAME**.

Heart Disease

Heart disease often has a genetic component. The psychological dimensions are the primary cause of the problem however. These are invariably grounded in a history of excessive love loss or chronic suffering in loveless relationships. Occasionally the problem is a fear of love itself because past encounters with love have been so painful.

Self-help Tip: If this is you, you need to heal from old love loss, become a lover of self and others, and find real love. Finding the love of God in meditation will go a long way toward liberating you from your illness.

Hypertension (High Blood Pressure)

Hypertension results from over-exertion of the heart (see HEART DISEASE). Similarly, the psychological and spiritual dimensions of hypertension are related to excessive love loss or chronic suffering in loveless relationships. However, with hypertension there is usually an anxious "pushing" in one's attempts to find love rather than letting love come more naturally and gently.

Self-help Tip: If this is you, you need to heal from old love loss and learn how to open yourself fully to the love of others.

Infertility

Infertility is closely associated with stress and more specifically: stressful or fearful concerns about sexuality, the process of giving birth and child-rearing or about bringing new life into this world. Often, at its root it boils down to "How could I do that to a child?" or "Will I be a good enough parent to shield my child from the harsh realities of life?"

Self-help Tip: If this is you, you need to discover the underlying fear that is fueling your problem and free yourself from it, as well as find healthy ways to deal with stress.

Injuries

Contrary to popular belief, injuries don't happen by accident. They typically occur in a part or parts of the body where we're holding a lot of stress to begin with. One tennis player will tear a rotator cuff while another stays healthy, largely because the first player stored too much stress in the shoulder, making it susceptible to injury.

If you have suffered injury look at the body parts that have been affected and ask yourself whether there is any obvious underlying symbolic meaning in the placement of the injury. Did you suffer from a lower back injury because you were "hefting" too many burdens, an injury to the hands because you were having trouble "getting a hold" of your life, a leg injury because you were having trouble "taking the next step" toward the future, an eye injury because you just don't want to see what the future holds? Keep in mind that while injuries may seem to occur by accident, they usually happen because of a subconscious desire to take ourselves out of the game, at least for a while.

Self-help Tip: If this is you, you need to find and release the negative emotions that are fueling your problem and find healthier ways of dealing with stress. Also see the content for **FEAR**.

Kidney Disease (or Renal Failure)

If you have kidney problems you should look to old unresolved anger for the underlying cause of your ailment – anger which is causing you to feel "pissed-off." Further, kidney disease is sometimes related to other illnesses like life-long hypertension. If you have a related diagnosis that is contributing to renal failure, look up the most typical underlying cause for that illness too and realize that whatever it is, you're angry about it. If you have both hypertension and renal failure for example, the likelihood is that you've suffered in love, strongly desire love, can't get it, and you're angry about it.

Self-help Tip: If this is you, you need to find and release the unresolved anger that is fueling your problem, as well as deal with the issues that caused the anger in the first place. Also see the content for **ANGER** and **FEAR**.

Migraines

Psychological stress (historical and present) is the most frequent underlying cause of migraines. For the migraine sufferer life has become one big headache. It's not that the psychological stress is repressed so much as that the person is trying to ride over it or through it. Migraine sufferers are typically trying to block their emotions. They tend to be strong-willed basically good-hearted people who are just trying not to give in to their underlying issues. For this reason the problems with eyesight frequently associated with migraines occur because the underlying cause is "blindingly obvious."

Self-help Tip: If this is you, your goal should be to find and release the negative emotions that are fueling your problem and find healthier ways of dealing with stress. Also see the content for **FEAR** and **ANGER**.

Multiple Sclerosis (MS)

MS typically arises in people who have very low self-esteem, to the point they feel so unworthy they deserve to be punished, which translates into a self-attack. The MS sufferer also tends to have a lot of repressed anger. These are generally folks who've suffered a lot of abuse or neglect early in life but they're too good-hearted to allow themselves to get angry about it. The combination of the two, low self-esteem and excessive amounts of repressed anger, turns into a self-attack on the central nervous system: the body's command central. If this is you, look to your early childhood history for repeated messages from your parents and significant others that you didn't measure-up and that no matter what you did, life would still be difficult.

Self-help Tip: If this is you, your goal should be to free yourself from the emotional pain and distorted thinking that keeps you locked in a cycle of self-deprecation. Also see the content for **ANGER**.

Obesity

The most frequent underlying psychological cause for obesity and excess weight gain is early life abuse or neglect which leads to self-deprecation and self-sabotage. If unresolved, the sadness, fear, anger, guilt or shame that arises in childhood can perpetuate a subconscious hunger for nurture and love that we satisfy with food. Old emotional pain of this type also fuels poor self-esteem and a sense of powerlessness, which can create a subconscious desire to appear less attractive in order to prevent yourself from getting involved and getting hurt. Those with a fear of relationships may overeat in order to create a barrier to human interaction. Alternatively, some people feel weak and small and weight gain makes them feel larger and more powerful. Others are so distressed at a subconscious level they eat for emotional nurture. And for some, an upbringing characterized by too much junk food and too little exercise ends up establishing a repetitive pattern in the subconscious mind that insists on maintaining an unhealthy lifestyle, no matter what.

Self-help Tip: If this is you, your goal should be to get at the underlying emotional causes of your over-eating and free yourself from them once and for all.

Podiatric Problems

Problems with the feet, including injury, usually occur in people who aren't well-grounded. Due to a history of abuse, difficult encounters with other people, places or events, poor self-esteem or a generalized fear, these folks just don't feel like they belong here. They don't feel connected (to the earth, literally) and they just aren't comfortable walking around on terra-firma anymore.

Self-help Tip: If this is you, your goal should be to get at the underlying emotional causes of your illness, free yourself from them and resolve your ambivalence about being here by finding a new sense of meaning and purpose in life.

Post-Traumatic Stress Disorder

People who suffer from PTSD have typically been over-exposed to life-threatening extreme trauma (as in the case of natural disaster, war or a long history of abuse). Their fear of being mortally harmed is so firmly embedded in the subconscious mind that it invades the conscious

193

mind: they have the conscious expectation that everyday occurrences will be life-threatening, are hyper-vigilant for this reason, and prone to sleeplessness, irritability, impatience, anger, depression, high anxiety and flashbacks.

Self-help Tip: If this is you, your goal is to free yourself from the underlying causes of your fear, which typically have a strong root in the subconscious mind (our storehouse of memory). Also see the content for **FEAR**.

Respiratory Illnesses

People who suffer from respiratory illnesses are typically uninterested in or ambivalent about living, so much so that they have a disdain for drawing in "the breath of life." These are folks who've typically had to endure a lot of suffering and carry a good bit of fear and anger as a result. They don't want to be involved in their lives anymore and they are trying to opt-out by withdrawing their connection to the basic rhythm that binds them to the world: the breath. Hard working people are often disproportionately affected because they feel as if they are being "worked to death" or like "life is a lot of hard work and then you die." People who carry a lot of repressed anger are more likely to smoke and suffer from smoking-related illnesses (i.e. emphysema, COPD). In extreme cases of anger these folks will often keep smoking even after they've received a life-threatening diagnosis. People who have more fear underlying their condition tend to develop things like asthma.

Self-help Tip: If this is you, your goal is to free yourself from old fear, anger and other negative emotions that are making you ambivalent about living and find new meaning and purpose in life.

Shame

Shame is a form of social censure. Its purpose is to control the behavior of people within a family, group or society so they don't selfishly act out in ways that are harmful to others. When it is used rightly, it is effective and necessary. A problem arises however, when censure is out of proportion or unfairly applied – then it is *very* harmful. Harmful censure is usually applied by someone who doesn't feel good about themselves and chooses to brutalize someone who is weaker. The recipient of this type of treatment, especially if it is severe or prolonged, ends up never feeling good enough and fearful about life and relationships. They will often develop anger in response to their torment and because of their low self-esteem, focus their anger on themselves.